Silas Deane,
Revolutionary War
Diplomat and Politician

Silas Deane,
Revolutionary War Diplomat and Politician

MILTON C. VAN VLACK

McFarland & Company, Inc., Publishers
Jefferson, North Carolina, and London

Frontispiece: Silas Deane portrait by Jared B. Flagg.
Courtesy of the Connecticut Historical Society.

LIBRARY OF CONGRESS CATALOGUING-IN-PUBLICATION DATA

Van Vlack, Milton C., 1931–
　　Silas Deane, Revolutionary War diplomat and politician / Milton C. Van Vlack.
　　　　p.　　cm.
　　Includes bibliographical references and index.

　　ISBN 978-0-7864-7252-9
　　softcover : acid free paper ∞

　　1. Deane, Silas, 1737–1789. 2. Diplomats — United States — Biography. 3. United States — History — Revolution, 1775–1783 — Biography. 4. Connecticut — History — Revolution, 1775–1783 — Biography. 5. United States. Continental Congress — Biography. 6. United States — Foreign relations —1775–1783. 7. United States — Foreign relations — France. 8. France — Foreign relations — United States. I. Title.
E302.6.D25V36 2013
973.3'85092 — dc23
[B]　　　　　　　　　　　　　　　　　　　　　　　　　2013001539

BRITISH LIBRARY CATALOGUING DATA ARE AVAILABLE

© 2013 Milton C. Van Vlack. All rights reserved

No part of this book may be reproduced or transmitted in any form or by any means, electronic or mechanical, including photocopying or recording, or by any information storage and retrieval system, without permission in writing from the publisher.

On the cover: Silas Deane portrait by Jared B. Flagg (courtesy Connecticut Historical Society); background *Signing the Treaties of Amity and Commerce and of Alliance between France and the United States in 1778*; mural painted by Charles Mills (courtesy Franklin Institute of Boston); banner © 2013 Shutterstock

Manufactured in the United States of America

McFarland & Company, Inc., Publishers
　Box 611, Jefferson, North Carolina 28640
　　www.mcfarlandpub.com

To the memory of
Janis Kisner Van Vlack,
1931–2009,
my beloved wife and partner
of fifty-four years

Contents

Acknowledgments	ix
Preface	1
Introduction	3
I. Influences on a Connecticut Youth, 1738–1761	11
II. Lawyer, Merchant, Politician, 1761–1775	20
III. Continental Congress Connecticut Delegate, 1774–1775	40
IV. Leading Connecticut Congressional Delegate, 1775	51
V. Secret American Agent to France, 1776	83
VI. American Commissioner to France, 1776–1778	115
VII. Franco-American Treaties at Last, 1778	146
VIII. Congressional Recall Debacle, 1778–1780	165
IX. Return to France, Exile and Death, 1780–1789	174
X. A Long Finale, 1789–1842	185
Appendices	
A: Key Personalities	189
B: Deane's Original 1776 Instructions	195
C: Deane's Unofficial Navy, 1775–1778	197
D: The Close Friendship Between Franklin and Deane	198
Chapter Notes	199
Bibliography	207
Index	229

Acknowledgments

My interest in colonial 18th century American history came about in the summer of 1939 when photographers from *House Beautiful* magazine came to my home for an article about our house. My parents had restored their 1738 Saltbox farmhouse during the early 1930s with "their own two hands." At 10 years of age I wanted to know why the photographers were so interested in our house. That was when the spark ignited.

While in high school, my fascination with early American history blossomed. In fact, my history teacher got so tired of me correcting some of his statements about the American Revolutionary era that he turned the textbook unit over to me to teach the class. I earned an A+. Since that time, researching the history of the American Revolutionary period has been my constant companion and hobby — no matter where or when.

This biography of Silas Deane is the culmination of more than five decades of reading, researching, lecturing and writing articles about Deane's life and careers. Its emphasis is on clarifying, in chronological order, the controversial charges and accusations made against Deane by his contemporaries and that were then carried through over 250 years by historians.

My specific interest in Silas Deane started in 1952 as a history major at Bates College. I was assigned "John Adams and the Peace Negotiations of 1783" as my senior thesis. In my research the name of Silas Deane kept coming up. I wondered why his name was not mentioned in most of my research sources. Later, in 1957, at Trinity College in Hartford, Connecticut, I was given an opportunity to satisfy my curiosity about Deane. Silas Deane's home is only about three miles from the Trinity campus. My history advisor assigned "A Survey of Writings Concerning the Controversial Envoy Silas Deane" as my master's thesis. From that study I learned much about the life of this man, but I continued to have more questions than answers as to his guilt for anything except occasionally being very human.

With the continued encouragement of the late and former Bates College and Vanderbilt University history professor, Douglas Edwin Leach, and the late Trinity College professor and friend Dr. Glenn Weaver, I launched into a lifelong hobby and companion quest for more detailed information about Silas Deane's life. The general purpose was to locate more positive aspects about the man's careers rather than just the two highly negative prejudicial classic sources accepted at face value by most historians right up to the present day.

Over the past 50 years, the following institutions deserve specific credit for allowing me access to their material sources: the Connecticut Historical Society, Trinity College Library, Bates College Library, Watkinson Library at Trinity, Yale Franklin Library; Webb-Deane-Stevens Museum and the Library of Congress.

In recent years since retirement, the Internet and haunting bookstores has kept me up-to-date with the latest related information to Silas's life.

Several close friends, and especially my daughter Tracey, deserve special credit for long years of locating source material for me hoping some day this writer would publish a book.

My wife and partner of more than 50 years deserves most of the credit for the existence of this biography. She located several rare references, listened time and time again to the various draft changes, criticized, praised and put up with a lot of complaining over the lack of more documented proof for a particular scenario.

Upon retirement in 1992, I felt I was ready at last to write an extended biography of Silas Deane. Thinking it might take me as long as two years to create a polished manuscript, I did not realize that retirement can be the busiest time of a person's life. Finally in 2003, I began to actually write a draft of the first chapter. In November of 2009 the fifty and lengthy final draft of the biography was completed. But, it just didn't seem to have a feel for the importance or uniqueness of Deane's abilities and accomplishments I originally hoped to portray.

After the Christmas holidays, I took a hard look at the chapters concerning Deane's activities in the Continental Congress and Secret Mission, and as commissioner to France. I decided to concentrate more in utilizing 20th and 21st century writings and their findings since their bibliographies were more extensive. Then I zeroed in on Deane's exact activities for which he deserves far more credit than he has ever previously received. Consequently, the sixth and final draft of Deane's biography flowed much more smoothly with the reality of events and situations of that time.

At the end of January 2010, knowing I could no longer physically type well enough to re-create 350-plus manuscript pages, I had to find someone to type the last draft from my scribbly handwriting. If anyone could know a person to contact it would be my friend, the editor of the *Boothbay Register*, Kevin Burnham. He said he would try, but in our relatively small community he doubted a person was available who had a background and an interest in the Revolution to help translate my scribbling. Kevin knew from articles I have written in the past for the paper of our Masonic Lodge activities that I had a somewhat erratic and rather blunt writing style similar to language I used in lecturing in the university classroom. Sitting back-to-back in their cubicles, Kevin and assistant editor Lisa Kristoff must have had quite a talk after my visit with Kevin.

In a couple of days I received a phone call from Lisa. She was interested and agreed to give it a try. It wasn't long before I realized she had a great background in journalism, was an author of children's stories, and best of all, had a passion for 18th century American lifestyles.

We decided we would meet for an hour or so on Saturdays to exchange newly typed material for another section of newly edited chapters. Lisa's abilities soon came to the fore. She could read my scribbling and quietly corrected phrasing and spelling as she typed; but at the same time, she kept my weird word usage intact.

After seven months, the last version of Silas Deane's biography was completed, in August 2010, and with many thanks to Lisa for all her efforts and continually asking why.

Finally, great credit must be given to writers George L. Clark, Helen Augur, Hilton Coy James, Robert Middlekauff, Walter Isaacson, Stacey Schiff and Joel Richard Paul for their extensive four-star works in locating and interpreting material of the murky period from early 1774 through mid–1778 in the European theater of the American Revolution.

My quest for locating additional sources concerning the man's life and career ends with the book you are holding.

Preface

When in 1952 my Bates American history professor assigned me "John Adams and the Peace Treaty of 1783" as my B.A. senior thesis topic, I came across a name that even as a history major I had not heard before. I was curious as to why the name Silas Deane seemed to have been practically erased from most American Revolutionary period texts. I asked my professor about him. He grinned and told me to worry about my thesis assignment. "Maybe someday in the future you can research this man and write your own biographical version of his very controversial career," he told me.

Life moved forward and starting my teaching career brought me back to Connecticut as a master's degree candidate at Trinity College in Hartford. I soon learned that Silas Deane came from the neighboring town of Wethersfield. For the next several years I spent countless hours in Silas Deane's Wethersfield home, the town library, the Connecticut Historical Society, and the Connecticut State Library, trying to quell my curiosity concerning this mysterious figure. My M.A. history advisor learned of my interest in Deane and, in 1957, made my master's thesis assignment "a comparative survey of writing concerning the controversial envoy Silas Deane!" After I completed the thesis survey, I was more confused about this man's life than before. Learning the "historically accurate truth" about Deane became a hobby which turned into a passion that has lasted over 50 years.

After retiring in 1992, I decided it was time to seriously plan and write a new Deane biography. Writing an accurate biography of a centuries-old subject is always a risky undertaking, but with over four decades of researching, I felt comfortable writing a continuous chronological version of Deane's biography.

The phases of his life known to be somewhat historically accurate are the years 1774 through 1783. Consequently, most of the controversy over Deane's behavior appears in the biography in that order. When the traditional stories arise in the biographic text, the specific (to quote historian Alan Axelrod) "approach is purposely concise and, while authoritative, it is non-academic — meaning that I do not hesitate to resolve controversies with straightforward explanations of the significance of the key events."[1] However, when very little verification is available, the descriptions of events or situations become educated conjectures derived from indirectly related source materials.

Many of the activities of the American commissioners in France in the years 1776–1778, performed for the good of the new United States of America, will remain unexplained. Due to its very covert nature, funding in the European theater of the American Revolution prior to 1778 lacks the pertinent written word by the key principals involved in the secret aid to America. Therefore, there is no valid argument that can be made against secret agent Deane concerning funding procedures.

Introduction

The life of Silas Deane is one of the most astonishing, controversial and mystifying of the mid–18th century American Revolutionary Era. The credo was the lifelong belief that middle class values of rights and power should always be based on merit and plain hard work, rather than on name and wealth. However, Deane did believe in society elitism based only as a reward for reaching success in a chosen field of endeavor.

The American Revolution was not a conservative affair. The North America of the seventeen hundreds was in fact a "churning cauldron of political and social discontent" regardless of race, religion, economic status or sex. Added to that description must also be the painfully slow, confusing, and sometimes outright dangerous conditions of transportation and means of communication.

The story of Silas Deane's life is a prime example of the ever-changing conditions of the time. His persona is one of the foremost enigmas of the Revolutionary period. Today, he is still considered by many historians to be "even worse than Arnold." Thus, the obvious question; why has this man's name been all but erased from American history? Name any aspect of the American Revolution, and Silas Deane was either part of it or indirectly involved. Unfortunately, Deane's contemporaries — and now modern-day historians, right up to the present writing — considered him one of the real bad boys of the Revolution, and a not too bright one at that.

Most of the derogatory evidence against Silas Deane is based upon the early nineteenth century biography of one Arthur Lee — Deane's nemesis — written by his famous brother, Richard Henry Lee. This biography is still the primary source for Deane bashing. It is accompanied by a mid–20th century article by Professor Julian P. Boyd entitled "Silas Deane: Death by a Kindly Teacher of Treason." This article has been generally accepted and recognized by most of today's leading historians as the ultimate proof that Silas Deane was far worse a traitor than his childhood and merchant friend General Benedict Arnold.

There have been only two previously published actual biographies of Silas Deane, one in 1913 and the other in 1975. Both are excellent accounts of his life but lack considerable crucial information and background. Rev. George L. Clark, the author of the 1913 version of Deane's life, was exceptionally fortunate in having direct access to many of the Wethersfield, Connecticut, lawyer/merchant's original personal papers and ledgers not found elsewhere. They were kept in the house that Silas built for his wife that was completed in 1766. The *Hartford Times* newspaper reported on November 16, 1932, that "the library of the Silas Deane house in Wethersfield was destroyed by fire last night. The house is now owned and occupied by the Honorable E. Hart Fenn, Connecticut Congressional Representative from 1921 to 1931. Some of the papers destroyed were unique and the information now lost forever."

For the 1975 publication by professor Coy Hilton James, the author located additional, previously unpublished, materials in the archives and files of various federal agencies and departments and the Library of Congress. Questions still remained, however, as to whether or not there might be more original papers of Deane's activities in the European theater of the American Revolution. In 2005, Stacey Schiff, in her book *The Great Improvisation*, decidedly put that possibility pretty much to rest. Her extensive research into the major archives and institutional files in the countries of England, France, Germany, Holland, Spain and Portugal showed no substantially new manuscript documentation.

Silas Deane was one of the top leading members of the First and Second Continental congresses from May of 1774 to January of 1776. Because of undeniable political foul play, Deane was not elected to a third term. But Ben Franklin and Robert Morris, respectively of the Congressional Secret Committee of Correspondence and the Secret Trade Commission, had, along with many other delegates, deeply admired the abilities and knowledge of the young firebrand patriot from Connecticut. Together, Franklin and Morris quietly pressured Silas into accepting a secret mission to France in order to seek financial aid and war supplies for the colonies. He was also to feel out the French ministry on the possibility of an open commercial alliance.

Squire/merchant Deane arrived in Paris in early July of 1776. After meeting with Foreign Minister Comte de Vergennes, he was told he could obtain war materials by working with their secret agent Caron de Beaumarchais.

Unfortunately for Silas, Beaumarchais had already been working unofficially with Arthur Lee, then a congressional agent in London. On their own, they had developed a plan to aid the colonies that would also greatly enhance their own finances. When Deane arrived in France as an official but secret representative of the Americas, Beaumarchais, at the request of Vergennes, turned and dealt directly with Deane. When Arthur learned of Deane's commission, he went into a rage and arrived in Paris only to find the two men fast friends and deeply immersed in drawing up contracts for military arms and supplies for Washington's army. From 1776 almost to the end of his life Lee hated Silas. With his noted miserable, rotten personality, Lee immediately started a letter and rumor campaign back to his brothers and other members of Congress, accusing Deane of embezzlement, profiteering, dealing with the enemy and a myriad of minor personal charges.

Arthur Lee's and his congressional allies' successful efforts to ruin Silas Deane is a black mark against the Continental Congress that simply cannot be excused or erased. In the Continental Congress, during the Revolution itself, there was an intense but rather impractical group of patriots centered around the leadership of the Virginia Lees and the Massachusetts Adamses, along with an assortment of individual allies. This group was definitely long on zeal but short on practicality and plain old common sense, especially when it came to how to fight a war. There were very few delegates with any real experience in diplomatic affairs, administrative procedures and military background. Opposing this highly philosophical faction was the famous pragmatic individual icons of the day, led by Benjamin Franklin: Robert Morris, George Washington, John Jay and Silas Deane. These individuals were far better qualified for turning a spasmodic rebellion into a successful revolution for independence than was the opposing group.

The philosophical group, however, was determined to keep their revolution pure and depend on as little outside help as possible. Realizing they could not go it alone, these men known as "radicals," decided that come what may they would make sure they had control over all congressional matters regardless of the long-term consequences. Known as the Adams/Lee Bloc, these delegates were able to penetrate and maintain control of most actions of Congress until Silas Deane exposed the entire conclave in late 1778 during the "Congressional Recall Imbriglio."

Unconsciously perhaps, our founding fathers, especially those delegates to the First and Second Continental congresses, were in some way involved in the preoccupation of the 1700s with speculation in North American western lands and properties beyond the boundaries established by the Proclamation Line of 1763. On the American coast, from the colonies of Massachusetts to Georgia, ownership of land dominated men's thinking. In the fast-changing lifestyles of the American 18th century, land was the key catalyst. Land ownership was the commodity upon which real wealth was based. It could determine the way an individual lived and his social standing within the community. From the beginning of the Revolutionary period, almost without exception, personal outside interests and agendas were directly affected. Speculation in western land was at the top of the list. Franklin, Washington, Thomas Jefferson and Deane were not immune.

Related to the acquisition of western lands was the propaganda rhetoric concerning the words "liberty" and "virtue," which were continually utilized to hide political philosophical differences in Congress. None of our revolutionary icons ever intended for their new country to be entirely democratic, and they definitely were not opposed to the concept of a new empire. In fact, their general and personal agendas revolved around the vision of creating a new land empire totally independent of England and France. Silas Deane's thinking was no exception. He was well aware of the empire concept. Silas, however, carried the idea a step further economically. He dreamed of an American commercial and land empire after the war that would include England and Russia as economic partners.

Over four decades of researching aspects of Deane's life I am continually amazed at the amount of interpretation variations of the same events, situations and issues involved in his careers. It is apparent that, most of the time, writers make little effort to go directly to Deane's own manuscripts. One common excuse has been that the word usage of the eighteenth century is quite different from the present. It is often stated that the word usage, punctuation and capitalization is confusing and hard to understand. Another reason is writers' use of tainted and obviously prejudicial material without having established verification.

In writing this biography, I have accumulated considerable specific correspondence of major players close to Deane. This correspondence has allowed for checking and verifying commonality of information and more accurate chronology not previously known.

The storyline of Deane's life is presented occasionally utilizing twentieth and twenty-first century vernacular in order to make events and situations more easily related to modern times.

Introduced in this volume are two facets of the American Revolution not ordinarily given much consideration by writers regarding concerns of the Revolutionary period. The subjects are Freemasonry and Secret Intelligence. Both give a different emphasis and imperative to Silas's mission as an agent and, later, as an ambassador to France. Strong attention is given to the sequence of events and accurate time lapse. The main focus is to keep the perspective centered around, and directly related to, America's first foreign intelligence agent operations. His exploits foreshadow today's CIA operations. Deane's actions have even been equated with Ian Fleming's James Bond (007) adventures, possibly excluding the girls and gadgets until Franlin arrived.

Secret intelligence gathering is as old as warfare and diplomacy. Sometimes it is referred to as the world's second oldest profession and the missing link in written history. Unfortunately, even long after intelligence itself ceases to be of any real value, governments tend to hold secret the means by which the information was obtained. Intelligence is often locked up in closed, classified government archive files. It is strongly rumored that the exact formula for the invisible ink used by Deane, Franklin and Washington in their clandestine operations is still sealed away in the CIA archives and unavailable to the public. Consequently, with certain secret materials inaccessible, the particular subject is usually ignored by historians, leaving any area in question open to wild, foggy and hazy conjecture.

The original ancestor of all American intelligence gathering systems is the Sons of Liberty organization formed in 1765 in violent opposition to the Stamp Act. By 1772, the American patriots began to establish Committees of Correspondence throughout the colonies with a more formal structure that quickly became a resistance shadow government network that was highly instrumental in bringing about the convening of the First Continental Congress of 1774.

At the start of the Revolution there was no system for accurate communications over great distances or any organized military intelligence gathering network. The most important factors needed were speed and accuracy. In early January 1776, realizing the desperateness of the situation, George Washington and Ben Franklin, independent of one another, started their own networks, thus becoming America's first spymasters — Washington on the home front and Franklin for Europe. In turn, the two spymasters chose individuals who were highly educated and well known for their administrative and organizational talents to be their chief intelligence agents. The assignments of the agents were to carry out the establishment of informational networks and intelligence stations from which clandestine operations could be carved out.

Colonel Benjamin Tallmadge served as chief agent for George Washington, personally operating the famous Culper Ring out of New York. Agent Silas Deane operated under chief of station Ben Franklin out of Paris. Deane became Franklin's diplomatic point man and sole coordinator of all secret aid to America through February 1778.

Historians of the American Revolutionary period largely ignore the contributions of Freemasonry to the actions and ideals of our founding fathers. The well-known Enlightenment Era of the eighteenth century was full of visionary thinking. Actually, there was only one place where basic democracy, along with religious and political toleration, was practiced to any great degree. In their lodge room meetings, Masons from all walks of life and political thought governed themselves without hatred or violence. As author Christopher Hodapp has stated, "Freemasonry was the firstborn son of Enlightenment, and it was a greater single influence on our Founding Fathers than any other."[1]

The language within the lodge was the same for businessmen, laborers, land owners, politicians and military officers. During the 1700s, Masonic ideals literally saturated American society, as well as the European salons of Paris and London.

As a young man, Silas Deane became well known for practicing the Masonic ideals of traditional dignity and exquisite manners. Consequently, his habitual congenial actions paired off well during his time in France while conducting secret aid operations for war supplies for America and the creation of intelligence network stations throughout the European continent.

With so many "word of mouth only," and "need to know basis only," the missing details known only by unrecognized individuals behind specific successful plans and operations need to be identified and rewarded for their contributions to the war effort. Silas Deane is such an individual.

Little is really understood or known about the involvement of, or initiatives by, Deane in the capture of Fort Ticonderoga in 1775, or the success and long-range results of the spectacular defeat of the British army at Saratoga. Returning from the First Continental Congress, in early 1775, Silas began worrying, concerned over the probability of British attack from Canada splitting New England off from the rest of the colonies. As a result, he turned his well-known planning ability to setting up a possible scenario to take Fort Ticonderoga on Lake Champlain.

During the Lexington alarm in April, Deane learned from his legislative friend Samuel Holden Parsons that his boyhood friend Benedict Arnold had told him that Fort Ticonderoga was ripe for picking with only a small contingent of soldiers, but it did have a lot of badly needed cannons for our colonial defense. Silas then obtained the backing of several prominent men and personally guaranteed the cost of an expedition against the fort by another family friend, Ethan Allen, and the Green Mountain Boys. Arnold independently got Massachusetts patriots to make him the commander of such a force. Eventually it worked out; both men led the successful attack on May 10, 1775. Silas became an overnight sensation in the Continental Congress as a result of his part, and audacity, in the capture of Fort Ticonderoga.

Although he did not receive much credit at the time, in 1777 the majority of arms used by the patriot army at Saratoga were almost entirely the result of Silas's efforts in France arranging for their purchase and shipping to America. Yet here was a man deliberately and methodically shafted and publicly humiliated by the tired, frightened, inept and vengeful Continental Congress of 1778–79, as well as being manipulated by the Lee brothers and their allies. The question still remains: why destroy Mr. Deane?

Part of the reason lies in a common issue of concern that runs rampant in any war, including the great American cause for independence. Old or new, every war sees massive private speculation and profiteering. The profit motive always seems to transcend any other agenda. Attempts at profiteering in military supplies was very common during Deane's time, and almost a necessity during the early years of the Revolution. Unfortunately for the profiteers, they more often than not ended up broke due to their lack of understanding of future ramifications of their individual actions.

Profiteering charges made against Deane by the Adams/Lee bloc have never held water. Basically, the charges were made due to the general ignorance of the mercantile economics of the eighteenth century at almost every level of society, except for merchants themselves. Simply put, to the agrarian society merchants were all crooks taking advantage of the public.

To the merchants, the physical manipulation of financial terms we call cash and credit was no mystery. The economic world, at that time, was in a whirling transition with little or no permanent stability. It still held largely to the age-old system of exchange called "swapping," or barter, which in itself changed by the day and season. When the war finally got underway after over a decade of festering, the young London stock market seemed to have gotten a handle on the ever-changing mercantile system by exploiting it with stocks, bonds and uninsured protection policies.

As a successful New England merchant with extensive knowledge of legal and illegal West Indies trade, Silas Deane was well-versed in the major aspects of Anglo-American and European economic trading systems of the period. By 1775, at the age of 40, Silas was experienced with, and worked in, high-risk land speculations, stockjobbing, credit holding and insurance gaming.

This biography gives a matter-of-fact coverage of Deane's various activities in those fields while he was in France. The explanations do, however, remind the reader that most of the money obtained from the various sources went right back into the commission's funds. Congress paid nothing for personal expenses or "salary" and relied upon the abilities of the American commission to obtain aid funds from France.

One can't help but wonder what might have happened if Silas Deane had remained on the American side of the Atlantic and had been reelected to the Continental Congress. Would he now be considered a "Founding Father," or would he still be a patriot almost completely erased from history receiving only an occasional backhanded compliment?

Welcome to Silas Deane Esquire's turbulent unforgiving eighteenth century world. He was no saint, but his political sins were far less than those of many of his contemporaries.

CHAPTER I

Influences on a Connecticut Youth, 1738–1761

In 1737, on the day before Christmas Eve, Silas Deane laid the cornerstone for his new house. He was an industrious and successful blacksmith in the colonial coastal town of Groton, Connecticut. The house was built, and still stands, in what was then the northern section of the town known as Church Hill. This area is now part of the present town of Ledyard.[1]

On the same day that Silas started their new home, his wife, the former Sarah Barker of Marshfield, Massachusetts, presented him with their first child whom they named Silas. Eventually young Silas became the eldest of seven Deane children: Barnabus, Barazillai, Simeon, John, David, and Hannah. Hannah, known as Sally, married a Josiah Buck. David died in infancy.[2]

The area histories of Groton and New London, the town across the Connecticut River Thames, both proclaim leadership in the colony's shipbuilding industry and shipping trade. This came about during the early part of the 18th century. A new socially elite class of men gradually appeared who used their Van physical and mental skills to become successful entrepreneurs. They were trader/merchants, shipowners, and tradesmen specializing in areas, such as sailmaking, related to the shipping and fishing industries.

Old records suggest that Silas Deane Senior was more than just another local agrarian village blacksmith forging and repairing farming tools.[3] Silas's father had joined the new social class as an ironmonger. Following the custom of the time, young Silas, as the eldest son, was learning his father's business. They were working with shipwrights up and down the Connecticut coastline producing needed specialized ships' iron hardware fittings. Who better than the local blacksmith, with the skills and the personal contacts in the colony's blooming iron industry, located in the northwestern towns of Salisbury and Canaan, to fill an important part of the shipbuilding industry.[4] Business was so successful that it has been recorded that Silas Senior was able to purchase a share and half interest in another slave to help with the heavy work.[5]

Such an enterprise brought the entire Deane family into ongoing contact with other local industrial families of higher social standing, wealth and educational background. A young Rev. Ezra Stiles of Norwich, future president of Yale College, was such a person and became a lifelong friend of the Deane family members.[6]

During the years that Silas Deane was growing into full manhood, the colony of Connecticut was going through several of the most tumultuous and drastic changes of its entire history. These included changes in population growth, politics, religion, economy and social distinction. In addition, there was the impact of the French and Indian War.

When Silas Deane was born, the colony of Connecticut was very independent minded. The population comprised largely moderate to small landowners whose main occupation was agriculture, with an occasional bent toward land development and speculation. The people had common interests and similar lifestyles and belonged to the same religious denomination. Connecticut was the envy of her neighboring colonies. The citizens enjoyed a relative high degree of freedom from outside interference due to Connecticut's famous sea-to-sea "Charter Oak" charter.

By the beginning of the mid–1700s, however, the accumulated effects of religious controversies sparked by the Great Awakening, along with new economic and commercial issues of the times, had made deep inroads into the land formerly known for its "steady habits."[7]

One of the foremost issues transforming the colony during this period was the rapid growth in population. According to the best estimates available, the population total more than tripled in thirty years. In 1730, it was about 38,000. By 1760 it was well over 130,000. On the eve of the American Revolution it was just under 200,000.[8]

As the population increased, agricultural resources failed to keep pace. The inhabitants began to demand more land and better economic situations. For a while in the 1730s, the thirst for more land was satisfied by the public opening and sale of some 300,000 acres in the northwestern area of the colony and part of the original Yale College grants from the king, now known as Litchfield County. The Litchfield area of northwestern Connecticut soon became thickly populated, largely by French and Indian War veterans who were paid in land for their military service. Many men then began to push their way into New York, New Hampshire and Vermont lands. So much so that Vermont earned the name "New Connecticut."

One of the major results of the growing interest in outside land development and speculation was the organization of the Susquehannah Company during 1752 and 1753 in the eastern town of Windham. Within a very short period the company became a great source of political controversy and division within the colony. In 1754, the agents of the Susquehannah Company signed a treaty with Indian chiefs to colonize the Wyoming Valley of western Pennsylvania, later known as Westmoreland County. The company was hoping the British government could be persuaded to support the treaty with the approval of the Connecticut governor and legislature. If the company received approval, it would literally give title to the investors of practically the entire northern third of the colony of Pennsylvania. Amazingly enough, at the ripe old age of 17, Silas's name appears on the company's list of investors. The Penn family proprietors of Pennsylvania strongly opposed the Susquehannah's group claims. An interesting sidebar during this period was the fact that Ben Franklin was Pennsylvania's colonial agent in England. Franklin was well known for his wide interests in the speculations of the colonies' western lands. Being at odds with the Penn family and in favor of Quakers fosters interest during those years. Franklin openly undermined the proprietors' objections to the Susquehannah Company's claims.[9]

From the actions of the colonial delegates at Albany, the congress's real concerns had more to do with inter-colony business than with any colonial plan of union actions the Colonial Board of Trades originally intended. The congress simply seethed with intrigue. The most important developments took place outside the formal sessions. Out in the "pucker bushes" (an old Yankee expression) a bitter conflict escalated between representatives of Connecticut's Susquehanna land speculators' group and agents of Pennsylvania's proprietary family. The company's scheme was to gain title somehow from the Iroquois Indian tribe for over five million acres in the Wyoming Valley on the upper Susquehanna River. All three Connecticut commissioners to the Albany congress were stockholders in the Susquehanna Company, including William Dyer, one of the originators of the company. He was to remain in Connecticut politics almost to the end of the century.

The conflict between Connecticut, Pennsylvania and the Iroquois Confederacy, including the Delaware Indians, would be a long, deadly struggle over the lands of the Wyoming Valley for years to come. The Connecticut assembly, whose members also included many stockholders of the Susquehanna Company, refused to agree to the Albany Plan of Union, along with other colonies. The plan would have nullified their colony's "sea to sea" charters.[10] Silas Deane's active interest and participation with, and for, the Susquehanna Company would continue until near the end of 1775. However, it did not end his lifelong interest in western land speculation.

A few years earlier, in the 1740s, colonial America was experiencing many dramatic and encompassing religious revivals known as the Great Awakening, extending into the 1760s. Connecticut's Congregationalism, however, was able to sustain an especially impressive establishment due to the colony's compact settlement by law-oriented towns and churches. Congregationalists strictly enforced the Sabbath, which restricted many activities just to the home and church. Arrests and fines were regularly imposed on those who worked, played or traveled on Sunday. As the waves of revivals continued, the evangelists became known as the New Lights, while their counterparts were known as Old Lights who defended established institutions and scriptural traditions.

The bitter controversy between New Lights and Old Lights split both the colonial elite and the common people. Both sides included ministers and magistrates, along with wealthy merchants, farmers, artisans, and common laborers. Basically, more men of education, prestige, wealth and influence chose the Old Lights' established forms. Any elevation of individualism was almost automatically seen as a threat to the socially elite, who felt their authority depended on the power to constrain religious choices. It was still primarily a male world. Slowly revivals cooled down as evangelistic groups institutionalized into Baptist or Methodist sects or dissolved altogether.

In the Connecticut colony, the Great Awakening years changed the face of politics forever. By the 1750s, it had become a social as well as a religious revolution that led to major political changes. Gradually an opposition party composed of New Lights grew in the Connecticut assembly and by the 1760s the New Lights party controlled the assembly and spearheaded resistance to the Stamp Act of 1765. The political shakeup went all the way to the state house, where Governor Fitch was called to account by the New Lights faction for refusing to convene the assembly in order to discuss the actions to be taken in relation to the Stamp Act.

Finally, the real turning point in Connecticut politics came in the colony-wide election of 1766. William Pitkin, and Jonathan Trumbull, a strong backer and stockholder in the Susquehannah Company and politically ambitious, were elected governor and deputy governor respectively. Three years later, in 1769, Governor Pitkin died and Jonathan Trumbull automatically became governor of Connecticut. One year later, in the hard-fought, bitter election of 1770, Trumbull defeated Fitch to become governor in his own right. From that period on, Jonathan Trumbull, Sr., would be an on-again-off-again political friend and ally of Silas Deane.

While the colony's politics were evolving in new enlightened directions, fundamental changes were taking place in Connecticut's general economic and commercial relations with Great Britain. During the 1750s, Connecticut was a land of relatively small-scale diversified farming, but surprisingly, the agriculture was not just subsistence farming. It was mainly commercial. Farmers grew large crops such as beans, peas, beets, squash, corn, onions, apples and tobacco. Increasingly, they participated in the wholesale raising of various livestock for export, primarily to the West Indies islands, but also to several European ports outside Great Britain.

Unfortunately, for years Connecticut had two major problems with its agricultural marketing. First, the colony had no major ocean port and thus had to depend on its neighboring colonies of Rhode Island, Massachusetts and New York for disbursement of this produce. Consequently, the ports of Providence, Boston and New York did a roaring business as "middlemen" on incoming and outgoing transactions at the expense of Connecticut merchants and farmers. The second problem came when Great Britain increasingly tightened regulations and policies of its colonial shopping with the West Indies — the one overseas area of the world over which Connecticut did have a direct and very valuable control. The key to Connecticut's general economic prosperity and growth prior to the 1760s was its trade with the West Indies, including both British and foreign-owned islands.

Silas was born into a world where England was perennially at war with France. In 1746, the hated French led Indian attacks against English settle-

Birthplace of Silas Deane. The house was built by Silas Deane, Sr., in 1737. The window panes were originally 9 over 6. It is located on Church Hill Road in what was formerly North Groton (now Ledford), Connecticut (courtesy Mrs. Anna May Capen, who gave the photograph to the author when the house was under restoration).

ments on the coast of Maine and then forged ahead from the French forts on Lake Champlain into the New York colony proper. The Abenaki made continuous forays into western Massachusetts and on down into Connecticut Valley. To live in New York, Massachusetts and Connecticut during these bloody years meant one had to be in constant expectation of an Indian attack. Then, in 1754, the French and Indian War broke out in full force.

In the first six years of the war, the colonies benefited handsomely in the field of economics. The British army and navy expenditures in the colonies from 1756 through 1762 came to over six million pounds, plus another million pounds paid directly to the colonial governments. This influx of credit and badly needed specie enabled the colonies to double their crucial imports from England. Then, in the last year of the war, a crisis in international finances shook up the London financiers and merchants to a panic level. English merchants trading with the colonies starting insisting that the colonists pay debts in specie. In 1764, the British Currency Act made the colonial government's currency no longer legal tender for payment of public or private debts. Now the big question became how the colonies, especially Connecticut, could ever help to pay for the French and Indian War, called the Seven Years' War in Europe. To add insult to injury, Prime Minister George Grenville taxed the colonists on anything he could think of to keep the utmost imperial control over England's colonies.[11]

Causing even more economic misery for Connecticut, the British government all but eliminated the direct overseas trade market available to the colony. For the sake of its economic survival, Connecticut, along with several other colonies, quickly turned to a highly systemized smuggling trade with the various West Indies islands regardless of ownership, owners which included the British, French, Spanish, Dutch and Portuguese. This outright necessary illicit trade was to continue throughout the entire American Revolutionary era.

While all the turmoil and changes were occurring in population, religion, economics, and politics in Connecticut, a socially positive entity was making its influence felt in the colony. The world's oldest secret fraternal organization, Freemasonry, had come to America from England in the early 1700s. As the age of Enlightenment succeeded the Great Awakening, it made its way into the North American British colonies. Pennsylvania, Virginia, Massachusetts and Connecticut were among the first. Freemasonry boasted such members as Ben Franklin, George Washington and Paul Revere.

Masonry itself was undergoing a basic organizational split during this period. It was primarily brought about by the themes of the Age of Enlightenment. In spite of its own schism, Freemasonry was flourishing in the colonies by the 1750s even though the schism would take nearly a half-century before it began to heal. Masons who wished to keep traditional ritual with inward-looking procedures were called "Ancients," while Masons who had joined Masonry mainly from the socially elite class were more open and turned outward into the community. They were, and are, called "Speculative" Masons. The Ancients' learning probably came from the organizations of the great stonemasons who built the beautiful edifices of the Middle Ages.

In the colonies, Freemasonry was embraced by gentlemen and artisans alike and, especially, the merchant class, who wished to be recognized as part of the socially elite. Masonry of the 18th century was starting to encourage upward social movement and a more inclusive elite class. It emphasized education, politeness, honor, mutual assistance, networking and tolerance in the delicate matter of religion. Masons are charged with a belief in the existence of a benevolent Supreme Being which they refer to as the Great Architect of the Universe.

Colonial Masonry helped to buffer and even blunt the various divisive forces of society by reinforcing the 18th century social system basically between gentlemen and "others." Masons often boasted that no one was excluded from the fraternity provided they were "duly qualified." In reality, however, the poorer classes rarely passed the proper qualifications. Masons never drew any sharp distinction between "the craft" and the standards of the elite society. The heart of gentility was the ideal of politeness. Unlike the "others," a gentlemen's manners were refined and showy, with consideration given for their equals.[12]

In the very early 1760s, Freemasonry began to soften on admission to Masonry. Many artisans, men like Paul Revere, were becoming leaders among the emerging working-class artisans; they were personally ambitious, upwardly mobile and patriotic, with a very strong regard for the general good. These men energized the American resistance to English oppression.

The common people also had their own agenda when it came to the use of the words liberty and freedom. Their interpretation of the words became very clear throughout the 1760s decade, but it was brought home to the colonial elite hard and fast with the Boston Tea Party episode. The "others" saw liberty and freedom required decisive action and not just being of a virtuous nature. Masonry soon welcomed men of this caliber regardless of their social rank.[13]

Somehow, in the year 1754, the Deanes were able to send their eldest son to Yale College in New Haven. The influence of a family friend, the Rev. Ezra Stiles, in New Haven surely helped in the admission process. The college had grown rapidly in the mid–1700s under the able administration of Rector Thomas Clapp. Yale was far more conservative in religion studies than Harvard during this period and maintained curricular emphasis in the classics. It never intended to be a college that trained only ministers. In the 1750s, more than half of its graduates were laymen.

Commencements had become very joyous occasions — sometimes so much so that drunkenness and rioting occurred. In 1758, the year that Silas graduated, Yale made a big step forward and listed students alphabetically in the catalog rather than by social distinction. The class stigma of being the son of a blacksmith was beginning to fade. From graduation on, Silas was continuously striving to keep his social rank moving ever upward into the American "polite society."

After graduation in 1758, with family blessings, Silas left the Groton/New London area and moved north to the colony's capital city of Hartford. With the aim of continuing his Yale studies in the field of law, Silas needed a means of supporting himself while he studied law. He contacted a Yale friend, Titus Hosmer, who was the principal of the five-year-old Hartford grammar school located near the corner of Main and Arch streets. Hosmer remained principal from 1758 until 1760, when he started practicing law in Middletown. Silas was hired as a teacher and succeeded Titus Hosmer as schoolmaster for a short time in 1761 just before being admitted to the Connecticut bar.[14]

During the years that Silas was teaching school, he had a very special pupil in fourteen-year-old Edward Bancroft, the stepson of Daniel Bull (proprietor of the famous tavern in Hartford known as the Bunch of Grapes located where the modern Gold Building now stands). Bancroft was destined to drastically affect Deane's life and political career some 15 years later. During the Revolutionary War era, Edward Bancroft became one of the most astounding double agents ever known. His double-spy career was never discovered or publicly known until the mid–1800s.

After being admitted to the bar, Silas was ready to hang out a shingle. Several of his fellow Yale graduates lived in the neighboring Connecticut River town of Wethersfield. Ever since the arrival of Silas in the Hartford area these graduates had been praising the attributes of the town. Silas was duly impressed and decided to personally investigate Wethersfield as a place to start a law practice. In the mid–18th century, Wethersfield was one of Connecticut's most economically thriving towns. Much like his hometown area of Groton/New London, Wethersfield was a highly successful commercial center.

The town's trade with the West Indies had begun in the 1640s and was only now reaching its peak. Citizens from all over the colony passed through Wethersfield to Hartford and tended to their personal business in Wethersfield, which continuously added to the economic, social and cultural growth of the town. Wethersfield was tailor-made for the young Silas Deane, Esquire. Consequently, the new lawyer came to town and hung out his shingle. With this background, Silas Deane launched himself into an elitist Connecticut lifestyle. He was a reflection and product of all the turmoil and change he had witnessed as a youth. His 18th century life and career would become a saga of ambition, success, intrigue, controversy and mystery.

It is unlikely that anyone will ever really know, or understand, Deane's true actions behind those secretive and murky times of so many social, philosophical, and economic uncertainties.

Chapter II

Lawyer, Merchant, Politician, 1761–1775

Once Silas had permanently settled in Wethersfield in 1762, he started doing what became a pattern he followed the rest of his life. He thoroughly checked out anything that was of interest to him and then set a plan in motion to accommodate whatever the particular interest required. The final thing he wanted to do was make a detailed analysis of Wethersfield's social structure being largely built around its commercial basis. His purpose was to decide just how he might become part of the community's elite. He learned that the Connecticut River Valley farmers were exporting bags of several different grains, cattle, horses, flaxseed, dried fish, pork, beef, tobacco and, from Wethersfield alone, its already famous onion harvests.

Wethersfield ship captains were shipping all of these items down the Atlantic coast, but primarily to the West Indies Islands. On their return voyage they would bring large quantities of molasses, rum, tea and coffee back home. What interested Silas most about the town's trading business was the fact that, of late years, a combination of local sea captains, merchants, and farmers were bringing into Wethersfield considerably sophisticated 18th century luxury items that included fine fabrics, ceramics, cutlery and books. Wethersfield trade was even more successful because the shipowner/sea captain was also likely to also be a merchant or farmer who personally manned the small river sloop that could easily navigate at sea as well. The successful commercial picture of the town fascinated Silas. He soon learned that the social structure of Wethersfield was quite typical of any Puritan-oriented Connecticut town, including his hometown area of Groton and New London.

From his childhood years to adulthood, Silas wanted to be on a higher social scale than just the son of a farmer, village blacksmith and ironmonger. In New England, the formula to be part of the socially elite always included

II. Lawyer, Merchant, Politician, 1761–1775

three measures: wealth, a career in the community or church service or both, and having the name of the community or colony founder.

After the young Mister Deane hung out his shingle, he immediately set out to obtain the first two steps to becoming a member of the socially elite in town. The new squire found the citizens of Wethersfield to be very close-knit, sharing some of the same ideals and moral convictions. The center of community and religious life was the Congregational church, then known as the Meeting House, a new unusual brick structure which had commenced construction the very year Silas came to town. It was destined to help Silas achieve his goal of being one of the local elite.

Official Seal of the Town of Wethersfield, Connecticut, designed by Jared Butler Standish (1866–1963). The Wethersfield Seal is quite unique. It not only tells a story of the town's early existence, but also shows several aspects of 18th-century lifestyle and technology. The geographic features of "Connecticut's Most Ancient Town" are also readily apparent (courtesy the Town of Wethersfield, Connecticut).

The Wethersfield Congregational Church, restored in 1973, was an ambitious undertaking in 1761, one of the few brick edifices of its time, and one of the largest. Much of the money needed to build such a church came from the sale of the famous Wethersfield red onion, given in lieu of a cash contribution. Consequently, it is often called the church onions built.

The church is patterned after the Old North Church in Boston of Paul Revere fame, but with a shorter spire. In 1938, after the "Old North" lost its steeple in the great hurricane, engineers and architects came to Wethersfield to use the church spire as a guide to rebuild the original design of the Old North Church.

In a short period of time, Silas became a very active church member. Pews were normally assigned according to social rank in town. Silas was determined to be placed in the first few rows. He took part in numerous church affairs and attended services not once but twice on Sundays. Silas served on many church committees, ranging from improving singing positions by setting up the stations of the parishioners who would carry the principal parts to fining members who were absent from services. Silas's church activities brought him notice from the church elders. Within a year, he was sitting on town committees. The young, ambitious lawyer was known to be interested in education, as well as having commercial interests. He soon found himself involved in helping to rearrange school districts, and, later setting up navigation markers in the Connecticut River for the commuters of Hartford, Middletown (Portland) and Wethersfield merchant sloops.

Silas became not only well known in town, but also well-liked and admired for his advanced educational background, especially after receiving his master of arts from Yale in 1763. Mr. Deane made a good personal appearance, though he was not particularly handsome. He was approximately 5'10" tall and had strictly good taste in clothing. He was a kind and pleasant man people enjoyed listening to. He always seemed to have rather expansive views on almost any subject and spoke with a clarity, force and frankness that sometimes bordered on bluntness.

Mr. Deane's new law practice took off. One of his new clients was the widow Webb. The household of her husband, the late Joseph Webb, was ranked as one of the most important in Wethersfield at that time. Webb had died in 1761 when only 34 years of age, leaving his wife, Mehitabel, with six children, a sizable store and a handsomely profitable mercantile trading business. Mehitabel hired Silas to settle and manage the estate. Surprisingly, or maybe not so surprisingly, although Mehitabel was five years his senior, Silas began to court her. On October 8, 1763, the couple married. Mehitabel was already part of the town's elite. Her maiden name was Nott, another successful West Indies trading family. Silas immediately joined his wife in managing the general store business. With his boyhood firsthand knowledge of the Connecticut shoreline shipping trade and the backing of the Nott family name, Silas shortly entered the West Indies trade to heighten their mercantile business profit.

For the American colonists, the series of Navigation Acts had made trade with any country other than England illegal. But, as a matter of sheer economic survival, merchants largely ignored the acts. The law was never vigorously enforced, but it did make most sea captains and merchants smugglers, which lasted into the Revolution years. Silas was now one of those smugglers. Smuggling would be a part of Deane's life for over the next 12 years. In 1764, while Silas became immersed in the commercial and mercantile world of trade, Mehitabel presented Silas with their only child, a son, Jesse.

The couple's business flourished with substantial profits. Mehitabel was used to the grandeur of the Webb house and she pushed Silas for a house of their own, as even the roomy Webb house was becoming rather cramped liv-

II. Lawyer, Merchant, Politician, 1761–1775

Left: Portrait of Silas Deane, ca. 1766, attributed to William Johnson. Willliam Johnson's style was definitely influenced by Joseph Blackburn's traditional English style. The painting shows a genteel but rather arrogant Silas Deane during the period that he was a successful young Wethersfield merchant involved in the West Indies trade. By the time of the Revolutionary War, artists had gained a new respect for the dignity of the individual and depicted their portrait subjects in a more realistic fashion. *Right:* Silas Deane's first wife, Mehitabel Nott (Webb) Deane, and their only son, Jesse, painted by William Johnson. This portrait shows the characteristic Pre-Revolutionary War portraiture style for the socially elite. Mehitabel was already a member of the genteel society (both photographs courtesy Webb-Deane-Stevens Museum and Kent Delord Museum).

ing. Since Mehitabel's oldest son, Joseph Junior, would be of legal age soon, the decision was made that when a house of their own was completed Joseph and the older children would remain in their family home. Mehitabel and Silas, with the younger children, would move into the new house. Silas was obviously delighted to build a home of his own as it would give him a chance to make a statement in, and to, the community. Because the Deane house is a mirror of the man's character, personality and wide body of knowledge in architecture and furnishings, it is necessary to describe the house in considerable detail.

The building reflects an original concept for an 18th century Connecticut house. It did not follow any common design of the day. From the beginning,

Wethersfield Congregational Church, brick edifice completed in 1764, exterior view. The Wethersfield Meeting House/Congregational Church was founded in 1635. The present church building is the third edifice, built in 1764, and restored to its original design in 1973. In the 18th century, the meeting house was the social, political, and religious center of Wethersfield. Its steeple is patterned after the Old North Church in Boston of Paul Revere fame. The present brick building earned the title "The Onion Church" because the famous Wethersfield red onions, sold in New York, were used to pay for the construction, at least in part (courtesy First Church of Christ in Wethersfield).

Wethersfield Congregational Church, interior view. The interior of the Wethersfield Meeting House and Church of 1764 is more or less a common design of the 18th century with the exception of the brick veneer. Toward the end of the century, however, the design was changed in several basic ways. The main door was moved under the steeple section and the pulpit and choir section was placed at the back of the edifice with rows of pews facing the pulpit area (courtesy First Church of Christ in Wethersfield).

it was considered a mansion. The house is a modified colonial designed around a huge corner hallway. As one walks in the large front Dutch door, on the right side is a wide staircase considered one of the finest in Connecticut during that era. The mahogany banister features balusters of three different turnings in each tread. The front parlor to the left of the hall is notable for the wainscoting and the paneled wall framing of the fireplace. The mantel is uniquely carved of Portland, Connecticut, brownstone in the Chippendale style then popular in Philadelphia. The entire house has elegance and dignity. Silas himself undoubtedly designed the entire building, as there were few professional architects in New England during that time. The building throughout shows Deane's knowledge of contemporary architectural styles from the colonies and England. While the house was under construction, a large ell was added for the kitchen and servants quarters. Also, the rear and front of the building had porches built into the house at the time of construction. They were unique appendages, almost unheard of in the northern colonies until the farmhouse veranda came along in the very late 1700s. The front porch was removed sometime in the first years of the 20th century. Unfortunately, no plans or pictures seem to exist as to its exact appearance. In 1766, the Deanes moved in. There was one more thing to make Silas's statement complete. It was his portrait and that was the most important possession concerning a man's standing in a community such as Wethersfield.

As life would have it, Mehitabel and Silas did not have long to enjoy family life together in their new home. Mehitabel died just a year later in 1764 of what then was called consumption. With Mehitabel's death, Silas buried himself in managing the store and contending with the many trading opportunities Wethersfield had to offer.

By 1765, Wethersfield had become the central supply depot and commercial center for the entire Connecticut River Valley. The prosperity produced a thriving local merchant class that was able to afford luxuries for themselves usually found only in larger cities, particularly in the southern colonies. One of the more prominent luxuries was the ability to own slaves. During the 18th century, slavery existed in all 13 colonies. In the northern colonies, slaves were domestics. The southern colony plantations depended on slaves for labor in the fields of tobacco, indigo and cotton.

Although there is no written record available of the original purchase or possession of slaves by Silas, there is considerable evidence that after his wife died and he remarried it is known that there were slaves taking care of the younger Webb children and his son, Jesse. Slaves definitely helped Silas with his social status and lifestyle. They also contributed to his further economic success as a merchant and shipowner. Deane is known to have owned, or shared ownership in about 12 ships during the mid–1760s. Although he never captained his ships (it seems he always had a very weak stomach), he often went on a quick voyage as supercargo to and from the West Indies to trade particular goods personally. Being involved in trade, Silas was well aware of the slave trade, but no evidence appears that he participated. He did, however, go along with 18th century Connecticut society's elite concerning the issue of slavery. Slaves were a mark of status, and Silas did own slaves, a subject he seldom made any comments about.

The years immediately before and after Mehitabel's death were hard and fast learning experiences for the young lawyer/merchant. Coping with the Navigational Acts took a lot of planning, and considerable risk if caught and prosecuted. But the 1765 Stamp Act was a lot more than just an annoying situation; it could bring many commercial activities to a standstill let alone bringing the political affairs to a boil. Finally, the Townsend Act of 1767 placed duties on paper, tea, lead and paint imported to the colonies, which would make smuggling even more complicated and dangerous for the sea cap-

II. Lawyer, Merchant, Politician, 1761–1775

The old Wethersfield Cove Warehouse utilized by Silas Deane illustrates the interaction of farmers, merchants, and shipmasters in the maritime trade that gave Wethersfield prosperity for over two hundred years. The lone remaining building (left, photograph by author) is one of six original warehouses in the cove which were destroyed by Connecticut River floods. The warehouse's history is symbolic of the area's role in the 18th century trade with the West Indies. The drawing (right) is artist William J. McKee's conception of how the Wethersfield area population utilized the cove's warehouses — for example, they were built on high ground in order to avoid destruction from the famous Connecticut River's spring floods. The drawing is part of a much larger rendering of the original six warehouses and was used in the 1991 Wethersfield Town Report and Calendar (drawing courtesy Town of Wethersfield, Connecticut).

tains/merchants. England was putting the screws to the American colonies to make sure they helped pay the cost of the French and Indian War and for the protection the colonies supposedly enjoyed.

As time moved forward, Silas's slow burn over England's oppression grew to a full flame. All these acts were curtailing his personal freedoms. Plus, he was getting unspoken pressure from his own community. In puritanical New England colonial times, widowers who did not remarry in a reasonable amount of time were looked at with a jaundiced eye. In fact, single, eligible men were so distrusted in many New England towns that they even had to pay a special bachelor tax. Silas decided to listen to his brother Barnabus, who was starting his own trading business. He was doing business with the Saltonstall family of Norwich, Connecticut, close to the Deane family's hometown of New London/Groton. Gordon Saltonstall was a successful and wealthy shipowner, owning several in fact. He also had a daughter who had lost her husband at sea. Silas was introduced to the widow by his brother, and in 1770, Elizabeth Saltonstall Erard and Silas were married. The Saltonstalls were not only wealthy, but were also a very influential Connecticut-wide political family extending into Massachusetts. Elizabeth's grandfather Gordon Saltonstall, Sr.,

Left, top: This portrait of Elizabeth Saltonstall (Evard) Deane was painted and signed by English artist Joseph Blackburn circa 1762 when several members of the Saltonstall family of New London, Connecticut, commissioned Blackburn to paint their portraits. Elizabeth's portrait shows the dedication of the times to the aristocratic society's ideal. She became Silas Deane's second wife in 1770. *Bottom:* Figure X. Portrait of Silas Deane, circa January 1776 and attributed to Charles Willson Peale, both of whom were in Philadelphia at that time (courtesy Connecticut Historical Society).

was a former governor of Connecticut. The family now opened Silas to an even wider world of politics and influence. Silas's new wife was also accustomed to having servants. She brought to their marriage at least two African slaves. Their names were Pompey and Hagar. It is assumed that Hagar helped Elizabeth raise her stepchildren and carry out domestic tasks in the house while Pompey took care of the family animals, gardens and general grounds. Sleeping quarters for the two were over the kitchen. Thus, Pompey and Hagar became part of the Wethersfield statistics of the 1770s where one of every 20 residents in town was a person of color — some slaves, some not. White domestics were less than half that number.

In spite of British attempts to control their activities in favor of the empire, the decade before the Lexington and Concord alarm of 1775 was the era of the merchant entrepreneurs who were, for the most part, involved in coastal, West Indies and foreign smuggling trade.

By the 1770s, Boston, New York and Philadelphia were major world

II. Lawyer, Merchant, Politician, 1761–1775

trading centers. Merchants were determined to carry on their legal and illegal import-export activities. They were insuring or financing various trading functions with an occasional participation in western land speculation. During all of these activities, merchants were quietly learning and accumulating knowledge and experience concerning British business practices in management and accounting techniques.

Meanwhile, the British government was making sure that any kind of mass manufacturing in the colonies was illegal, unless carried out only for England. In the colonies, manufacturing of goods was limited to a rudimentary fashion in farmhouses, household industries, yards, shops or furnaces. On the other hand, shipbuilding became one of the most important industries exported to England from the colonies. In colonial America, and especially in Connecticut, the related iron production industry was exporting over 15 percent of the entire world's output, some of it legal and some not so legal. In Connecticut, the Salisbury Iron Works were doing a brisk business with its own local shipbuilding connections.[1]

In the 1700s, Connecticut had two capitals, on alternating years, one in Hartford and the other in New Haven. It was during that strong trading period that we first see evidence of a friendship between the infamous and famous Benedict Arnold and Silas Deane, although they had been relative boyhood neighbors.

Both men were successful merchants by 1765 and were advertising their goods in the *Connecticut Courant* (now the *Hartford Courant*) and the *Connecticut Gazette*. Silas was advertising choice brandy, which he would sell by the hogshead, barrel or keg. He also had hemp at 20 shillings a bushel.[2] Arnold was advertising genteel horses, barrels of pork, bales of hay and bags of oats. At 24 years of age, Benedict had three ships and an apothecary shop. These two men had specific ships sailing to St. Kitts, Martinique and Honduras, trading livestock, lumber and several other goods for Spanish gold specie or cargoes of salt and cotton, both of which were in short supply in Connecticut.

Silas and Arnold did their business with each other personally. When Silas was in New Haven on political business they met at Arnold's home. The key trading item, however, that Connecticut merchants needed most was hard, cold specie from any country. Great Britain was now making the colonies pay their bills only in specie. It would not accept any colonial printed money. Little is known about just how the colonial merchants did personal business during that decade before the revolution, but according to the Colonial Office records in London, every Connecticut and Rhode Island merchant was considered a smuggler. For any merchant to keep accurate records was simply self-destructive. To not engage, to some degree, in smuggling was all but impossible if a merchant's business was going to survive. Smuggling became a necessity not only for regular merchants, but also for shipowners/captains, farmers, and virtually anyone doing business in colonial America.

The year 1765 was when Silas, now seven years out of college, was truly baptized into the real-world difficulties of carrying on a career as a merchant trader under the continuing business impressments of the English government. The Stamp Act set off a chain of events for the fading lawyer turned merchant. Although Silas was not in town when the resignation of the Stamp Tax agent Jared Ingersoll took place under the famous Wethersfield elm, forced onto Ingersoll by the newly formed Connecticut Sons of Liberty, merchant Deane was quick to be aware of the political potential of their group in the resistance movement against the English crown. Actually, the passage of the Stamp Act led directly to the creation of America's first intelligence service. The Sons of Liberty, sometimes known as the Liberty Boys, sprang up throughout the colonies. They were a federation of dissident political groups known to employ a variety of tactics, most of which were rather violent. The Connecticut New Haven Sons of Liberty quickly fell under the leadership of Silas's friend Benedict Arnold. With the cooperation their New York counterparts, they set up a sophisticated military resistance movement in the event that England might attempt to enforce the Stamp Act with British troops. By the late 1760s, the organization became, in fact, a shadow government that not only kept Tories under control but also helped organize the Whig Party of the Connecticut assembly, procure arms, train farmers and tradesmen in the military arts, and basically prepare for an eventual armed conflict, which, of course, led to all kinds of intrigue and espionage.

In early 1768, as Silas began to give increasingly more time to Connecticut politics, he brought his brother Barnabus into his Wethersfield-based trading business and operation. Barnabus had made several trips to the West Indies as supercargo and was now master of his own vessel. He was already trading with Silas's father-in-law, Gordon Saltonstall, and two close lifelong Yale friends, Thomas Mumford of New London and Jeremiah Wadsworth, later of Hartford. Wadsworth was doing Silas the favor of introducing Silas's favorite stepson, Samuel Blanchley Webb, into the West Indies trade to follow in his own father's footsteps.

Like most other New England merchants, Silas highly resented the 1767 Townsend Acts, especially the Duty Act, which forced duties on importation of all kinds of essential goods. The following year, Silas was one of the leading Connecticut merchants who made a compact with Massachusetts and New York merchants to unite in stopping importations of general goods from England in retaliation for the Duty Act. As a result of his action, in 1769 he was appointed by the town to work with other Connecticut towns to enforce

II. Lawyer, Merchant, Politician, 1761–1775

The Silas Deane House in Wethersfield, Connecticut, was completed in 1766. Architecturally it is very unusual for its time and location. It has been said to be a hundred years ahead of other New England architectural styles up and down the Connecticut River Valley. It is thought that because of his knowledge from many trips to North Atlantic seaports Deane probably designed the entire house himself as a showplace to impress the Wethersfield society elite. Instead of the typical Georgian/Federal central hall with the four-over-four window arrangement, it has an off-center split up and down front Dutch-style doorway with a wide entrance hall beyond, giving a feeling of great spaciousness. Although no longer part of the house, there was a wide veranda-type front porch running the width of the building when it was built. The house is now part of the Webb-Deane-Stevens Museum (photograph by Charles Lyle; courtesy of the Webb-Deane-Stevens Museum).

the nonimportation agreement. With such resistance throughout the colonies, the act was repealed in April 1770.

As Silas's personal activities widened, his social and political life and contacts grew. By 1770, he had reached a point in his life where, as a man of his prominence and connections, he found it quite difficult to stay clear of the world of politics. Mr. Deane, of course, had no such desire. His life had become far from narrow, whether working in the store or loading his trade vessels in Wethersfield Cove. Merchant Deane was continually corresponding with other merchants up and down the Atlantic seaboard, West Indies, and the European ports of Bilboa and Texel. He also had a steady trade with Ireland. As a merchant he was well known as a protestor and financial contributor

Top: The Deane House front parlor. *Bottom:* The Deane House eating parlor (photographs by Charles Lyle; both courtesy of the Webb-Deane-Stevens Museum).

Top: The Deane House kitchen (photograph by Charles Lyle; courtesy of the Webb-Deane-Stevens Museum). *Bottom:* (two different versions; one a close-up). The Deane House stairway. The three different balustrade turnings on each riser is unique (photograph by Charles Lyle; courtesy of the Webb-Deane-Stevens Museum).

against any trade restriction placed on the colony by England. Consequently, he sought a seat in the Connecticut General Assembly and was elected in October 1772 by his friends and neighbors as a Whig. Silas entered Connecticut politics primarily with a merchant's point of view. It was during the next two years that trade became one of the prime reasons for increased difficulties with England. But once he was a member of the assembly, Silas realized trade restrictions were only part of a much bigger picture of colonial impressment.

In the legislature Silas waded into any colonial problem related to Connecticut's interest. At age 35, his background was well known by his fellow representatives. With his strong leanings toward physical resistance to Britain's controlling policies, he was recognized by Governor Jonathan Trumbull as a key individual to help deal with other royal governors who were of the opposite views and opinions.

In May of 1773, the Connecticut assembly, as a result of urging by the Virginia House of Burgesses and Connecticut's neighboring colony of Massachusetts, voted to establish a standing committee of nine to be appointed called the Committee of Correspondence. The mission of this committee was to obtain intelligence and maintain continuous correspondence with the other colonies. Silas was appointed its secretary and General Israel Putnam its chairman. The two men and the other seven members soon became a zealous cadre. Silas kept up a continuous correspondence with merchants and politicians in at least ten of the thirteen American colonies. Although many of his correspondents had never met him personally, his zeal earned him a reputation as a real firebrand.

Later in 1773, a 15-year-old interest in the Susquehanna Company came to light again. Silas received an appointment as a member of a commission nominated by the Governor's Council "to assist Governor Trumbull, in stating and taking proper steps to pressure the claims of this colony to said western lands."[3] He earned Governor Trumbull's admiration for "collecting and preparing all exhibits and documents necessary to pursue and prosecute the claim and title."[4]

The Committee of Correspondence created a more formal structure for conducting resistance to England's colonial policies. While the Sons of Liberty's membership was usually made up of artisans and tradesmen of towns and cities, the correspondence committees were set up in the countryside as well. This created a parallel rural and urban resistance movement to any British restrictions on colonial freedoms.

While events were taking place during the late 1760s and the mid–1770s, Connecticut Freemasonry lodges were increasing and growing in membership. The colony now had four very active lodges — the Hiram Lodge #1 in New Haven, the Saint Johns Lodge #2 in Middletown, Saint Johns Lodge #3 in

Fairfield; and the Hartford Lodge #4, which later changed its name to Saint Johns #4, F&AM (Free and Accepted Mason). Freemasonry in 18th century Connecticut was attracting men from all walks of life who were intellectually philosophical but who also felt a Masonic lodge was an excellent gathering place for developing social and business contacts.

The ideals of Freemasonry promote brotherhood, unity, family and community. Under Masonic general law, a man must ask to become a Mason and place his name before a specific lodge for acceptance or rejection. Until very recently, under no circumstance could a Mason ever ask another man directly to consider becoming a Mason. It is interesting to note that during that time period the average membership makeup for a lodge by social standing just before the revolution was running 60 percent merchants, 20 percent professionals, 10 percent shipowners and sea captains, and 10 percent artisans and tradesmen.

No Masonic records have ever been found that prove Silas Deane was ever a Freemason. Masonic historians and researchers have not been able to locate any evidence of specific Masonic activity related to lodge rituals or officer positions. Those facts stand to be true. However, the situation of continuing circumstantial relationships concerning Silas's activities, associations, and close friendships with well-known Masons throughout his business and political careers make it almost impossible not to believe that he had to have been a Mason in order to carry out many of the activities with which he is credited. His writings and use of Masonic words and phrases alone indicate that he was at the very least associated with Freemasonry.

Masonic ideals and purpose were always part of Silas's prime interests and goals in his personal and public life. The Masons feature of stressing good manners was of the utmost importance in Deane's early life and is often mentioned in many other sources. The Hartford Lodge kept few records between the years 1769 and 1779 due to the "chaotic uncertainty of the times."[5] In the published history of Saint Johns Lodge #4 (F&AM) there is also a very curious single sentence unrelated to the preceding or succeeding paragraph that states "1761 was the year that Silas Deane moved to Wethersfield."

If Silas was a Freemason he probably joined in late 1772 or early 1773 when his close friend Benedict Arnold was already an actual member of the Hiram Lodge in New Haven and local leader of the Sons of Liberty. Both organizations were sympathetic to outright resistance. It would have been just at that time that Silas was becoming known as a fiery patriot.

Whatever the lack of written evidence, Silas was accepted and trusted as a Mason by many known American and European Masons. In the coming years, Brother Deane would be closely associated with more than two dozen famous revolutionary era Masons, including Franklin and Washington.

There is another very possible reason why no written records of Masonic membership for Deane exist. From 1781 until his death and to the present day, Silas Deane was considered by many to be an outright traitor. Supposedly, in Freemasonry, if a Mason is found to be a traitor by his fellow Masons all evidence of his very Masonic existence is expunged from his lodge and Grand Lodge records. This was done with Benedict Arnold, but not all records were destroyed completely.

Without question, in 1774 Silas Deane was one of the most influential politicians in Connecticut. In response to the Boston Tea Party, Parliament passed a series of measures to punish Massachusetts known as the Coercive or Intolerable Acts. As a result, on May 27, 1774, the Boston Town Meeting called for the immediate economic sanction against all English trade and asked for all colonies to support them.

Several of the colonies immediately agreed, but felt an intercolonial congress should be called to coordinate such actions. On June 3, as secretary of the Connecticut Correspondence Committee, Silas wrote, "Resolves of merchants of any individual town or province is unworkable ... [but a] congress is absolutely necessary previous to almost any other measure, since the injury is general, the mode taken for redress ought to be commensurate, which is not probable to be obtained short of a general conference and union ... the earlier ... the better."[6] Silas also wrote that he thought perhaps New York City would be an appropriate location for a congress, but due to the oppressive summer heat it might be better for such a congress to meet in a country town on the Connecticut coast.

On the very same day that Silas was doing his job as correspondence committee secretary, the Connecticut assembly empowered the committee to "appoint a suitable member to attend such a congress or Convention of Commissioners or Committee to the several Colonies of British America,"[7] the obligation being to consult and advise, for the good of the colonies in general. Connecticut became the first colony to authorize appointment of delegates to such a congress. It was understood the delegates were to periodically send dispatches to Governor Trumbull informing him of the business at hand with personal views and attitudes of other colonies. In return, the governor advised the delegates of his opinion and, sometimes, gave very specific instructions. Eventually, a special colony, and later state, messenger was employed specifically to relay communiqués between the colony and the congressional delegates.

On July 13, of the nine-man Committee of Correspondence, eight met in New London to appoint delegates. The committee then appointed three of its own members — Eliphalet Dyer, Silas Deane and Erantas Wolcott, with William Samuel Johnson and Richard Law as alternates. Within a week, Wolcott, Johnson and Law refused to serve. In the meantime, the committee divided into two basic factions with the young versus the older members, except for General Israel Putnam, the actual chairman. The three young men were the active 37-year-old Silas Deane, Captain Joseph Trumbull, the governor's son, and a very active Mason, Samuel Parsons, both of them close friends of Silas. Because it took three delegates to represent the colony, the committee met again on August 1. In a letter to William Samuel Johnson, another longtime friend, Silas gave an interesting account of the second meeting. Evidently, one of the older members opened the meeting with the demand that if the committee nominated a man from the eastern part of Connecticut then a man from the western section must also be nominated. A vote was taken and the committee split four and four. After several more votes a compromise was reached that two could be nominated but only one should attend. Soon to be famous as a signer of all three founding documents, Roger Sherman and the governor's son Joseph Trumbull were both nominated. As Sherman was nominated first it was left to him to decide whether or not he would attend. Sherman decided to accept.

Deane's letter went on to say he hoped that Johnson would talk Sherman out of the post, thinking that Mr. Sherman probably did not want to be a delegate anyway. Silas did not know Sherman that well; but he knew if Trumbull became the third delegate, the Connecticut delegation would be solid phalanx concerning the acquisitions of western lands for Connecticut through the Susquehanna Company. As it eventually happened, Sherman was an extremely strong proponent of Connecticut's western lands interest. In mid-June, the colonies finally decided a colonial congress should be held in Philadelphia sometime in September.

During that summer Silas was one busy guy. He and Barnabus, anticipating a possible non–export-import agreement by the Continental Congress, pushed their trading business hard to stock up on essential imports not manufactured in the colonies. Facing the possibility of open hostilities with the mother country, Silas made arrangements for gunpowder runs by his friends and relations in New London. Planning with the Governor's Council, Silas identified issues that needed to be addressed in congress that could possibly help Connecticut retain her famous "darling charter" with all its freedoms against a British takeover.

Deane's continual correspondence with other colonies and communities over the previous two years gave him a clearer view than most of his contemporaries concerning just what was the real thinking of others. Avoiding all-out warfare with England was going to be a real challenge. The colonies had already stepped too hard on the lion's tail. Another direct insult could definitely lead to war. In Massachusetts, even Sam Adams had come to the same conclusion; he realized he didn't want to be known as an open radical wanting full independence now. He was beginning to act like Teddy Roosevelt's motto, "Walk softly, but carry a big stick." Silas reinforced the feeling when he wrote Sam saying the colonies had to stand together "in the common cause" before any drastic overt action could take place.

Although it wasn't written down or spoken out loud to any great degree during the First Congress of 1774, most delegates did realize that they probably had only three basic options in the current crisis dealing with King George III and Parliament. One, they could secretly seek outside aid for complete independence regardless of circumstances; two, they could stand firm on an all-out embargo against England; or three, patch up everything with the king for complete reconciliation.

Leaving the Boston area on August 10, the Massachusetts delegation arrived at the Hartford Meeting House on the evening of Saturday, August 13. John Adams already knew Silas from his 1772 visit to the Stafford Springs spa and town of the upper Connecticut River Valley (which he proclaimed a living paradise). While on his tour in Wethersfield, John was a guest at Silas Deane's home where he announced he was entertained most genteelly with punch, wine and coffee.

Sunday the delegation went to church, not once but twice. Between services Silas proudly showed off the Wethersfield "onion" church. John Adams remarked, "We went up the steeple of the Wethersfield Meeting House from whence is the most grand and beautiful prospect in the world, at least, I ever saw."[8]

Sam Adams was more basic in his thoughts. He asked Silas point-blank what would happen to Connecticut's commerce if the congress declared a full embargo of goods to and from England. Silas replied that Connecticut shipped 30,000 bushels of flax to New York for export annually in exchange for salt. The flaxseed could easily be made into linseed oil and sold locally at a profit. He explained that would be just one example of exchange that could be made, but the livestock trade with the West Indies and Central America being cut off would be an individual economic disaster.

Before the Massachusetts delegation continued their journey, Silas gave them a briefing on the New Yorkers they would soon meet. He told them who the lawyers were, who the merchants were, and which individuals were the most popular.

Sam Adams' question about Connecticut commerce prompted Silas to obtain more specific information on the colony's trading business. Immediately, on Tuesday, August 16, Silas wrote to Governor Trumbull asking for a general statement of Connecticut's import and export accounts to take with him to Philadelphia. Concerned about the protection of the colony's coastal towns from possible British naval attacks, Delegate Deane also asked the governor for an accounting of the number and size of the colony's ships to offer protection and harassment from privateers.

Ending his letter, Silas informed the governor that he would be leaving for the Continental Congress on the following Monday, August 22. He said he would pick up Dyer and Sherman on the way.

CHAPTER III

Continental Congress Connecticut Delegate, 1774–1775

On Monday, August 22, 1774, Silas did indeed set out for Philadelphia in his status symbol gilded carriage. Entertaining the Massachusetts delegates had slowed down his departure. But after receiving the data and statistics he had requested from the governor he was on his way.

The Connecticut delegate from Wethersfield was a man halfway through his 37th year, well known, with a wide acquaintance among men throughout the colonies. Squire Deane was recognized as a successful merchant entrepreneur with tremendous energy. He was of medium height (5' 8") with a pleasant appearance and exquisite taste in clothing. Silas was well-mannered, living in the style of a gentleman of his well-earned social status. Being highly educated he was intellectually active, with a wide and varied range of interests, especially in world history. On any subject his opinions were known for their clarity, forcefulness, frankness and honesty. However, now at the prime of his life, he did have the reputation of talking and writing to excess.

The Connecticut delegates to the First Continental Congress of 1774 were the most talented men the colony could offer. They would become known for their unity of purpose with respect to commerce, currency, and western lands. Perseverance made up for what they lacked in colony power. The personal agendas closely corresponded to the concerns of the colony. As Governor Trumbull often observed, "The art of government is to render individual and public good inseparable, and to lead men thro' their own interests to advance the interests of their colony."[1] In Congress, Silas Deane would become Connecticut's leading and influential delegate through January 1776, when he was forced to give up his seat.

But the day he left in 1774 was not only a great day for Connecticut but also for Wethersfield. A crowd of townspeople, neighbors, friends and fellow assemblymen turned out to see Silas off to Congress. Also, a large number of socially prominent men, most of whom were Sons of Liberty, escorted Delegate Deane as far as Middletown (Portland) some 12 miles down the Connecticut River. Silas was accompanied to Philadelphia by his favorite stepson, Samuel B. Webb. They continued on to New Haven where Silas had arranged to pick up Judge Sherman.

Approaching New Haven they were met with bells ringing and crowds of people in the streets or peering from windows as they rode by. Silas was openly pleased that the people of New Haven had felt Connecticut made a good choice of delegates to attend Congress. His long-time friend Benedict Arnold was so grateful he decided to accompany his friend to Philadelphia as New Haven's local leader of the Sons of Liberty.

The next day, the entourage proceeded to Fairfield where Silas had agreed to meet and pick up Colonel Eliphalet Dyer. The trio and company crossed over the Connecticut boundary on August 24 and arrived in New York City, where they met the Massachusetts delegates and two from South Carolina. Silas personally sought out other men of considerable reputation in the city, especially those involved in trade. In New York Silas made it a definite point to learn how individuals really felt about current situations with Great Britain. He found that their men were very fond of, and admired, the colony of Connecticut for its "charter freedoms" and its stand on the Navigations Acts.

On their way, Silas was constantly irritated by Roger Sherman's personality. In a letter to his wife while they were in New York, Silas explained that "Mr. Sherman is clever in private, but I will only say he is as badly calculated to appear in such a Congress as a chestnut burr is for an eye stone."[2] (This statement almost defies 21st century translation, but many historians have considered it quite insulting.) Silas also reported that "he occasioned some screwed countenance among the company, and not a few oaths, by the odd questions he asked, and the very odd and countrified cadence with which he speaks; but he was, and did, as well as I expected."[3]

While in New York, Silas and Colonel Dyer bought some clothes but were both dissatisfied when they found them not of very good quality. In the same letter about his clothes, Silas stated something to his wife that would definitely be a hard fact of the delegates' congressional relationships with a few short months. He wrote Elizabeth that "the more I converse in the City, the more I see and lament the virulence of party."[4]

Getting ready to leave New York on Monday morning, August 29, the hair on the back of Silas's neck was still straight up. On Sunday evening he wrote to his wife: "Mr. Sherman (would to Heaven he were well back at New Haven) is against our sending our carriages over the ferry this evening."[5] The next day, Silas wrote, "As I expected, our delay, or rather superstitious neglect of getting over our Carriages the preceding evening, brought us under the mercy of the ferryman, who kept us until after ten that excessive hot day and then part of us ... assisted in rowing over, as it was calm."[6] It is left to the reader's imagination when Deane was asked to row.

Monday night the Connecticut delegates stayed at Elizabeth Town. The lodgings were tolerable and the group was on its way at four o'clock the next morning. Silas was still suffering from dysentery that had plagued him from the time he left Wethersfield. They passed through Prince Town, which impressed no one, and ended their day in Trent Town where Mr. Deane had one rough time with his dysentery. He told his wife, "The night and bed were worse to me than to have proceeded on my journey. I turned and groaned while Judge Sherman, who lodged in the same chamber, snored in concert."[7]

Nevertheless, the delegation continued on its way the next morning, passing through Bristol only 17 miles from Philadelphia. In the extreme heat of that day they stopped at a tavern just six miles from Philadelphia. Silas was in misery and immediately swilled down six bottles of cider, which, according to Colonel Dyer, didn't help his "ailment" much.

At five o'clock the next morning (Wednesday) the Connecticut delegates and their "company," set out for Philadelphia while it was still cool. They drove up to Biddle's Tavern where Colonel Dyer and Samuel Johnson had previously made reservations. Silas grabbed a quick cup ("plate") of coffee and went off to a prearranged meeting with a Mr. Galloway and a Dr. Smith. When Silas returned, he took the bed reserved for Samuel Johnson, who had refused to be a delegate. Mr. Gadsen and his son, from South Carolina; Samuel Webb, Silas's stepson; Dyer, Benedict Arnold and Silas were now all lodged in the same building.

Writing home on Thursday, Silas told Elizabeth that his brother Barnabus had arrived in Philadelphia on business. He wrote that the Connecticut men spent their time visiting other delegates who had arrived. He said he was particularly impressed with the men from the Jerseys and South Carolina, as well as the men from Virginia, Maryland, New York, and what was called the lower counties. That evening about 30 of the delegates present gathered at a coffeehouse and talked over some preliminaries, but they agreed to wait for other men to arrive, at least until the next Monday.

By Friday, Silas's close friend Captain Jeremiah Wadsworth arrived. Silas was impressed with all the new arrivals. On Saturday, he continued his exploration of the city, with which he was not overly enraptured. Interesting enough was the fact that the always socially status-minded Mr. Deane "went this day to a noted coach maker and viewed his work, and asked his prices. A sulky 34 pounds, without a top; a full-back carriage like mine, fitted with one horse, 60 pounds; and he asked me five pounds to new paint and gild like mine, for which reason I shall bring it back in status quo, as my money will hardly hold out at such a rate."[8] In the same letter, Silas made note that his father-in-law, Gordon Saltonstall, and stepson John Webb had arrived. He wrote, "I inform my friends that we are in high spirits, if it is possible to be really so when the eyes of millions are upon us, and who consider themselves and their posterity interested in our conduct."[9]

Sunday morning the Connecticut group took a pleasant ride about six miles outside Philadelphia to the falls of the Schuylkill River which they found to be exceedingly beautiful. To their surprise, they met several other delegates there, including George Washington and John Jay.

Later in the day on Sunday, September 4, the remainder of the New York delegates arrived. They immediately met with the Connecticut delegates and the Sons of Liberty from other colonies. The meeting was held to deal with a very irritating problem. They wanted to decide what to do about the most widely read and influential Tory newspaper in America, James Rivington's weekly, the *New York Gazette of New York City*.

Isaac Sears, New York's toughest radical, hated James Rivington. In his paper in 1773, Rivington had called Sears "a tool of the lowest order," a political crackpot and laughingstock of the town. Sears had promised himself that the first chance he got he would "scatter Rivington's type and wreck his office."

The "Sons" and delegates realized that something had to be done and soon, before Rivington's paper grew even stronger in its influence on the populace. The group decided on a Connecticut-based expedition on the paper. After the meeting, Silas wrote to Elizabeth to pass the word on to his stepson Joseph Webb, who was Wethersfield's local Sons of Liberty leader. His stepfather wrote that a group of gentlemen at Philadelphia agreed that Rivington's paper had to be stopped, that subscriptions of money were being taken to promote a raid from Connecticut and Joseph should "put it forward."[10] Nevertheless, Rivington's *Gazette* blasted the Continental Congress all during its 1774 sessions. Finally, in November 1775, Sears, one victim of many, got his revenge when the paper's office was destroyed in a raid of some 150 Connecticut Sons of Liberty.

On one of the shorter sightseeing junkets that September weekend, the Connecticut delegates visited the Jersey-covered market on High Street. Silas was not overly impressed since the produce also varied and was not of the quality he was used to in the Wethersfield/Hartford area. But when Doctor William Shippen invited the Connecticut men to visit the Pennsylvania Hospital and the insane asylum in the basement of the hospital, Silas was very interested to see a modern facility. He was even more impressed when the doctor showed them the latest anatomical drawings from, and researched in, London. The future world was fascinating to Silas, regardless of the topic.

In the next few days, Silas was accompanied by his friend Arnold to a whole series of political-type caucuses. Much of the advised planning of the First Congress was also done over an endless round of dinners, luncheons, and coffee and teas in that first week before the formal opening of Congress. The leading Philadelphia elite fell over themselves to play host to the delegates, for obvious reasons.

Then on Monday, September 5, forty-eight of the delegates gathered at the now famous City Tavern. The division between conservatives and radicals was quickly apparent. The split was immediately defined over the routine question as to where to convene. The state house (now Independence Hall) was offered by the Pennsylvania speaker, Joseph Galloway, but the radicals, led by Sam Adams, pushed for Carpenter's Hall as their choice. The hall was also very agreeable to the mechanics and citizenry in general. It had a library on the second floor available for pleasant retreats and research. It was situated well back from the street and had a circular garden. The trees allowed for private conversations and exercise. Its "perfect" location resulted in Carpenter's Hall winning the vote, which gave the radicals their first victory. Silas wrote, "It was downright mortifying to the last degree to Pennsylvania elite who in turn tried to boycott the opening of Congress."[11]

The next order of business was the need to appoint a recording secretary. Within a couple of hours of the start of Congress, Silas's name was at the top of the possible candidate list. His name was well known by most delegates for his fiery writings as secretary of the Connecticut Committee of Correspondence. The question that became a matter of dispute was whether the delegates should choose a secretary from within their membership or from outside it. The conservatives put up the name of Silas Deane, knowing his popularity with the radicals. The radicals, however, put up the name of Charles Thompson, known as the "Sam Adams" of Philadelphia. Silas quietly made it clear, and in the right places, that he didn't really want the job and the radials had their second victory. Charles Thompson was called back from his honeymoon to take on his duties as congressional secretary, a position he would hold through the darkest days of the Revolution.

Silas knew only too well that a secretarial position allowed for a wide interpretation of events and situations that could come back and bite you at a later date. He wrote to his wife that he doubted the wisdom of having one of their own as secretary. He explained that if he had opposed Charles Thompson, in all likelihood he would have been elected secretary. Even though the division of thought among delegates remained very clear, the unopposed nomination of Peyton Randolph as chairman of the Congress was a hopeful sign of outward unity. The delegates decided to call him president.

The next issue that had to be settled before the delegates could carry out business was the weight of each colony when it came time to vote. Should it be by colony population or a more equal method of one vote for each colony? Connecticut was the swing vote on the question. All of its delegates couldn't have been more vehemently together in insisting on one vote for each colony with a majority rule.

Patrick Henry helped the Connecticut delegates stand when he told the delegation that he was strong for the weight of population when voting, but if he was overruled he was willing to submit to the majority. He said he wanted the delegates to realize they were no longer just New Yorkers, New Englanders or Pennsylvanians. They were Americans. The Congress did agree to one colony, one vote, but that decision was not to be irreversible.

Then a unique issue arose when Thomas Cushing, of Massachusetts, moved that each session be opened with a prayer. John Jay of New York and Edward Biddle of Pennsylvania (the tavern keeper in Philadelphia) quickly opposed the idea. The delegates came from so many faiths — Episcopalian, Anabaptist, Presbyterian, Congregationalist, and Quaker — there was no way could they worship together. After a few minutes of comment and confusion, Sam Adams stood up and stunned the body of delegates. Sam announced he was no bigot and could hear a prayer from any virtuous man from any sect. He went on to say that although he was a stranger to the city he had heard (from Silas) a Mr. Duché was such a man and moved that Duché read a prayer to Congress the next day. Because Sam was so widely known by the New Englanders, and by his radical reputation throughout the colonies, Reverend Duché, on the morning of September 6, gave an opening prayer. Silas told his spouse the praying was worth a ride of 100 miles to hear and that even the Quakers shed tears.[12]

The following morning, Silas again wrote his wife a disturbing description: "The city is in the utmost confusion, all the bells toll muffled and the most unfeigned mark of sorrow appear in every countenance."[13] General Israel Putnam had ridden into the city with the rumor that the British had shelled and burned Boston. The story was proven false on Wednesday when it was learned that the British soldiers had only seized stores of gunpowder at Medford, Massachusetts.

The real division among the delegates at the First Congress was actually how to deal with the king and Parliament. Should they write grievance petitions alone or make a plan of action to back up the petitions? Throughout the entire session delegates differed on three basic areas of approach. The first basic issue was the theoretical grounds for resistance. Second was the question of whether should there should be trade restrictions set up against England by the colonies. Third, was what to do about the Suffolk Resolves from Massachusetts that Sam Adams had James Otis write and drop in Congress's lap.

As the congressional session and committee groups got underway, the delegates approved several procedures they would follow. For Silas, from the very first days in Philadelphia, he did what mattered most in his trading world of business: he got to know with whom he was dealing and the possible agendas involved. Today we would call it profiling. Silas was a man who took a direct interest in every delegate, putting a name to every face. Who was he, where was he from, what was his character and background, and, for influential reasons, what was his occupation, wealth and social status? Both Silas and fellow New Englander John Adams kept detailed notes on the actions of every delegate during various sessions. The Connecticut merchant wrote home to his wife detailed descriptions of many delegates. He often gave particular attention to those delegates known to be Freemasons. A select few included Captain Edward Biddle, John Dickinson, Peyton Randolph and George Washington. Sometimes it would seem Silas had visions of the future for these men.

Most delegates were, or had been, legislators in their own colonies. All except possibly Sam Adams — although two of his biographer agree that many stories about Sam were purely hearsay legends — were moderately to extremely wealthy. Washington was a prime example. He owned 8,000 acres of tobacco and wheat, over 100 slaves, a lumber business and title to 60,000 acres of western lands in Virginia and the Ohio River Valley area. Thirty delegates were known to hold a law degree or to practice law or both. Fifteen members were businessmen or trading merchants. Silas, of course, was in the first two groups of delegates. Twelve members fell in the agrarian group, five being southern planters and six northern farmers. Six delegates were also doctors or clerics.[14]

Neither Silas nor the quill pen-addicted John Adams ever completed their profiling of the delegates of the First Continental Congress of 1774. Although they both kept copious notes on specific members during daily debate sessions, their observations often did not agree or match up. But they did give deeper insight into the agendas of several of the leading delegates. Their profiling served two major purposes. It gave history a firsthand, detailed account of sessions, rather than just dry motions from the sessions recorded by the secretary. Best of all, this information made it easier for these men to plan their own future strategies concerning their respective viewpoints. They had, as a result, a much deeper insight than most as to why the Congress as a body behaved in a particular fashion on specific issues.

As Congress plodded along, the oppressive Philadelphia September heat caused considerable irritability and discomfort among the delegates. They had trouble concentrating on the work before them. Delegates from the northern colonies were throwing off their coats and pushing up their ruffled, cuffed sleeves. Some delegates took off their wigs, revealing a lot of shaved heads. However, most southern delegates remained relatively comfortable in their light silk coats and breeches. Pleas were made to move someplace further north. Delegate Lynch of South Carolina even went so far as to ask Silas to book him reservations in Hartford, Connecticut. Fearing the middle colonies would become more involved with Massachusetts and Connecticut's affairs, the conservative faction vehemently squelched the idea of any move northward.

Congress early decided on meeting in secret sessions and committees, thereby hoping to hide their division from both the American public and England. At first they met six days a week, from 10:00 A.M. to around 4:00 P.M., and then again around 7:00 P.M. to 9:00 P.M. The evening hours after 9:00 P.M. became an informal round of feasting and drinking in various private homes and taverns. Each location had its own clientele. Freemasons met at the Indian King on Market Street. First and Market streets were favorite locations for merchants and sea captains, while the new and larger City Tavern became the gathering place for the delegates when they first became aware of each other's identity. Silas first met George Washington at the City Tavern. At this location delegates felt they could speak more freely and directly to each other about possible strategies and the negotiation of compromises. The late night gatherings were also known for their lavish rich food, including jellies, sweetmeats, truffles, creams, cheeses, almonds and raisins drunk with a strong punch or a rich red wine. It's interesting to note that Silas and other New Englanders complained of the inferior quality of the cider compared to that back home.

Without much of a surprise to anyone, the radical Sam Adams and conservative Joseph Galloway emerged as the leaders of the two major factions in the 1774 Congress. The situation between Sam Adams and Joseph Galloway in 1774 turned into a desperate struggle to control all congressional actions. Adams wanted a tough embargo and stand against England, even if it meant war. As a basic result of this position a close partnership between Adams of New England and the powerful Lee family of Virginia developed. It became known as the Adams/Lee Junto, which literally controlled Congress over the next five years until Silas, in December 1778, blew the whistle on them publicly in the *Pennsylvania Gazette* as a result of his congressional recall.

Sam Adams was a tough throwback Puritan to Boston's very early days. He was profoundly religious and would have liked to have seen the Massachusetts colony returned to the cheerless, Bible-oriented, stern world of

Puritanism. Sam liked to work behind the scenes. Like a kid in a classroom, he made the spitballs but had some other kid throw them. In the congressional case, it became the Lee brothers stepping out front. Adams didn't care about getting credit for anything, but he wanted the power to make things go his way.

The very first fundamental issue the delegates had to agree upon was what rights the American citizen truly had and from what source. Joseph Galloway, leading the conservative faction, declared they intended to define American rights and petition the king for a solid constitutional union between the American colonies and England.

More than three months earlier, the trio of radical delegates from Connecticut, in their general assembly, had backed a declaration of allegiance to the king; but they also recognized that the rights of Englishmen were theirs by natural law, which included freedom from taxation — except by England. Unfortunately, the final draft of the Declaration of Rights that was passed by Congress fell far short of the Connecticut delegates' position. But Sam Adams, Silas Deane, Dyer and Sherman were willing to wait until the other colonies caught up with reality. As it stood, the Declaration was by no means a weak document. It still claimed all traditional rights of Englishmen, including life, liberty and property, plus freedom from standing armies or arbitrary proclamations.

Things had plodded along for some, but moved too fast for others. Sam and the New Englanders kept the pressure on. Suddenly, from the county of Suffolk, in Massachusetts, came a set of resolves delivered to Congress by Paul Revere, written by Sam Adams' close friend, Dr. Joseph Warren. The rhetoric in the Suffolk Resolves absolutely disgusted the conservatives. To them, the real danger in the resolves was the total ignoring of the Intolerable Acts, reorganizing all militia, purging all officers holding commissions from British governors and immediately disregarding all compromises made with England. Regardless of these difficulties, the congressional majority did eventually support the resolves.

The radicals wanted, and finally got, a total boycott and the following dates were set: December 1 for nonimportation; March 15, 1775 for nonconsumption; and September 10, 1775, for nonexportation. To make sure the boycott was enforced, the Continental Association, as it was called, required that a committee be set up in every county, city and town in the American colonies. Silas personally promised Sam Adams that Connecticut would "pay the most sacred regard to the resolutions of the Congress."[15] Despite the Tory county of Fairfield, and the temptation to trade with Long Island, Connecticut did make a strenuous effort to abide by the association's resolutions, and did so as well as, if not better than, most colonies. Fortunately for Connecticut, it did not normally trade directly with England to any great extent, but rather through New York, Newport or Boston, making the boycott easy to follow without much suffering, a fact that Silas had earlier told Sam on the way to Congress.

In his diary, notes and letters home, Silas made many shrewd and biting observations and remarks about many of his fellow delegates' abilities and work. Silas often used the phrase "seems confused" when he was not particularly impressed with an individual's comments. He watched with a merchant's trained eye the practical side of situations and let the recognized leader handle the questions as to why. Silas, like Sam Adams, had earlier come to grips with the fact that, all things considered, sooner or later the colonies were going to war with England unless she totally gave in to independence.

Silas wrote home after only a few weeks of sessions that "business is slow from the vast extent and lasting importance of the questions."[16] During those long arduous days, the Connecticut delegates' unity of purpose and interest, new knowledge, and awareness characterized their actions. They kept their personal antagonisms (and there were quite a few among the trio) at a bare minimum for the sake of their colony and America's future.

Just as Congress was considering adjournment, Joseph Galloway objected strongly to the nonimportation agreements and announced a plan of his own. His proposal called for an "American Grand Council" that would represent all colonies. The British Parliament would be a check on its regulations and laws. The king would support a general leader, who was to be called "Resident General."[17] Sam Adams and the New England delegates blew a gasket. After all New England had been through they were not about to go home as second-class citizens.

By this time, Sam was no longer a "stranger in Philadelphia." He, along with "other radicals," delegates (unnamed), put the word out on the street that Galloway was selling out the colonists' liberties. Fearing a physical attack by an angry mob, Galloway called for a vote. His proposal failed, but only by one vote. The rejection meant Joseph Galloway's swan song as the conservative leader. Actually, the plan failed more because it addressed the British-American issues only on constitutional grounds. But by mid–October, the delegates were much more concerned and involved with economic, as well as some social and religious, issues. An example of the latter is that Sam Adams wanted no dancing or drinking to be allowed in the colonies.

With all the individual new experiences and knowledge occurring from so many sessions, the delegates did finally accomplish three major hurdles toward becoming a unified force. They accepted the Suffolk Resolves, created the Congressional Association of Trade and produced a Declaration of Colonial Rights and Grievances. All fourteen individual articles pertaining to these resolutions were signed by 53 delegates on October 20, 1774.

As the Congress got ready to close, it wanted to leave the king and Parliament some wiggle room, but reconciliation would definitely have to be on the colonists' terms. At the same time, it wanted to avoid the appearance of hardball provocation. The delegates felt if war came, it would be necessary that the American public believe the British were solely responsible. Upon adjourning, the majority of the delegates truly believed they had left the door open for reconciliation.

The First Continental Congress formally adjourned on October 26, 1774, but not before they voted a Second Continental Congress to convene in Philadelphia on May 10, 1775. Connecticut's congressional delegates returned to their colony and immediately went right back to the work in Connecticut's general assembly. Being one up on the other members of the assembly, the trio pushed hard and long for the Boy Scout motto: "BE PREPARED."

Many Connecticut Yankee military officers had been trained by the British in the French and Indian War. Governor Trumbull and the New Light majority in the assembly mobilized these men that were true patriots into top command positions within the Connecticut militia and ousted Tory sympathizers.

During the 1750s and 1760s, Connecticut endured the French and their Indian allies swooping down from Canada and attacking New England towns, cutting them off from the middle and southern colonies. The governor and the assembly were sure the British would now do the same if hostilities broke out. Silas was so certain he even published, along with the editor, such a statement in the *Connecticut Courant*.[18]

In December of 1774, the general assembly concentrated on being militarily ready for the worst. It ordered ships to be dispatched by leading merchants, including assemblyman Deane, to the West Indies to purchase weapons and gunpowder. Also during December, the assembly commissioned two independent military companies and then added four more in March of 1775.

In New Haven, Silas's friend from childhood Freemason Benedict Arnold organized a group of 65 "gentlemen of influence and high responsibility."[19] They petitioned the general assembly to be known as the Governor's Second Company of Foot. The company was granted a charter in March, with Benedict Arnold being made its captain. All militia were then ordered by the assembly to train for 12 days before May 1.

Patrick Henry once asked Roger Sherman why Connecticut Yankees were so much more ardent in the cause of their liberties than others. Sherman replied, "Connecticut had more to lose — its precious charter."[20] The charter had given Connecticut virtual autonomy for more than a century and represented a tradition of self-government stronger than any sister colony. Connecticut did not intend to lose it.[21]

CHAPTER IV

Leading Connecticut Congressional Delegate, 1775

On the morning of the April 19, 1775, in Watertown, Massachusetts, Colonel Joseph Palmer of the Massachusetts Committee of Safety received the first reports of fighting in Lexington and Concord. Palmer immediately called for Israel Bissel, a professional express rider from East Windsor, Connecticut. He ordered Bissel to give the alarm down his regular Boston Post Road route and on to New York and Philadelphia.[1]

By 3:00 P.M. that same day, Bissel reached Pomfret, Connecticut, where he found the chairman of the Connecticut Committee of Correspondence, General Israel Putnam. Putnam immediately issued an order calling out the militia. Then, on horseback, Putnam hurried to Cambridge for verification. He did not want the same mistake of the rumor he carried to Congress the previous September.

On the following morning of April 20, Silas, as secretary of the Connecticut Committee of Correspondence, was the first to receive Putnam's message from Bissel. Silas quickly copied the message and sent Bissel on his way. Like Putnam, the energetic secretary had trouble believing what he had just received and copied. He, too, remembered what had happened after the false alarm reached Congress and Philadelphia in 1774.

Silas wrote in his diary that he had dinner first and then went to Hartford for a meeting with the members of the Correspondence Committee where he presented a copy of Putnam's message. The committee had the same doubts as Silas and decided to take no immediate action until further verification. The next morning around 10:00 A.M. Silas's brother Barnabus was able to verify the news from a second express rider.

April 21 was a day of cautious acceptance of the fact of real hostilities that were leading to war. Men were drummed to arms and provisions were gathered. As the hours passed and word spread throughout the colony, militia units from all over Connecticut began to arrive in Hartford. They came to the capital to receive their orders.

By noon of the 21st, Bissel was in New Haven. Benedict Arnold, hearing the news, did not hesitate to take action. He called out the Foot Guard and any volunteers that wished to join them on a march to Boston. The next morning after a little difficulty with the town fathers over the releasing of a gunpowder supply, Arnold, with the scarlet-coated Foot Guard, Yale students and Sons of Liberty, set out for Hartford to receive orders and additional supplies.

Arnold had just left Hartford on the 23rd when he met Colonel Samuel Parsons — of the New London militia — who was a member of the general assembly and another close friend of Silas. Parsons and his men had answered the alarm and had seen the conditions around Boston. They told Arnold the patriots were in desperate need of supplies. The makeshift army was going to need quantities of food, blankets, and ammunitions. Most of all, they were going to need cannon if they hoped to keep General Gage bottled up in Boston.

In his trading business over the previous 12 or so years, Arnold had traded extensively over colonial North America. He had seen the deterioration of British forts after the French and Indian War. Arnold told Parsons there were two forts in particular, located at the southern tip of Lake Champlain — Fort Ticonderoga and Crown Point — that as well as he could remember contained over 100 cannon, if not more. Only 50 or so old soldiers had been left to guard them. The forts certainly could be easily captured.

Returning to Hartford on the 27th, Colonel Parsons could not help thinking about what Arnold had told him and the great need for cannon and the immediate ability to eliminate the possibility of a British rear door attack on New England out of Canada. An even more immediate concern for Connecticut was the vulnerability of its coastline to British naval bombardment. Connecticut had no shore cannon to respond. Parsons asked for a meeting with the Committee of Correspondence. With the information from Arnold, both Parsons and Silas pushed the committee hard for an immediate attack on Fort Ticonderoga. With the general assembly not in full session, the Connecticut Committee of Correspondence had almost unlimited powers. On their personal notes, Silas Deane, Samuel Parsons and Samuel Willys borrowed £300 in tax money from the treasury for expenses against an attack on Fort Ticonderoga. The next day the three men, and several other committee members, sent six recruiters under the command of Captain Romans of Wethersfield with £100 to western Connecticut. Both Parsons and Silas knew Ethan Allen from his earlier activities in the Salisbury Iron county of western Connecticut. Allen now was heading a vigilante group operating to keep New

York out of New Hampshire grants in what is present day Vermont. The day after they had spoken to Herman, Ethan Allen's brother, Silas and Parsons sent two more veterans, Captain Edward Motts and Noah Phelps, with 17 men to overtake Captain Romans. Additionally, Romans had orders to rouse Ethan Allen and his Green Mountain Boys with the hope that Allen would agree to lead an attack on Fort Ticonderoga. Knowing his reputation, Silas and Parsons were quite sure it was a done deal.

Benedict Arnold had also kept thinking about his conversation with Colonel Parsons and decided while at Cambridge that he would try to convince the Massachusetts Committee of Safety to finance an attack against Fort Ticonderoga with "Colonel" Arnold in command. The safety committee agreed and Arnold set out to recruit men and head for Lake Champlain.

The rivalry that resulted between Ethan Allen and Benedict Arnold over who was actually in command of the expedition is well known and countless stories have been written about their encounters. However, it is worth noting that Ethan Allen reported back to the Connecticut committee, after the capture of the fort, that "Colonel Arnold entered the fortress side by side with me."[2]

Like many Connecticut towns, Wethersfield had its own militia detachment. Immediately after the April 21 ten o'clock confirmation of the fighting at Lexington and Concord, an all-out call to arms was sounded. One hundred men of the contingent were chosen to go to Massachusetts under the command of Colonel John Chester. As town assemblyman, and secretary of the Connecticut Committee of Correspondence (now calling itself the Committee of Safety), Silas wrote the agreement which each man signed, promising to "refrain from drunkenness, gaming and profanity."[3]

On August 26, the Connecticut General Assembly was called to full session by Governor Trumbull in order to meet with delegates from the Massachusetts and Rhode Island assemblies to hear of further reports and orders. Thus, according to Silas's diary, by May 1 the Connecticut Assembly was "busy making out Commissions and arranging their officers & Men."[4]

The events of April 19 reinforced the reelected Connecticut congressional trio's enthusiasm for the issues that lay ahead. The state of events would now be changed when the King declared the New England colonies in a state of rebellion. As far as the Connecticut patriots were concerned, violence must now decide whether they remained subjects of the king or became an independent people. Silas's carriage carried the Connecticut delegates from Wethersfield to New Haven and on to Stamford where they picked up an escort of the Governor's Horse Guard to New York City. In the city, they were once again joined by the Massachusetts delegations, who, in many eyes, were now considered heroes.

From there, the two delegations went from town to town being entertained at each stop and greeted by happy and noisy crowds. Silas wrote to his wife that they reached Philadelphia on May 10 and "were met at about six miles on this side of the city by about two hundred of the principal gentlemen on horseback with their swords drawn.... At about two miles distance we were met by a Company on foot, and then a Company of Riflemen.... Thus rolling and gathering like a snowball, we approached the City, which was full of people and the crowd was as great as New York, the bells all ringing and the air rent with shouts and huzzas.... The scenes before us are so vast ... and I tremble when I think of their vast importance, May the God of wisdom preside."[5]

The capture of Fort Ticonderoga took place on May 10, the same day Congress was scheduled to reconvene. News of the capture arrived in Philadelphia just one week later. It was the first order of business the next day. The event showed just how ambivalent the delegates still were about what direction they should take. To Silas and the New England delegates' utter amazement and disbelief, Congress resolved that the fort should be abandoned. The guns and stores were to be removed, but a detailed inventory should be taken in order to be returned safely when harmony with England was restored.

Silas and the entire New England delegations simply would not accept the weaseling of the majority and finally made them change their minds under the threat that the Connecticut Council of Safety would go ahead and secure the fort on their own under the direction of Barnabus Deane. As a result of all the planning and pressure of the capture of Fort Ticonderoga, Silas earned the nickname "Ticonderoga Deane" from his fellow delegates.

After the impact of the capture settled down a bit, Congress began to fully realize the importance of their cause. Silas and his Connecticut colleagues now started to enjoy a reputation second only to the Massachusetts delegates. Also, as a result of the fort episode, Silas was recognized more readily as somewhat of a military strategy expert; a reputation he enjoyed from that time on until he was forced to leave Congress as a delegate by vote of the Connecticut General Assembly. In the interim, however, Silas sat in on over 40 different congressional committees.

In its early days, mainly 1775 through late 1776, the Second Continental Congress was virtually a repetition of the first in its personnel. Fifty-four delegates had served in the first, and only four did not return. Silas was personally appreciative of the new members' political support. He was particularly glad to meet and work with the famous old Ben Franklin and his merchant friend of many years John Hancock. James Wilson and Thomas Jefferson were the other two replacements, both of whom had wide supportive patriot backgrounds and leaned toward the radicals' viewpoints. This time Georgia did send one delegate, Lyman Hall, formerly of Wallingford, Connecticut.

Congress was still a little squeamish over the capture of Fort Ticonderoga and its possible aftermath. To cover a potential forceful reaction from Canada, the delegates appointed a committee to write a letter to the Canadian people. On May 26, Silas and his New York delegate friend John Jay were two of its members. Jay was well known for his moderate views concerning the colonial troubles with the mother country and was selected to write the actual letter. Delegate Jay assured the Canadian people that the Americans did not intend to use the forts to threaten Canada: "You may rely on our assurances, that these colonies will pursue no measures whatever, but such a friendship and a regard for mutual safety and interest may support."[6]

During the first week of June, Congress received an invitation from Massachusetts for the formation of a unified army. Silas was cautiously optimistic about its actual reality. He wrote, "Congress is an unwieldy body but unanimity hitherto prevails to a most surprising degree."[7]

On June 10, after a week of debate, Congress voted to raise £6,000 to purchase gunpowder. Then, on June 14, the body agreed to raise an army drawn from those colonies able to provide men immediately. Twenty thousand troops from Pennsylvania, Virginia and Maryland were ready to march to Boston.

For the provincial-minded Connecticut colony, there were a lot of problems to overcome. Local politics and aggressive and arrogant personalities would have to be dealt with before any agreement as to a unified fighting force could be wholly accepted. The first point involved the troops around Boston from Massachusetts, Connecticut, Rhode Island and New Hampshire, who decidedly needed a unified command. Who could lead such an army? Colonial politics definitely called for congressional supervision of the New Englanders if the Boston siege was to be a continental war.

John Adams had quickly supplanted his cousin Sam as the radical leader in the Second Congress. As to who should lead the primarily New England army surrounding Boston, John had a brilliant idea — if he could only pull it off with his fellow delegates. To cement relations between northern and southern colonies, he proposed, why not choose a man from the southern colonies to be the commanding general. Hearing the idea, Roger Sherman hit the ceiling: it had to be a man from New England.

Almost immediately after the vote to form a Continental Army, George Washington and Silas were appointed members of a committee to draft rules and regulations for a standing army. The next day, John Adams felt he was ready to recommend the Virginian George Washington as the man to be the commanding general of the new army. Roger Sherman still strongly objected, but Dyer saw the merit in the idea after working closely with Washington over the previous 24 hours and heartily agreed to such an appointment.

Silas found that the more he got to know the man, "the more he esteemed him."[8]

After more hours of political arm-bending of delegates, George Washington was unanimously appointed Commander-in-Chief of the Continental Army. Within the next few days Silas got to know Washington even more as the two men worked hard on the regulations and organization of the Continental Army.

Silas realized the need for speed and convenience in seeing that the new army commander took charge at the Cambridge army headquarters as soon as possible. Silas offered his home as a resting place on his journey to the Boston area. He wrote to Elizabeth on June 16, 1775:

> George Washington will be with you soon; elected to have that office by the unanimous voice of all America. I have been with him for a great part of the last forty-eight hours in Congress and Committee, and the more that I have become acquainted with the man, the more I esteem him. He promises me to call, and, if it happens favorably, to spend the night with you. I wish to cultivate this gentleman's acquaintance and regard, for the great esteem I have of his virtues, which do not shine in the view of the world by reason of his great modesty, but when discovered by the discerning eye shine brighter. I know you will receive him as my friend, and what is more — his country's friend, who, sacrificing private fortune, independence, ease, and every domestic pleasure, sets off at his country's call to exert himself in her defense without so much as returning to bid adieu to a fond partner and family. Let our youth look up to this man as a pattern to form themselves by, who unites the bravery of a soldier with the most consummate modesty and virtue.

On June 18, Deane wrote again to his wife: "General Washington sets on Thursday of this week. I have a strong temptation to accompany him to the camp. This morning, Colonel Schuyler and I rode as far as the Falls at Schuylkill; our ride was to consult a plan we are forming for another bold stroke like that of Ticonderoga (which is become my nickname at times.) People here, members of Congress and others, have unhappily and erroneously thought me a schemer; this has brought me rather more than my share of business in a commercial way." He adds with a premonition of coming troubles: "I find, however, that he that has the least to do in public affairs stands the fairest chance at happiness. If General Washington sets out on Thursday, he will be in New York early on Saturday, where affairs will doubtless detain him until Monday or Tuesday, and in that case he will be with you on the Friday following. He is no lover of parade, so do not put yourself in distress. If it happens convenient, he will spend one night with you; if not, just call and go on. Should he spend a night, his retinue will doubtless go on to Hartford." On June 22, Deane wrote again to his wife: "This will be handed you by his Excellency, General Washington, in company with General Lee and retinue."⁹

Next came the problem for Congress of appointing four major generals under Washington's command. Artemus Ward, who had been superseded by Washington as Commander-in-Chief, got one, and another, under Washington's insistence, went to Charles Lee, a former professional British army officer. One each would be awarded to offices from New York and Connecticut. Philip Schuyler, a veteran of colonial wars and a congressional delegate from New York, got New York's award. After much hassling, Israel Putnam received Connecticut's slot.

Israel Putnam was as authentic a military hero as Connecticut had ever produced. He was a huge man of tremendous strength and energy. His courage was unmatched and he had legendary physical powers. While at Cambridge, he was everywhere during the fighting. He even "liberated" hundreds of pigs, sheep and cows for the army's food from a British-held island in Boston Harbor.

Putnam's unanimous congressional appointment mortified Connecticut's commanding general, Daniel Wooster, and second-in-command Joseph Spenser. The colony almost produced the colonial equivalent of a mushroom cloud over the situation. Spenser, who had been Putnam's immediate superior, immediately left his troops at Roxbury and went to Governor Trumbull and the Committee of Safety to complain. At age 65, Wooster, as Connecticut's mayor general, stayed behind in Connecticut during the Lexington alarm, planning and launching the expedition to hold Fort Ticonderoga. The General Assembly immediately requested Governor Trumbull to write a letter to Connecticut's congressional trio asking them to persuade Congress to devise some method of reinstatement of Wooster over Putnam.

The Connecticut delegates split wide open over the issue. Silas supported Putnam all the way and damned "the slavishness to traditional seniority." Sherman backed, and made a strong fight for, his New Haven friend Wooster, while Dyer tried to convince Congress to follow Connecticut's arrangements. Silas pushed hard for Putnam's promotion. He wrote the general "is not adept either at political or religious canting and cozening; he is no shapehand body; he therefore is totally unfit for everything except but fighting; that department; I never heard that these intriguing gentry wanted to interfere with him in."¹⁰

Silas described Wooster as an old woman unfit for the Major Generalship of Connecticut forces. While Silas declared Wooster unfit for the position, Dyer was won over for Putnam; besides, he figured, being a colonel himself, he might even be considered for Wooster's position. As to Spenser, Silas was disappointed in a man he once admired when he heard he had left his troops in such a manner to complain. He wished the man would simply retire and let someone else take his place. Putnam's fame was so well known throughout the continent and abroad that it automatically gave him preference in the general opinion of Congress. His appointment remained unanimous among the delegates.

The appointment of Putnam, however, continued to hinder relations among the Connecticut delegates. Silas wrote his wife at home to "pray listen to the reports (about the general) and inform me how far I am charged with being active in this arrangement. I have various reasons to expect their friends will father it all on the old scapegoat...."[11] He also wrote a little later that he was "well aware that the storm is raised, or at least blown up by others ... but, I am determined to do my duty, and will on no occasion sacrifice the good of my country to the whim of an old man or old woman, rather, or their sticklers."[12] Deane knew he had gone against the Connecticut General Assembly's wishes, but he was looking at the bigger picture of possible military success. He further realized the more individual friends in high places the better the chance he had of convincing Congress to get on the ball and move forward toward an independent nation, no matter the price. Nepotism was only a secondary act, but convenient. Therefore, Silas didn't hesitate to recommend his stepson Samuel Webb to be Putnam's aide-de-camp. He wrote to his close friend Joseph Trumbull, who had several good friends in Congress: "I have some little right to place as I was the General's friend in the Assembly, I have not been idle here (Philadelphia) of which I make no merit, & only wish I may not be censured by certain persons."[13] The plea was unsuccessful, but Silas, with Dyer, entered Joseph Trumbull's name as one of Connecticut's prizes from Congress. Joseph was soon to be Dyer's son-in-law. Surprisingly, Sherman also pushed the young Connecticut Lebanon, and Joseph Trumbull was unanimously given the post of commissary general. The governor's youngest son, John, and also Silas's friend, was given the position of paymaster for the New York Department.

July found the radicals bending over backward to accommodate the more timid or moderate delegates by permitting them to write and send to King George III another conciliatory offer. This was the so-called Olive Branch Petition, adopted on July 5, 1775.

Over the previous six weeks, Silas had been so busy with committee meeting after committee meeting he had found little time to keep up with his correspondence back home, but he did keep a running diary of people and events. When Ben Franklin appeared at the Second Continental Congress, Silas wrote Elizabeth on July 1: "Doctor Franklin is with us, but he is not a speaker tho' we have I think his hearty approbations of and assent of every Measure."[14] Almost from the day they met they were impressed with each other and soon became friends despite the age difference (see Appendix C).

IV. Leading Connecticut Congressional Delegate, 1775

On July 21, as an entire body Congress decided that it had better take time out to see just what was the actual state of the thirteen colonies. A few weeks earlier, Connecticut had taken its own stock of where it stood in this astonishing era. The fast-growing concept of nationalism was found among a few other colonial assemblies who were basing their approach on Connecticut's own charter and brought the nationalistic theme to the floor of Congress in the form of a generalized plan of union. Franklin then presented a draft of a document called the Articles of Confederation and Perpetual Union. A few days later, Silas followed with his own version of the Articles of Confederation. Unfortunately, most delegates were still under the illusion of reconciliation and the movement died. Congress still needed more petitions to the king. Regardless of this state of affairs, Franklin and Silas had led the message that "shook up the troops" enough to make the delegates start truly thinking ahead in a more pragmatic fashion rather than spending all its time worrying about America's virtuous image in the eyes of Great Britain.

What happened in May, when the delegates returned to Philadelphia, was the beginning of a definite split in philosophies within the Continental Congress which was to grow stronger with every situation that came along through 1778. During the last day of July, both Franklin and Silas were appointed to a committee to locate sources and manufacturing locations of lead and other ores. They reported back to Congress with extensive knowledge, but very little physical help to fight a war. They told, and warned, Congress it desperately needed help from outside the colonies for the quantities needed. Silas had previously written Governor Trumbull asking that the Salisbury Iron Works and related territory be placed under government control.

Of all the British West Indies, the northern-most island of Bermuda was the most closely tied to mainland America. Bermuda exchanged her famous cedar sloops and salt for the mainland's food, without which the island would quickly starve. The Bermudians lived in terror of going hungry—a well-founded possibility. Aside from the resources of salt and sloops, Bermuda was desperately poor. Over the years, many islanders had taken up illicit trade as an occupation.

Silas, as well as any other merchant in Congress who had experience in the West Indies trade, knew the Bermudians' skill for brilliant seamanship, knowledge of coastlines, hidden caves, and all sorts of other means of collusion. He fully realized Bermuda would make an ideal ally for the Americans. During the mid-to-late 18th century, Bermuda was more or less controlled by the Tucker clan and its leader, Colonel Henry Tucker. The colonel was thoroughly indoctrinated with the ideals of the American cause. In fact, midway through the Revolution, he wrote a letter to Washington begging him to "capture" Bermuda, as he would be happy to capitulate.

In July, the head man himself, Colonel Tucker, arrived to try to persuade Congress to rescind its resolutions stopping the export of food to the British West Indies. For Bermuda, the food problem was becoming acute. Franklin, Silas, Robert Morris, and other pragmatic delegates had quickly recognized the suicidal effects that the nonimportation/exportation act was causing. They were determined to get it annulled. Together, Franklin and Deane were very anxious to meet with Tucker and learn what he might offer in return. Tucker confided that in the Royal Arsenal at St. George's there was a substantial supply of unguarded gunpowder.

With their appropriate illicit merchant trading contacts, Robert Morris's reputation, and Silas's West Indies background, the duo took over the necessary "arrangements" to acquire the gunpowder. Franklin then used his powers of persuasion on Congress for backing. On Saturday, July 15, Franklin presented a resolution using the gunpowder as bait; it was an inclusive order to exchange food for guns with any vessel arriving on the North American coast and it neatly sidestepped the issue of trading with the enemy. The resolution passed Congress and a special concession was granted to Bermuda — a promise to supply the island with other goods besides food, such as candles, soap and lumber.[15] Colonel Tucker rushed home to carry out his side of the bargain.

On the night of August 14, a "raiding party" acquired the barrels of gunpowder from the arsenal without a single problem. Twelve days later the *Lady Catherine*, one of the two ships involved in the "raid," arrived in Philadelphia with 1,800 pounds of gunpowder. The second ship, *Susquehana Paquet*, delivered her cargo of gunpowder at Charleston.

Thus began close amiable relations between Bermuda and America, which was supplied well with sloops and salt for the entire war and beyond. Several times during the struggle, Bermuda, with strong backing from Franklin and Deane and several others, came close to becoming the fourteenth state and a war base for the American mainland.

Congress had now been in session continuously for 80 days without a break. The delegates were hot, tired and often verbally abusive to one another during debates. Silas stated, "The Congress has now sat without a day's respite since the 10th of May, and consequently are much fatigued."[16] The body adjourned itself on August 2, to reconvene on September 12.

Roger Sherman had borrowed Silas's carriage in mid–July and had an accident that badly damaged the chaise. In fact, "it broke entirely." Silas wrote his wife about it: "I lent my chaise to Mr. Sherman yesterday and it is broke in pieces; but shall repair it, I believe by a new one for the old one is totally broke and destroyed."[17] Silas decided to have his chaise made over into a phaeton. This made the trip more comfortable than earlier trips had been. The Connecticut trio traveled together for the five-day ride, sharing expenses as they went. All personal animosities were temporarily suspended, as any good politician can do when it is convenient.

Back from its much needed respite in late September, Congress showed some signs of a different frame of mind and mood. Yet it was still waiting for an answer to the Olive Branch Petition, an answer that would never come. Various members had learned by the first week in October, from a London newspaper and many sea captains, that it was thought beneath the dignity of the British government to answer any petition from Congress as it was an unrecognized and illegal body. On August 23, King George III had declared the colonists to be rebels and by December all ports would fall under the extended Boston Port Bill.

Franklin and Deane, along with several other eager patriots, kept telling Congress it had better prepare for the worst. They became very important to Congress in the need to prepare for all-out war. The big problem was that Congress had to contend not only with organizing an army, but also with the fact that the British navy controlled the world's oceans.

Privately Franklin told Silas, who had been loudly pushing from the floor of Congress some kind of united colonial navy, "I lament with you the Want of a naval Force. I hope next Winter we will be employed in forming one. When we are no longer fascinated with the idea of a speedy Reconciliation, we shall exert ourselves to some purpose. 'Til then Things will be done in Halves."[18]

On September 18, Congress finally resolved to organize a method of obtaining supply aid and, as usual, appointed a committee. This action followed the realization by Congress that France and Holland, through their merchant houses, had already secretly provided the colonies with war supplies to the estimated value of well over eight million in the new American dollar. These supplies were coming mainly by the West Indies islands of Santo Domingo and St. Eustatia (often called Statia by colonists).

The Secret Committee, or as it was later known, the Commerce or Trade Committee, was one of the most effective operations of Congress, although Congress didn't realize it until midway through the Revolution. It was given wide powers and large sums of money and kept its transactions quiet, even destroying many of its original records. Its first chairman was Thomas Willing of the house of Willing and Morris. The original members were Franklin and Deane, Robert R. Livingston, John Alsop, John Dickinson, Thomas McKean, John Langdon, and Samuel Ward. The basic aim of the committee was to make sure to keep men on the committee who were experienced in trade. It was specifically supposed to be just an importing body that could make contracts for arms and ammunitions (especially gunpowder). The Secret Committee was also allowed to draw on the congressional treasury for advances to contractors. By November, the committee was empowered to export produce to the West Indies in exchange for war materials.

Then in December, enter Robert Morris as the new chairman. Up to this time the house of Willing and Morris of Philadelphia and Silas Deane, along with his Connecticut merchant friends and relatives, were the chief suppliers of munitions. Robert Morris was well known as the greatest merchant of the American business community. With a winning personality he endeared himself to all sorts of people. He was a man noted for his honesty whose signature or verbal promise was his bond — but the delegates with the congressional "buzz word of virtue" seldom thought so. Morris was keenly aware of national and international affairs of a political, economic and maritime character. He would have made a good 21st century baby boomer. Everything had to be immediate and he was known to have the temper to go with that expectation. He had the all–American "I want it now" syndrome. All through the war, George Washington, when in desperate need of something, could always turn to his close friend Robert Morris, not only to get it but often furnished to Washington out of his own pocket with no strings attached.

With a shove by both Silas and Franklin, Congress allowed the new chairman to import all kinds of supplies, including medicine, blankets, cotton goods, and the like. The Secret Committee by January 1776 controlled virtually all foreign trade.

Several members of the Secret Committee, but especially Morris and Silas, acting for Congress, had earlier, and privately, contracted in the West Indies to obtain gunpowder and arms for an army. With the expansion of powers of the Secret Committee much greater, contracts now went to Willing and Morris and Deane's friends and relatives. Nepotism was simply a way of life for any merchant if he was to succeed and it boiled down to "blood was thicker than water" for obvious reasons of expediency in the 1700s (not in the 21st century). It must be pointed out that several firms connected with other members of the committee also received generous contracts and those included Alsop and Livingston.

The throw-back Puritan Sam Adams and the powerful agrarian bloc led by the Lees, immediately upon learning of "delegate contracts," started sounding off that the committee members were making fortunes off of Congress — a very nonvirtuous thing to do. Nevertheless, the committee continued to make contracts right and left: the Browns of Providence; Livingston & Trumbull of New York; Blair McClenachan and George Mead of Philadelphia; and Carter Broxton and Benjamin Harrison of Virginia. What was the *real* chief reason? The answer is simple. The committee needed merchants experienced in foreign trade with fast ships and courageous captains ready for dangerous voyages. These were the only men with committee contracts. Everyone knew there would be sizable profits if they were successful — a success called profiteering — but the bottom line was the fact that Washington's army got badly needed supplies.

Independence was still an unpopular issue with many delegates, but to any merchant it had long been a done deal. After bucking England's economic rule for so long, merchant/sea captains had formed an efficient but highly dangerous system of free trade throughout the entire Western world (more on this system in the next chapter). Any successful merchant knew he could not survive if he actually followed England's regulations on trade.

Having the knowledge, background and experience, Silas took the lead, along with Robert Morris, in issuing contracts for gunpowder. One of the first contracts of 1775 from the Secret Committee went to Silas's wife's brother-in-law and his friend Thomas Mumford, the (up to then) too-highly successful and wealthy merchant from Deane's hometown of Groton. The contract involved "Statia" for 50 tons of gunpowder. Unfortunately, there were several misunderstandings on how the international merchants and their agents operated to protect themselves from political "problems." It turned into a fiasco that took over one year to straighten out, by which time only less than half the amount could be delivered — a prime example of merchants' risks, financial and personal.

In the early 1770s, when the socially elite patriots in the Boston area started organizing the middle and lower classes against the trade regulations of the English government, they soon discovered that these "people" had agendas of their own regarding British colonial rule. The area revolutionary leaders from then on realized they needed men whose socioeconomic and cultural background outlook allowed them to move among the various classes below the elite society of the 18th century. In other words, they were looking for individuals who could bridge the gap between the waterfront traders and the Harvard graduates.

Not being Masons, the Adamses and the Boston area revolutionaries at first did not realize the Masonic Brotherhood, with its enlightened ideals, was made up of such men. And who else stood out as one of these individuals but the man soon to become famous for his exploits, Paul Revere.

In Connecticut, many Freemasons with the background needed to cross socioeconomic lines were merchants struggling to be accepted by the local social elite class. In a few short years Silas had become a worthy member of his community and a workaholic lawyer/merchant who inspired loyalty from friends and neighbors from all walks of life. Silas Deane was an outstanding choice for the best "class" communications. Fortunately for Congress, Silas was already in Philadelphia as a delegate. He could easily become available for reaching "the people" where they lived and worked as one of them. He was being watched by delegate revolutionaries as just such a man. In congressional session Silas was constantly jumping to his feet to defend the people's interest as well as his own.

On September 23, after Roger Sherman suggested the Continental soldier pay for his own equipment, Silas stood up and said, "The army must be clothed or perish. There is no preaching against the snow storm. We ought to look out that the men are kept warm and the means of doing it be secured."[19] Then again, on October 12, he stated, "We must have trade; I think we ought to apply abroad; we must have powder and goods; we can't keep our people easy without."[20] Meanwhile, Franklin tucked away this verbal profile of Silas for future use. He did respond to some delegates that Congress was fortunate to have such a valuable and knowledgeable man.

The biggest problem of the Secret Committee's job was not dealing with foreign countries, but was rather the fact that Americans in the 18th century were addicted to the agrarian lifestyle and prejudices. It included over two-thirds of the Congressional delegates. Being a merchant making a living through the trading business was considered by most of them to be hardly an honorable vocation. The profit motive was not a good moral approach to life. Instead, sacrificing all individual interests to the greater common good formed the essence of republicanism and would remain the idealistic goal of the Revolution in the eyes of the agrarian patriot. The American agrarian society never fully understood that profit was a merchant's source of income and pay for taking all the risks in obtaining merchandise to sell. Silas and most merchants could never buy the concept that economic freedom most be subordinated to the good of the general 18th century society (as is the case in the 21st century).

Next after the major problem of agrarian economic acceptance came the responsibilities of the individual merchant himself and his role as an agent for Congress, a role that became a constant issue throughout the entire war. The vocation of a 1700s merchant was intricate and complicated. The agrarian delegates, and the general society, never really had a clue concerning how the system and risks involved operated in the trading business. Most merchants' business connections remained closely guarded secrets, making their actions obscure and complicated. They operated through a hidden network of personal contacts fostered by mutual patronage and trust.

These men were desperately needed by Congress. They and they alone, had the knowledge, skills and connections to transact business for Congress. Merchants felt no obligation to give up their own private affairs while taking on contracts for Congress. In fact, it was not expected. Merchants considered themselves commission agents and the Congress their principal. They received commissions rather than salaries, worked under their own names and incurred their own debts and liabilities. Moreover, they were expected to advance their own money for public purposes. Therefore, merchants did not hesitate to mix Congressional business with their own private dealings, something, again, that the agrarian could never seem to understand. Furthermore, the 18th century merchant had to be his own marketing agent, shipper, wholesaler, retailer and banker, plus quite often, insurer. Contrary to verbally negative revolutionaries, most merchants were loyal to their own professional standards of the day and had a high regard for their own personal reputations if they wished to remain in business.

The Secret Committee (of Trade) kept its members and merchant contractors straining to obtain gunpowder for Washington's army and colonial militias throughout the thirteen colonies. The "powder cruises," as they were called, were the prime reason why the patriots kept the Revolution alive for the first three years of the war.

Not too unexpectedly at the end of the First Congress, a longtime personal interest of Silas's came to the forefront. In May of 1774, the Connecticut General Assembly assumed full jurisdiction over the Susquehanna Company's claim to the Wyoming Valley of Pennsylvania, causing the Connecticut trio considerable embarrassment, especially since Connecticut had established the town of Westmoreland there, and, in turn, incorporated it into the colony's government. Hard feeling between the Pennsylvania and Connecticut delegates was the obvious result.

The Pennsylvanians asked the Connecticut Yankee trio to please calm down the strife in their doubtful western appendage of the Wyoming Valley. The merchant, the judge and the colonel wrote a mutual letter to their western leadership stating "that there is great danger of discord and Contention if not Hostility & Bloodshed between the People sitting under Connecticut Claim & those under Pennsylvania which would be attended with the most unhappy consequences at this time of general Calamity & when we want our whole United Strength (against) our common enemy."[21] The letter didn't work; fighting on the frontier border between colonists continued.

The Pennsylvanians finally submitted a resolution to Congress asking that something be done about the Connecticut intrusion. Sherman considered arbitration. Dyer, being the principal founder of the Susquehanna Company after some 16 years of trying to make the company's claim legal under English rule, caused the founder to go off the deep end in a barrage of abusive verbal protests which soon made him virtually useless in coming to any kind of settlement with Pennsylvanians. The initial reaction from Silas came as a surprise to everyone. He called the Connecticut settlers activities a "mad frolic" and seemingly sided with the Pennsylvanians. Of course, the non-pragmatic delegates immediately saw his action as cozying up to "buy time" for merchants and their personal interests. Actually, he felt at that point in time that his interests in western lands should be relegated to a backseat until unity could become a reality.

With Dyer's zeal against the Pennsylvanian claims, Sherman and Deane took quite different tacks. Silas explained: "I avoided the dispute wholly and when forced upon it expressed my warmest wishes for a friendly Settlement. By this means I stood well with the more dispassionate of the other party...."[22] Sherman, on the other hand, continued to push hard for a legal settlement through the courts. In the Connecticut General Assembly, the Susquehanna party, long a supporter of Silas and Dyer politically, dropped their backing of both men. The legalities would drag on for another six years.

A few days after the Second Congress convened in May of 1775, the success of Fort Ticonderoga's capture, and the major role that he played in bringing it to fruition, caused Silas to be considered a master schemer and persuader. The last Sunday in May, General Schuyler and Silas took a ride in the country to discuss another plan Silas had to surprise and harass the British. As he wrote his wife, the idea could be another possible "bold stroke."

Having spent his boyhood on the Connecticut coastline communities from New Haven to Stonington, Silas was well aware of the importance of the fisheries of Greenland and Hudson Bay trade to England's economy. He wanted to convince the members of Congress to attack and capture the fishing fleet and raid the Hudson Bay Trading Posts. Schuyler felt it far too risky for Congress as a body to even consider the idea without armed continental ships. The general told Silas, too, that the "Indian Problem" in and around New York and New England was becoming much worse. Having been appointed by the local government to take charge of keeping the lid on the problem, Schuyler said he would not dare to spare the men needed for such an expedition.

Silas still wanted to shake up the British in their own backyard. Back in Congress, he cornered his friend and fellow delegate John Jay and presented him with yet another daring plan of harassing the British Lion. This time the plan (which became a favorite of Silas's) was to attack the English coastline, plundering and burning Liverpool and Glasgow as a "most glorious revenge." Jay held back any opinion for over a year. By that time, Silas was in France.[23]

In September, when Silas became a member of the Secret Committee (of Trade), he continually hounded the committee members with his plans. Franklin would listen but remain silent while other members simply shook their heads. They knew Silas was angling to get Congress to authorize privateers, but in 1775, Powder Cruises were first priority with the colonies, to which they provided ships and men on a private basis.

On October 3, Rhode Island, after months of having her shoreline pounded by the British navy, introduced a resolution calling for a Continental Navy at congressional expense for a fleet sufficient for the protection of the colonial coastlines and employ the ships in such a way as to annoy, "annoy" being the operative word. Opposition to the resolution was loud and strong. It was considered by many delegates a wild and crazy idea. The formation of an American navy to take on the world's greatest naval force was like "an infant taking a mad Bull by the horns."[24]

Regardless of the strong opposition, a positive vote resulted and, as usual, Congress appointed another committee. The initial work by the new naval committee was begun by two of the most vocal, skilled and delighted men, Silas Deane — of course — and John Langdon of Portsmouth. Then, on October 13, Congress commissioned the purchase of four warships. Silas and Langdon went to work searching out and acquiring ships. Silas personally purchased the first ship on the 15th of October. It was the *Alfred,* formerly the *Black Prince,* a Philadelphia merchantman thought to have been one of the many Willing & Morris House ships; it has been rumored, but not substantiated, that Silas actually persuaded Robert Morris to donate the *Alfred.* No matter, the *Alfred* was immediately outfitted with 21 guns (canon) and commissioned on December 3 as the first ship of the Continental Navy, which was officially established by Congress on November 25, 1775.

Silas was working far beyond his usual hours. By now he had been in over three dozen congressional committees. He was constantly going "six ways to Sunday" every day, but rumors were flying around Philadelphia that a new flock of delegates would soon be in town replacing original delegates.

Back on November 3, 1774, the Connecticut Council of Safety had reappointed Deane, Dyer and Sherman to Congress along with Titus Hosmer and Jonathan Sturgis as alternates. After a year, however, the Connecticut General Assembly took the election of the delegates to Congress upon itself. Thus on October 12, 1775, Sherman and Hosmer were reelected and Oliver Wolcott, Samuel Huntington and William Williams were elected. Sherman, Wolcott and Huntington had the highest votes and Hosmer and Williams were the alternates. The new delegation would take their seats in January of 1776; four days later an express rider brought the official news.

Silas's reaction was rather quiet, partly from disbelief and disappointment. The reasons for Silas's dismissal were many. Deane was never trusted by several of his Calvinistic fellow politicians. William Williams and Sherman were afraid that Silas would use his position in Congress to promote his private interests. To a Calvinist that was always a no-no and they made it a point to cabal against Silas during the 1775 September congressional recess, with other members of the Assembly joining them. Silas had also antagonized the Susquehanna group. In addition was the fact that the assembly itself was still quite upset with Silas for his stand in supporting Putnam as a major general in the Continental Congress over the assembly's choice of David Wooster. Of course, there is no doubt that Silas saw the Revolution primarily from a merchant's economic point of view first and from a republican philosophy second.

At first Silas and Dyer pretended they were glad to be replaced. However, Silas did write a letter to Governor Trumbull explaining the reasons for the actions he had taken in Congress. Governor Trumbull was not sympathetic. He wrote back saying, in rather official terms, that Silas had screwed up by not following the party line and the true interests of Connecticut.

The month of October turned out to be a personal and political disaster for the Wethersfield merchant. He would never again trust the arrogant elite or New England's religious zealots. He wholly understood from that time on, through the rest of his life, that friendship was to be valued far above wealth, power and position.

Silas was not a vindictive person as so many of his political colleagues were. That is not to say he allowed himself to forgive the actions of those politicians. He was not that much of a Connecticut New Light Congregationalist, either. To Silas such individuals no longer existed and he had little or nothing to do with them. As a highly educated and successful person he understood the trait of arrogance, but he never quite got the hang of being vindictive himself.

Silas's patriotism always came first and his personal life and interests second. His personal priorities always shifted easily with the times and events. He seldom kept any tunnel vision. He was not afraid to take an all-out risk of changing his mind while involved in the Revolutionary struggles even to making turns of 180° (some contemporaries and many historians still maintain he did so only if the risk was going to be personally beneficial if successful — a fallacy of the nth degree).

Silas bared his exact feelings and attitude concerning his true reactions to his dismissal from Congress to his wife. It gave a very clear picture of his personality and character that would be hard for any of his contemporaries to refute. He wrote on November 26:

> Believe me, my Dear, my long and thorough acquaintance with the genius of our Assembly prevents my being surprised at any sudden whim they take, or uneasy at any of their Resolutions, so far as they respect myself individually. On a review of the part I have acted on the public theatre of life, and examination of my own genius and disposition, unfit for trimming, courting, and intrigues with the populace, I have greater reason to wonder how I ever became popular at all. What therefore I did not expect, I have too much philosophy to be in distress at losing. I only wish that my friends felt as easy on this occasion as myself. If they knew what fatigues I have undergone, and the disagreeable prospects before me, as to public

affairs, they could wish me here, only in confidence that my abilities might be of service to the public, rather than to myself. But of this the Supreme Assembly are best judges, and to them I must submit, sincerely praying that the consequences which I think I foresee, necessarily flowing from this measure, may be averted. I should be sorry that you or my friends should manifest any uneasiness on my being superseded; for they who affected it will find, and that soon, the mischief intended recoil on them to their shame and disgrace, or I am greatly mistaken; and at present, God knows I wish the worst of them no other punishment than a consciousness of the low, envious, jealous and sordid motives by which they actuated; as, on the other hand, one of the greatest pleasures I enjoy is a consciousness of the rectitude of my intentions and conduct, and the pleasing reflection of being superior to such motives and those actuated by them. I have wrote a long letter, and on a review it is too much about myself. I will write of some thing of more importance in my next. My compliments to all Friends.[25]

Silas knew he was no outright genius and he certainly did not fit the mold of a typical Connecticut assembly politician. But he was certain the neo-Puritan zealot's philosophy time was passing and a new era of strong, creative, materialistically self-interested individuals was emerging. Like his mentor Franklin, he foresaw a different society constructed that would someday be the wealthiest and most powerful in the world without equal.

Thus, the fiery merchant patriot took a deep mental breath and reconsidered his options. Silas openly decided he simply could not stop what he was doing just because he was not reelected. To him, his responsibilities to his country for its future's sake were far too great to let some conspiring self-righteous republicans and land-hungry speculators control his actions. As he wrote Elizabeth, his country's liberty for now would have to come first over family, wealth and reputation. He felt strongly that somehow the colonies had to get out from under the yoke of the English king and Parliament.

When the Naval Committee's membership list was completed, it had added John Adams, Richard Henry Lee, Joseph Hewes of North Carolina and Governor Stephen Hopkins of Rhode Island. Knowing his waterfront and naval background, the committee asked Silas to write a first draft for rules and regulations for the Continental Navy.[26] Silas realized that they would be needed almost immediately so that future crews could be persuaded to join. The rules and regulations he wrote were quite harsh. He knew from his experience as a youth that naval crews were not of the highest caliber and needed strict discipline if they were going to win any battle. It has often been thought, and is probably true, that the real reason Silas wrote such tough terms was to protect the draw of crews from privateers. Every colony had merchant ships that were being converted and commissioned as privateers. Already by 1775, privateers were taking a real toll on British shipping — both military and private. Privateers were a ready-made fighting force on the sea and all Congress had to do was issue commission. This was another favorite wish that Silas had, but unfortunately Congress did not issue commissions for privateering until early 1777.

The Naval Committee approved Silas's draft in mid–November, but made it even tougher to recruit seamen by adding the use of the cat-o'-nine-tails and lowering the pay to eight dollars per month and only a small portion of the prize money given the crew, and then only if it was a British warship. Meanwhile, a privateer paid $30 a month and a larger share of prize money for any captured ship, and rules were also far less harsh.

Two weeks after the creation of the Continental Navy was official, the Naval Committee had to work fast. They needed a ready-made fleet to take on Lord Dunmore, the loyalist governor of Virginia who was raiding and terrorizing coastal towns and capturing their rebel privateers. Silas and Langdon were put in charge of finding such a fleet, then having only the *Alfred*.

To find officers to command the ships they hoped to acquire they turned to personal friends and relations they knew had some appropriate backgrounds. Ezek Hopkins, the brother of Stephen Hopkins, was made commodore. As captain of the *Alfred*, the committee picked Silas's brother-in-law, Dudley Saltonstall. Through the network of fellow Freemasons, John Paul Jones got Joseph Hewes to introduce him to the Naval Committee. Silas, in turn, as the most influential Mason on the committee, recommended Mason Jones as the first lieutenant on the *Alfred*.

On December 3, 1775, the Rattlesnake flag with the yellow background with the words "Don't Tread on ME" was hoisted at the main mast of the *Alfred* as the first ship of the Continental Navy. At the same time, First Lieutenant John Paul Jones hoisted another Rattlesnake flag with 13 red and white stripes at the ship's stern as the Continental Navy's Jack.

The following day, Silas wrote Elizabeth that naval preparations were getting underway with enthusiasm. He told her on that morning, a standing committee had been appointed by Congress to oversee the Continental Navy. Silas informed his wife that he had the honor of being chosen a member of the new Marine (maritime) Committee replacing the Naval Committee. In fact, Silas had also been asked to be the chairman of its ways and means subcommittee, in charge of obtaining provisions of all types for the new navy.

As a last act of the Naval Committee, Silas was sent to New York to purchase a ship to carry 29-pounders and a sloop of 10 guns. He was told to then send them through Long Island Sound to the New London/Groton area ports to be fitted out with crews and guns. The two ships are thought to be the *Columbus*—24, a converted merchantman and the sloop *Hornet*—10; both were commissioned in January of 1776.[27]

The reasons for sending newly acquired ships for converting and outfitting with guns to the Connecticut coast was basically two-fold. First, New London/Groton ports had continually been the leading ports for successful privateering and powder cruises to the West Indies. And the Connecticut ports were already known for their eager seamen and available seafaring supplies. Second, Connecticut had one of the three major iron foundry locations in the thirteen colonies, at Salisbury. And the surrounding area of iron mines in the very northwest corner of the colony, extending into New York, which had been taken over by order of Governor Trumbull with considerable pushing by Silas, and a few other dynamic patriots, in the Connecticut assembly.[28] The final week of December saw Congress move even further in creating a viable navy. It ordered each of the thirteen colonies to build a frigate.

As chairman of the Ways and Means Committee, Silas made a request of his brother Barnabus, who was in Philadelphia on the family's business. He asked Barnabus if he would become the Marine Committee's agent in Connecticut, in the construction of one of the frigates, for which he would receive a 5 percent commission on the total cost of building. The frigate *Trumbull* would be equipped with 28 guns. Barnabus accepted Silas's request, but took Silas's close friend Jeremiah Wadsworth as a partner. Wadsworth could help only with the initial capital. He was immediately appointed by Congress as commissary general of purchases for all American armed forces.

Before Silas's delegate term ran out he made sure that he obtained plans for the *Trumbull* from the famous designer Joshua Humphrey. In March, as Silas headed for Paris, work started on the *Trumbull*. Like so many other canons produced at the Salisbury Iron Works, *Trumbull's* 28 twelve-pounders were taken by oxcart overland to Portland on the Connecticut River. Unfortunately, without Silas's influence and because of the war in general, Barnabus ran into endless delays trying to get the ship fully outfitted. It was finally ready for action in 1779, but it had to wait at the mouth of the river until the British blockade of Long Island Sound was relaxed a bit. Knowing that Congress would always be short of cash, Silas made arrangements before he left, with his merchant friend President John Hancock, that $31,000 in payments be released to Barnabus by Continental treasurer Hillegar. During the remainder of the month of December, Silas and Langdon got the Marine Committee's acquisitions ready for action.

On January 3, 1776, five desperate ships, newly outfitted and commissioned in the Continental Navy, sailed down the Delaware headed for the open sea but were forced to turn back because heavy ice had frozen over parts of the bay. The brave little contingent of five ships called the Continental Navy were the converted merchantman *Alfred*, with 30 guns; the converted merchantman *Columbus*, with 28 guns; the brig *Andria Doria*, with 16 guns; the brig *Cabot*, with 14 guns; and the *Providence*, with 12 guns. These outfitted first five were joined later in January by the sloop *Hornet*, with 10 guns, and the schooner *Wasp*, with eight guns.

Writing to his wife on January 21, 1776, Silas told Elizabeth that it was necessary for him to stay in Philadelphia a while to close the naval accounts under his responsibilities and assist in getting ready the preparations for the little fleet's spring offensive. That is the last time anything was heard from Mr. Silas Deane until March 2.

All the time that Silas was involved with the Secret Committee (of Trade/Commerce) and the Naval and Marine Committee, he was constantly kept informed by Franklin and Morris of the actions of the Committee of Secret Correspondence, formed on November 29. Franklin and Morris were on both "secret" committees. The new committee of November 29 was supposedly created "for the sole purpose of Corresponding with our friends in Great Britain, Ireland and other parts of the world"[29] with Franklin at the helm—well, not exactly. The committee had a number of functions. It was the first American governmental agency ever to be established to collect foreign secret intelligence; thus, without much of a stretch, it was the predecessor of today's CIA. As the committee members were neophites in the art of secret diplomacy and the collection of intelligence, their skills in diplomacy would be harshly tested. But soon, as a result, with Franklin and Deane on the foreign side and Washington and Benjamin Tallmadge on the home front, American innocence was shortly overcome as they mastered what has been called the world's second oldest profession. The Secret Committee of Correspondence is considered the forerunner of the United States State Department.

Franklin loved intrigue, and under his direction the Secret Committee of Correspondence (its name was changed in April 1777 to the Committee of Foreign Affairs) used secret agents, couriers, ciphers, codes, invisible ink and covert operations. Little was known about just how the committee operated, even years later after the war; one invisible ink's formula is reportedly still in the archive vaults of the CIA. Silas Deane would have the honor of being the first American ever to use, or be involved with, all of the above spy elements.

It is necessary here to return to the creation of the Secret Committee of Correspondence. Its members were men of considerable prestige whose names would go down in history after the war was over. Franklin, as the most knowledgeable, became the self-appointed and accepted unofficial chairman. By careful maneuvering he was able to get his personal allies and friends on the committee, but that by no means meant they always agreed with him. The members were John Dickinson, leader of the conservatives and Franklin's close friend; John Jay, Silas's friend and a brilliant New York lawyer; Benjamin

Harrison, a major Virginia merchant and silent partner of Robert Morris who strongly admired both Franklin and Washington; and Thomas Johnson, a Marylander and eminent jurist.

Congress had been stunned by the king's reaction to the Olive Branch Petition. The committee decided they had better find out just what had been the reaction in Europe. It made inquiries on an informal and confidential basis with representatives of European power. Letters were sent by a special courier across the Atlantic (the first diplomatic courier being Thomas Story). Orders were given to the captains and Story to destroy the letters if the ship was in danger of capture — verbal instructions were also given to the courier and various captains.

The first letters that went out were written by Franklin to two old and trusted friends in Europe. He opened his correspondence with his literary friend in the Hague, Charles W.F. Dumas, and resumed his years of constant correspondence with his publisher of scientific experiments, Dr. Jacques Barbeau Dubourg in Paris. Franklin asked them both straight out if they would check to see if there were any European powers that would be willing to enter into an alliance with the colonies for the benefit of their commerce. In these first letters was a seed of serious and continuous trouble for Silas down the road. Franklin, on Washington's request and need, asked in the letter for two military engineers before the spring campaigns of 1776, one familiar with fieldpieces and strategy and the other experienced in seaport fortifications.

Before Franklin heard back from his letters, France stepped into the picture. Foreign minister Vergennes hated England and was always looking for a way to exploit England's trouble with the colonies as long as it could be done discreetly. For direct information he needed a spy, one that was well informed. Chevalier Julien Archchaud de Bonvouloir was selected. Bonvouloir had been to America before and wasted no time heading to Philadelphia posing as an Amsterdam merchant. Once in the city, he sought out a French bookseller in Philadelphia, feeling that he could have dealings with Franklin on science, especially electricity. Bonvouloir was right; he had the good luck of locating a bookseller who was actually the librarian taking care of Franklin's own library volumes. The bookseller quietly told Franklin of the spy's desire to meet with him.

Franklin met alone, and secretly, with Bonvouloir until he thought it was time to arrange a secret meeting with his other colleagues on the Committee of Secret Correspondence. Since meeting with Bonvouloir would be the first contact with a foreign agent (from experience Franklin knew the signs that would give them away), the members of the committee took precautions against being found out by British agents and sympathizers. On the night of December 18, each member went to the meeting place by a different route.

Vergennes had told Bonvouloir to let Congress know that France sympathized with the American cause and would not intervene in the question of Canada. He could offer the Americans free use of French ships and ports to carry their war supplies after they had declared independence or had become independent from Great Britain. For the Americans that was going to be the same as the "damned if you do, damned if you don't" syndrome. The Americans were not able to get foreign aid without declaring their independence, and they couldn't declare independence without foreign aid. The discussions continued but were very delicate on both sides. Dickinson and Jay were hesitant and resisted any rash claims toward independence, but they did admit the colonies couldn't win without foreign aid. But, in turn, it was obvious that France was concerned about openly committing itself to the patriots, who might then give in to England and turn on France.

At first Franklin and the rest of the committee doubted that Bonvouloir carried much authority. Over the course of the next three meetings they continued to probe for explicit answers. From the committee, up came that dangerous request that would affect Silas's future politically and personally again. General Washington required two competent military engineers. How could they get them? Would France accept American products in trade for military supplies? Of course the patriots knew they were already getting older French arms by way of the West Indies, but the profiteering merchant/captains were making as much as a 350 percent profit on a single cargo. Congressional finances could not hold out.

Finally, Franklin, with his "negotiating skills"—which were actually just a line of cock-and-bull anecdotes on how well prepared the Americans were—convinced Bonvouloir, who went beyond his instructions, to promise two French military engineers, but Bonvouloir balked at committing France to any alliance. After the last meeting on December 27, Bonvouloir dashed off a glorious dispatch to Vergennes, stating, "Everyone here is a soldier. Troops are well clothed, well paid and well armed. They have more than 50,000 regular soldiers and even a larger number of volunteers that do not wish to be paid. Judge how men of this caliber will fight.... Independence is a certainty for 1776."[30] What a "snow job" Franklin and the committee pulled off. Some six weeks later Bonvouloir continued his report in person. Vergennes was impressed, but by his nature he was still cautious over the American situation.

After Bonvouloir's visit, Franklin met with Robert Morris to go over the information obtained from the French spy. They immediately agreed with each other that they had better get an American representative across the Atlantic to France as soon as possible. America needed someone to deal with the French government firsthand. That person had to be a man with merchant trade skills, highly educated, and with wide experience dealing with world conditions, rather than just provincial knowledge. He should also be an individual with high personal ambition with political and administrative skills to match. Most important, he would have to be willing to take the high personal risks with a strong commitment to American independence.

When Silas learned he had not been reelected to Congress, he knew he was going to have to make some hard decisions concerning his future political and private life. Being so close to all of the major issues facing Congress, he realized that many crucial events were taking place at the same time or in tandem that were both of a positive and a negative nature in relation to the war effort. He had committed himself to the cause of American liberty far more than most delegates. Silas knew he had a clearer big picture of the colonies' entire situation more than most did.

Groups in Congress were beginning to solidify into definite politically and philosophically oriented forces. Belonging to the Morris-dominated Secret Committee of Trade (Commerce), and having worked closely with Franklin, Silas was already aware that the two secret committees were looking for an individual who could represent America in a secret mission abroad. At first Silas gave the idea of volunteering for such a mission little regard. It could be just one of many options open to his future.

When the news got out to the body of Congress that Silas was now a free agent, it took many delegates by surprise and chagrin. They needed this guy in Congress. He was well known for his prodigious work habits, resourcefulness and incessant pushing of the envelope to get a committee, of which he was a member, to take some positive action over inactivity.

Franklin felt strongly that Silas was the man for the job, especially after learning about the positive intentions of France and the Indian crisis in the "colonial" west. After all, like Silas, Franklin had personal stakes speculating in western lands. Knowing the 38-year-old's background, Franklin admired Deane's popularity in Congress among the mercantile delegates, his social graces and impeccable manner and dress, and, above all, his administrative and persuasive abilities when working with all classes of men. Yes, Franklin was sure he had the right man for the complicated mission he had in mind. Robert Morris agreed whole-heartedly because he knew Silas's merchant contacts were not only on the American continent. Silas knew businessmen in Ireland in the trade of flaxseed, in Gibraltar on the Barbary Coast in flour and lumber, and the ports of Lisbon and Bilboa in fish.

Franklin approached Silas "officially" just as Silas had finished getting the little new Continental Navy outfitted and ready for action the first week in January. When Silas was asked to take the mission he was flattered but hesitant. He would be separated from his ill wife and frail 11-year-old son for a long period of time. There was also the rough sea voyage with the danger of being captured and imprisoned. He told Franklin he didn't have any diplomatic background and he didn't speak French, although he could stumble along to read and write the language in the simplest of terms. But Franklin told him he need not be too concerned; nobody in America had any true diplomatic background, except Franklin, and his own knowledge of French and European diplomacy were at best minimal. Franklin played on Silas's ego hard. He told Silas that he possessed a broad background of historical knowledge, had a pleasing vibrant personality, and the ability to converse on dozens of subjects clearly with force, frankness, and, above all, honesty.

Morris's committee of trade offered Silas a 5 percent commission incentive on all mercantile committee contracts as the sole American purchasing agent in Europe. Morris was well aware that Silas was fairly well financially independent and the offer was "nice," but not what interested Silas the most. So Morris even offered a personal partnership of Morris's overseas contracts, which did get Silas's attention.

After much deliberation the young firebrand just couldn't let go his strong sense of duty to his country. As he had told his wife earlier, the cause of liberty had to come first; but if he failed the chance of future personal financial gain was still there.

As soon as Silas accepted the mission, Franklin began to brief him on what the real conditions were in Europe up until the time he left for America. There were two areas of which Franklin wanted Silas to be sharply aware. The first was how Franklin had been working quietly setting up gunrunning operations for the colonies on the continent since late 1773. And, second, the issue of one Arthur Lee was discussed. Franklin filled Silas in on the kind of personality he would have to deal with in Lee and the trouble Lee had caused Franklin while Lee was the "assistant" colonial agent under Franklin. Franklin wanted Silas to understand that no matter the circumstance, Arthur Lee always had an exaggerated impression of his importance on the world stage.

It occurred to Franklin while he was bringing Silas up to date that he had better let Silas know that Lee was somewhat aware of the colonial agents' gunrunning contacts and arrangement. He told Silas that all of his contacts were Freemasons and merchants. In France, he dealt with Sieur Montaudoin of Nantes and Dubourg in Paris; Dubourg got the supplies together and Montaudoin shipped them out to the West Indies. (What Franklin did not know at the time was that both Dubourg and Montaudoin were under Vergennes' personal protection.)

Besides the contacts in France, Franklin had direct relations with the Crommelins of Amsterdam, Diego Gardoqui of Bilboa, and several other merchant houses up and down the European coast that were sending supplies, including Bordeaux. Franklin told the Connecticut Yankee that, to his knowledge, there was no paper trail. Silas agreed. He rather stunned Franklin by telling him he had been dealing, on a personal basis, with Amsterdam and Bilboa for several years and had never heard of Franklin's involvement "in trade." Silas said, however, he would like to know some details on his "supply laundering" operations with the English merchants he had mentioned.

The cities of Nantes and Bordeaux were strongholds of Freemasonry, which had become a powerful influence throughout France during the second half of the 18th century. For Freemasonry, it was an easy transition from the ideals of Voltaire and Rousseau to becoming warm sympathizers with the rebellious Americans. The merchants had needed little prodding from Franklin. Even by 1770, there was a great increase in commerce between those ports and the colonies, and the American business agents who were settling in French ports to expedite goods across the Atlantic made big commissions. In 1775, just six months before Silas arrived in Bordeaux, the port of Nantes had become the main port and base for "secret" aid to America in war supplies.

After Franklin made sure Silas was aware of and understood the intrigue, dirty tricks and diplomatic espionage that was currently taking place in Europe, he turned Silas over to Robert Morris for further briefing in current happenings in the international mercantile world. During the years 1775 through 1776, Morris was truly considered the most powerful, rich and influential merchant in all North America. He introduced Silas to his personal trade network and personality contacts in New Orleans, the West Indies islands of England, Spain, Holland, and the North Sea coastline (notice the absence of France), all by letters of introduction to be kept and delivered independently by Morris. Thus no paper trail was left by Silas in case of capture.

The hope and purpose of Franklin and Morris was that, if Silas, as America's first foreign secret agent, could pull it off, there would ensue the largest and most coordinated commercially based diplomacy and intelligence gathering network of the 18th century. To organize a secure intelligence system was a tall order. Franklin knew how efficient the British Secret Service could be.

While Silas was busy with the detailed preparations for his mission, the two secret committees (with their dual memberships and chairmen in both committees) led by Morris and Franklin put strong pressure on Congress to obtain funds to be used for the importation of goods to help the friendship of the Indian tribes. Franklin was on the Indian Affairs Committee and knew all too well the English were presently buying up Indian loyalty at a tremendously fast rate.

The last week in January, Congress voted Morris's committee the whopping sum of £40,000 sterling for "Indian goods." After voting such a sum, Congress stipulated that the goods purchased and imported should be divided between the Indian Affairs Department, north, middle and south. The Secret Committee (of Trade) would export goods to cover its purchases. The "Indian goods" contract was made by the Secret Committee (of Trade) with four merchants, and not surprisingly, three of them were committee members: Robert Morris himself, John Alsop, Francis Lewis and Philip Livingston.[31]

Franklin and the rest of the Indian Affairs Committee realized early in their deliberations that the need for Indian goods was very real and crucial to the war effort. Conflicts between Indian and European cultures had been steadily increasing by the eve of the Revolution. The growing pressure on the loss of Indian lands had eroded previous peaceful coexistence. North Carolina's population, for example, jumped from 45,000 in 1750 to over 275,000 by 1775.

The colonial frontier had come to believe that the English government, and its various agencies, favored Indians over settlers. By the beginning of the Revolution the backcountry was ready to explode. The American patriots called it a war for liberty and independence. The Indians knew that for them it was the same old struggle for their lands.

For the Indians, in this new war, it was crucial that they pick the side that could keep them supplied with the most goods of all kinds to help their chosen allies. To the Indians victory was not a possibility. The best they could hope for was damage control over their lands. For the Americans, as well as the British, the shifting fortunes of war meant constant attention to the supply of Indian gifts to their Native American allies, lest they change sides. To the Americans, the war was a fight for freedom and the creation of an empire of their own which included Indian lands of the West. For the Indians, it was a no-win situation: they were excluded from American society.

In the Indian contract with Silas, as part of his mission, the Secret Committee of Trade/Commerce was to ship cargoes to the appropriate markets in Europe. The cargoes would be assigned to various commission merchants in the European ports. The merchants were to sell the cargo goods and give the proceeds to Samuel and J.H. Delap in Bordeaux and Clifford and Tysett or John Hodgon in Amsterdam. In turn, these men would account to Silas, who would then purchase from the list of various Indian goods approved by the committee.

Although Franklin was never very handy in their use himself, his love of intrigue and his years of experience with the secret power struggle of European nations made him feel it was necessary for Silas to have a working knowledge of some secret ciphers and codes. Franklin hoped it would help protect congressional correspondence crossing the Atlantic in both directions.

IV. Leading Connecticut Congressional Delegate, 1775

It so happened that Silas's friend, and member of the Secret Correspondence Committee, John Jay had a brother, James, who, while practicing medicine in England, developed a formula for invisible ink. It was quite different from the ones used in Europe and worked by wetting the written words on paper with a fine brush dipped in a reagent that caused the original straw-colored ink to turn a deep black. John Jay obtained a supply of the ink and reagent and, acting like a modern "CIA control officer," trained Silas in its use along with several different codes and ciphers.

Peculiarly, in the years 1778–1780, Deane's friend and former Wethersfield school superintendent, Major Benjamin Tallmadge, Washington's chief secret agent, also used the very same formula ink for secret correspondence in operating the famous covert operation of the organization known as the Culper Ring. The relationship and correspondence between Silas and Tallmadge as spies from 1777 to 1780 is interesting. And, in several ways, it is quite suspect. Considering Silas's sometimes unanswered actions, it is of special interest due to the fact that both individuals were number two men under the Revolution's two chief American spymasters—Franklin in Europe and Washington in America.[32]

Suddenly, toward the first of February, Silas disappeared under the radar. He did not reappear until the first week in March. At that time, both secret committees gave him written and word-of-mouth instructions on the 2nd, 3rd, and 4th of March along with his commission and portfolio. There is a very long letter on March 3 to Elizabeth explaining a variety of family and personal situations. It tells her what to do "in case of," plus a few hints about his mission, but nothing explicit.

The letter is important in explaining Deane's future problems and actions. It is quoted here in part to show the reality of Silas's private concerns:

> I have, in one of the most solemn acts of my life, committed my son and what I have to your care and the care of my Brother, confident you will be to him a real mother, which you have ever been, and for my sake, as well as from the truly maternal affection you have ever borne for him, guard his youth from anything dangerous, or dishonorable. I can but feel for the pain I must give you by this adventure, but on all occasions you will have this satisfaction, that let what will happen, you have in every situation discharged your duty as one of the best partners and wives, while on my part, by a peculiar fatality attending me from my first entrance into public life, I have ever been involved in one scheme and adventure after another, so as to keep my mind in constant agitation and my attention fixed on other objects than my own immediate interests. The present object is great. I am about to enter on the great stage of Europe, and the consideration of the importance of quitting myself, well, weighs me down, without the addition of

more tender scenes; but I am, "Safe in the hand of that protecting Power, Who rul'd my natal, and must fix my mortal hour." It matters but little, my Dear, what part we act, or where, if we act it well. I wish as much as any man for the enjoyments of domestic ease, peace, and society but am forbid expecting them soon; indeed, must be criminal in my own eyes, did I balance them one moment in opposition to the Public Good and the Calls of my Country.

P.S. Confident this letter will go safe, I venture to say that a Concern, different from my contract is to support me. I have agreed that all expenses of every kind shall be paid, and referred my salary to be determined hereafter, in consequence of which it is agreed that I have Five hundred pounds Sterling to carry with me for that purpose, and the same sum is to be remitted to me at the end of six months. Should any accident happen to me, you will find this entered on the Committee of Secret Correspondence's Books. The members are: Dr. Franklin, Mr. Dickinson, Mr. Jay, Mr. Morris, Col. Harrison, and Mr. Johnson. But you must not communicate this to any one, except my Brother. This will explain my saying that I have a commission of two thousand pounds free of charge, as my charge will be amply provided for by the other way. And now, my Dear, are not the ways of Providence dark and inscrutable to us, short-sighted mortals? Surely they are. My enemies, tho't to triumph over me and bring me down, yet all they did has been turned to the opening a door for the greatest and most extensive usefulness, if I succeed; but if I fail,—why then the Cause I am engaged in, and the important part I have undertaken, will justify my adventuring.

Several papers I have mentioned were inclosed in the packet to my Brother, as will be found on the opening. I shall leave with Mr. Morris, Eighteen hundred dollars to be called for by my Brother, as he will find a reference in my Cash Account No. 2, sent him by Capt. Wadsworth. The sum I left Mr. Marshall, I sent a receipt for. I have not been able as yet to make any insurance, and if you think prudent to do it, you must advise with Mr. Jno. Alsop and Mr. Morris, upon it, as it may be dangerous to have the matter made public.[33]

For more than two centuries, historians have made dozens of conjectures as to what Silas was doing, why and where, besides being briefed for his mission. At present there is still no written evidence of any kind that has been located. The same kind of blackout appears again from early April until Mr. Deane arrives in Bordeaux on June 4. The one known exception to total disappearance is one letter to Robert Morris dated May 26 that gives no pertinent information. Such a voyage, all things considered, normally would take no more than a maximum of 45 days from Philadelphia to the French coast.

There are some obvious reasons for such silence as to what and why. In diplomatic situations during wartime among and between nations, they automatically became adversaries in both foreign policy and military decisions. Sources and methods then of obtaining information must be protected by secrecy if intelligence is to continue. Secret intelligence by its very nature is obscure and inaccessible, given out only in the old adage "on a need to know basis." Consequently, its role in the scheme of things is largely overlooked or ignored by historians.

Silas, with his more than a dozen years of merchant smuggling background, Franklin, with his long colonial agent experience, and Morris, with his command and financial expertise, all recognized the fact that the business of American secret intelligence activities would have to remain a hidden subplot in the American Revolution. They, and George Washington, fully understood the "honorable treachery" of secret agents, and the part they played during the war would unfortunately have to stay cloudy and fuzzy to future generations. These men knew that the most secret and covert operations of a war probably never see the light of day from a nation's archives until, perhaps, sometime far in the distant future, if ever. Suffice it to say the patriots were neophytes at the beginning of the Revolution in obtaining and utilizing secret intelligence, but they quickly mastered the "art."

Silas's mission's written instructions (see Appendix C), were generally outlined by Franklin. It definitely was supposed to be a secret mission, but since Congress still had several halfway patriots and wavering individuals physically situated in close proximity to Congress, England heard about Deane's mission months before Congress as a body even knew he was gone.

Basically Silas was to act only as a private merchant to avoid embarrassing the French ministry. In his instructions were several definite "orders": contact Dubourg who could get him an audience with Vergennes. Silas was to offer the minister the benefits of American trade in exchange for help in obtaining war supplies. He was also to ask Vergennes whether, if the colonies declared independence from England, France would recognize them and under what basic conditions she would consider receiving American envoys to enter into a treaty of alliance for commerce or defense or both. If he could arrange it, he was to go to Holland and get in touch with Dumas. Silas was also told to get in touch with his former student, Dr. Edward Bancroft in London, and ask him to come to Paris and update him on European situations. Lastly, Silas was to initiate correspondence with Arthur Lee in London.

After receiving his direct orders in writing from Franklin, now acting as the "Company's chief of station," in modern CIA terms, Silas, on March 8, took a pilot boat to Chester, Pennsylvania, on Delaware Bay and boarded a merchant brig, but the winds forced it back to shore, damaging the bottom.

Silas then waited near Cape May, New Jersey, for a sloop that was being outfitted in Maryland. In the meantime, the two secret committees sent a guard of 20 soldiers to protect Silas from capture by loyalists as nothing remained a secret for long around the Philadelphia area. Nearly a month passed before the Bermuda sloop *Betsy* was fully outfitted. Silas talked one Captain Johnson of the Bermuda Tucker clan to take him to Bermuda. Once in Bermuda, Silas renewed his acquaintance with the Tuckers, whom he had known from the previous summer's "gunpowder raid" arranged by him, Franklin and Morris. Silas had been directly involved because he knew Bermuda customs. Consequently, he bought the sloop *Betsy* outright, with Johnson as captain to take him to either Nantes or Bordeaux. The exact date Silas left Bermuda is not known, but it was early April.

From that time on, it has always been only theory and conjecture as to where Silas was and what he was doing for two months before arriving at Bordeaux to start his mission. The answer remains another secret.

CHAPTER V

Secret American Agent to France, 1776

By many reliable accounts Silas Deane was a brilliant and perceptive individual of the 18th century world. But he, and undoubtedly almost every other colonial, had little knowledge or understanding of the real politics and values of the European societies. Even the famous "First American," Ben Franklin, with his long tenure as a colonial agent in London and known throughout Europe for his scientific achievements, could not fully realize what all-inclusive situations Silas was about to enter.

By its very nature and location, early America was isolated from European life. Occupied by incessant colonial wars for more than two centuries, Americans had definitely become a different people (a point Silas was to use several times in the coming two years). Yet, they were still quite provincial in their knowledge of the world across the Atlantic.

After the French and Indian War, (known as the Seven Years' War in Europe), the North American colonies were preoccupied with a general economic slump, worsened by the British ministry's oppressive trade restrictions upon the colonies in order to keep its own economic strength after the strain of its war with France. In 1763, the Peace of Paris ended the Seven Years' War between England and France. The French had virtually accepted defeat in order to plan their revenge.

By the end of that year, France was already thinking in terms of an independent North America as far as the colonies were concerned. All during the next decade the French government kept a very close eye on what was happening in the North American British colonies. France had spies in all major American cities and the countryside sending back detailed reports concerning American defenses and, especially, its trading routes. The French ministry was particularly interested in the colonists' reaction to the 1765 Stamp Act and the punitive measures that followed. By the year 1768, the French ministry was actually ready to aid the colonies if they should openly break with England.

The famous Baron De Kalb of the Revolution years was sent to tour the colonies for France in 1769. He reported back that the colonies were not yet ready to declare anything close to independence. They were still highly suspicious of the French monarchy as a result of the French and Indian War and the fact that it was a Catholic country. The Americans were also wary of France because the peace treaty had allowed the French to retain the West Indies rich sugar islands of Guadeloupe and Martinique, which gave it both commercial riches and suspect naval bases that could threaten the colonies at any time.

The year 1770 brought a new French foreign minister to power. His name was Charles Gravier Comte de Vergennes and he caused a deep desire for revenge against the British. However, at that time, the young and new King Louis XVI was not yet ready to take on England. Vergennes decided it was crucial to beef up his intelligence network any way he could to keep more abreast of what the British were doing about the continuous unrest in the American colonies.

Hopes for the future King Louis XVI's France were accompanied by the phenomenon of Freemasonry. In 1775 there were over 1,000 Masonic lodges throughout France comprising upward of 100,000 Freemasons. Masonry was seen at that time as a society of beneficence and pleasure. There were bishops and monks in Masonry's ranks who ignored the pope's prohibition in membership and preferred the conviviality of a lodge to the spirituality of a religious fraternity. Over 75 percent of Masons were commoners and from the professional class, including lawyers, medical doctors and governmental employees. Over one-fifth of the total membership was drawn from the trades and business world, along with military officers and students. Shopkeepers and artisans were also found in the fraternal ranks. French Masons were both Protestant and Catholic. Freemasonry, however, faithfully held to elitism with a claim to moral and virtuous respectability. The "vulgar" were definitely excluded, along with women of any background.

From the early 1770s, and especially after the accession of Louis XVI to the French throne, the nobles and savants sought to create a national network of intellectual sociability, while the "second estate" Masons of professionals and merchants extended their networking into the commercial world of commerce and trade.

When America began to seriously squabble with England and its empire, the second estate Masons saw a chance to covertly enhance their business and trade with colonial America at British expense. Although it was not their primary reason for their interest, in the process they would be aiding America in its fight with England over the loss of its chartered liberties.

Their network included the major French coastal interior cities. These urban centers were rich in all types of goods needed by Americans. The two coastal cities of Bordeaux and Nantes were the major strongholds of Freemasonry, but their influence included a long string of other French cities and towns. Rouen, Marseilles, LeHarve and Dunkirk were primaries, but inland there was Strassbourg, Dijon, Metz, Besançon and Charterville.

Before Silas ever set foot on French soil he would unknowingly be working with a stacked deck in his favor, if only events would let him play his cards right. When Silas sailed into Bordeaux harbor, America's first foreign secret agent and emissary to France would quickly become the only American who had some understanding of the governmental and economic circumstances in France.

Even though the new king and his ministers knew they needed to use restraint in their goal of revenge against the British, they were working hard to prepare for eventual war. Intelligence gathering was highly improved in the spring of 1776, and Sartine, the new naval minister, was rebuilding the navy.

Suddenly the French ministry had a big, but rather welcome, problem. An unofficial American envoy arrived on the scene. The ministers began to wonder how long, if they aided the Americans, they could hold off on the colonials — until France was truly ready for war and without the "rebels" reconciling with England.

While Silas was doing a long disappearing act on the high seas for almost three months before finally making landfall with the sloop *Betsy* at Bordeaux, Congress had become quite concerned and worried with the buildup of French warships in the West Indies. It had only been a little over 12 years before that France was the enemy.

Congress asked the Secret Committee of Commerce (Trade), with Robert Morris now chairman, to investigate. Morris supported William Bingham, his second protégé (Silas being his first), to sail to Martinique in the West Indies as a private businessman and to report back what was going on with the French. Born wealthy, young Bingham was well-educated, worldly and known for his efficiency in most matters. Arriving on the *Reprisal* under Captain Lambert Wickes at the port of Saint-Pierre on Martinique in July, Bingham had the pleasure of seeing Wickes go after the Royal Navy sloop HMS *Shark*. But the harbor port fired on the *Shark*, making it break off the engagement and withdraw. In a few days, the British launched a major complaint with the island governor followed by vague threats, which were happily ignored.

Within a couple of weeks the now congressional agent Bingham had secured a large cache of military supplies for shipment to Congress and informed it that the French were there to protect and aid the Americans, not hurt them as feared. The network of intelligence and arms trade that Silas hoped to set up between America and Europe now had a beginning point on the Atlantic side. Bingham wrote Silas to ship all his goods through him rather than straight to American ports that were heavily blockaded by British warships. He would then reload them in smaller ships that could hide along, and hug, the North American coastline where the Royal Navy could not go. For the entire war period, Bingham would be the key link in successfully getting much of the network commerce to America.

As Silas made his way in the *Betsy* to the French coast, several very specific situations were taking place that would have a direct bearing on the course of his mission both in America and across the Atlantic. In London, Arthur Lee and Caron de Beaumarchais had become very chummy. The two men had met at several of the famous John Wilkes dinner parties. Beaumarchais was in London as a French secret agent for Vergennes, gathering intelligence and trying to convince one Chevalier d'Eon — who was owed in today's buying power about $2.5 million for heading up a spy ring in the 1760s for King Louis XVI's grandfather, King Louis XV — not to release his correspondence to the English press. The situation would develop into a long and drawn-out blackmail affair involving the cross-dressing Chevalier d'Eon, or Cheralière d'Eon, that would ultimately have an indirect connection with the signing of the Franco-American Alliance of 1778.

Beaumarchais knew Lord Rockford, the former secretary of state for the Southern Department who had very loose lips, as the source of British planning activities with the colonies. While Beaumarchais was in the city he made it his personal business to make contact with Americans who were active in advertising the American colonial unrest. There are several versions of the plans and agreements made by Lee and Beaumarchais to aid the colonies at a profit while they both were in London, but whatever the case may be, Lee did not inform Congress of his contact with Beaumarchais for more than 18 months.

In February 1776, Thomas Story arrived in London with Arthur Lee's appointment as America's agent in London. From the Committee of Secret Correspondence, Lee received verbal orders through Story. Immediately Lee objected to Franklin and Jay as members of the committee. Writing his brother Richard Henry Lee, Arthur said they are "men whom I cannot trust. If I am to commit myself to an unreserved correspondence they must be left out, and the L's and the A's put in their place."[1] But, within a couple of months, he changed his mind and wrote the committee anyway. Although no record has appeared, Franklin had likely told Bonvouloir to inform their agent in London, Arthur Lee, of his meeting with the Secret Committee of Correspondence and the information exchanged.

In early February, Bonvouloir reported to Vergennes the news that a declaration of independence was forthcoming (courtesy of Dr, Benjamin Franklin and still six months away). Ben often stretched the truth. Almost immediately, Vergennes received a letter from Arthur Lee urging straight out that France should aid the colonies in their struggle with England and send two urgently needed military engineers to Washington. The phrase "two engineers" would become the basis for much of Silas's trouble with Congress in the future. At Cambridge the previous fall, Franklin had been on a mission to learn exactly what the general's needs were. Washington told him he urgently needed at least two qualified military engineers. Washington wanted one for fort building and one for battlefield issues. Franklin passed it on to Lee and later to Silas as the "official" unofficial American representative.

Vergennes' reaction to Lee's letter was "diplomatic irritation." He resented Arthur's audacity and the fact the letter did not come through secure diplomatic channels but direct mail prone to interception. The foreign minister was beset by Beaumarchais at the same time pressing both him and the king with a plan to aid the Americans.

Finally, on March 2, 1776, the French monarch agreed to the plan that Beaumarchais had been pushing.[2] The translated secret instructions given Beaumarchais at the time by Vergennes for organizing a pseudo firm were as follows: "You will found your house, and at your own risk and perils you will provision the Americans with arms and munitions and objects of equipment and whatever is necessary to support the war. You shall not demand money of the Americans, because they have none, but you shall ask the returns in commodities of their soil, the sale of which we will facilitate in our country."[3]

From May 3 through June 14 there was a flurry of letters back and forth between Beaumarchais and Lee. But on June 12 Beaumarchais wrote a letter to Arthur stating that, because of his difficulties with the French ministry, he had determined to form his own company to supply Congress with war materials in return for tobacco and other goods. He did not tell Lee that the French government was going to back him. Two days before that, the author of the *Barber of Seville* had already received one million livres from the French treasury. The translated receipt read:

> Received from M. Duvergier, in conformity with the orders of M. de Vergennes, dated the 5th instant, which I have handed the sum of one million, of which I am to render an account to the said Sieur Comte de Vergennes
> Caron De Beaumarchais.
> Good for a million of livres tournois.
> Paris, June 10, 1776.[4]

Almost two months later to the day, with a lot of arm twisting by King Louis XVI, Beaumarchais received another million from the Spanish government. That receipt read:

> Received from His Excellency M. De Comte de Vergennes the receipt of one million livres tournois, given by M. Duvergier to the Spanish ambassador, with which receipt I am to receive from the said royal treasurer the sum of one million tournois, the use of which I am to account for to his said Excellency, M. le de Comte de Vergennes.
> Caron De Beaumarchais.
> Versailles, August 11, 1776.[5]

Thus, there can be no doubt that the two million livres addressed by France and Spain for use in obtaining secret aid and war supplies for America prior to the 1778 alliance was a gift.

The controversy, started by Lee in late 1776, that the money was a French loan was always an absolute falsehood. Unfortunately for Silas, Beaumarchais and Franklin, the accusation still lingers on into the 21st century. Silas often receives a bashing from modern-day historians for using government money with Beaumarchais for private gain. Actually, the two million livres would act only as an insurance and security against loss for Beaumarchais and his merchant associates (investors). Never during the period of 1776 through 1778 were the Americans told officially that Beaumarchais' assistance was gratuitous.

While Silas was still on the open ocean, events back in Philadelphia were taking place rather quickly. After bitter and long debates, Congress authorized a committee headed by John Adams, with Franklin's stiff but cooperative input, to draw up a plan of treaties with France. Few delegates truly wanted a political alliance with any European country; they wanted to be free of all political entanglements with foreign powers. Most members, however, did realize that they would have little chance of winning independence if they continually tried to go it alone.

Then, on June 7, came Richard Henry Lee's famous resolution for independence from Great Britain. John Adams, Franklin, Jefferson and Roger Sherman were appointed to a committee to compose a declaration of independence, which finally passed Congress on July 4.

In mid–September, Franklin received correspondence from Dubourg dated June 10, 1776, saying he had met with Penet, with whom Franklin and Silas had secretly made arrangements to procure arms and war supplies in France. He took Penet to Versailles and introduced him to Vergennes, who sent them to a Monsieur Dupont. Dupont said France was sympathetic to the American cause but was afraid their struggle might collapse due to the lack of money. On a pleasant note, Dupont did say the French government was considering the opening up of credit for the colonies that would not be readily apparent to the British. It's interesting to note the parallel dates with Beaumarchais' undertaking. Penet told Dubourg he was headed back to his company's offices in Nantes to start looking for the "goods" that the Secret Committee for Correspondence had commissioned.

In the same letter to Franklin, Dubourg said he had already negotiated a deal from the king's own arsenal for fifteen thousand 1763 rifles with the promise that he personally would eventually replace them with newer models. He said the rifles had been shipped to Penet's company in Nantes and were waiting for the Secret Committee's ships to arrive. Dubourg continued, saying he had also made a deal with the Farmer's General (the French Royal Tax Collection Agency) for Virginia's entire year's supply and had hired two outstanding military engineers that Franklin had asked him to get for Washington. Obviously Dubourg had to be exaggerating his accomplishments just a little bit.[6]

After over three months out of Philadelphia, Silas sailed into the Bordeaux harbor aboard the Bermuda sloop *Betsy*. Mr. Deane was full of the whole broad range of human emotions, but two held his constant attention; namely fear, primarily for his family and events back home, and worry, concerning the success of his mission. He had no idea of what lay ahead, but he hoped for the best and would definitely give it his best whatever happened.

Events did not start off well. There were no Secret Committee ships in the harbor. Hoping the tobacco ships would arrive any day, Silas decided he would move ahead with his and the Secret Committee's plan to set up a secret trading and intelligence network to coordinate commercial and political activities throughout Europe, the West Indies and the Atlantic coastal ports. Now all the Connecticut Yankee had to do was use his convivial, easygoing personality, which really didn't expect much from people but was delighted when they exceeded his expectations.

By late June, through obvious methods of written and unwritten communication techniques and with the help of the Bordeaux merchant house of S.& J.H. Delap and merchant Masonic brothers, Silas had made initial contact with merchant houses up and down the European coastline, including Texel, Rotterdam, Amsterdam, Dunkirk, Nantes, Bilboa and Lisbon. Several of the contacts he had known previously.

According to his instructions, Silas sent off a note to Dr. Edward Bancroft, Deane's student in Hartford 18 years earlier, asking for a meeting in Paris and including 30 pounds for his expenses. After more than three weeks of waiting for the "Indian trade" committee ships that would never come, Silas knew he had to get busy with the political and diplomatic part of his mission. (The *Charming Polly*, with a cargo of 3,000 pounds of sterling for

Silas to use in the "Indian trade" was captured along with the *Adrian* and the *Peggy* bound for Bordeaux.)

Before leaving for the rough 300-plus miles to Paris, Silas showed the socially pleasant and patriotic side of his personality. He sent his sloop *Betsy* back to the West Indies to join the American privateering fleet harassing English trade. With the sloop he sent presents home to his family and close friends, especially those who were fellow merchants like Hancock, whom he had known from the mid–1760s. Silas was openly excited about the trip to the great city of Paris, but quite wary about his future in the French "capitol." Writing back to the Delap brothers about his 300-mile trip, Silas showed another side of his social personality and character. He wrote, "We drank plentifully on the Road, paid Duty for 2 doz. and smuggled in 2 doz. more, which was brave doings, but you know Am-will smuggle."[7] Silas was always willing to take a risk, but it had to be reasonable or, at the least, somewhat salvageable if things went wrong; total failure was not an option, there was always another way to go. "Definitely don't take yourself too seriously" seemed to be his motto, "everyone can be replaced."

Silas arrived in the grand city of 18th century Europe during the sixth of July and immediately started looking for suitable lodgings for a "Bermuda" merchant. He settled on Hôtel Villars just as Bancroft came calling, having arrived in Paris the day before. The two men quickly renewed their teacher-student acquaintance of 12 years earlier. Silas had been briefed by Franklin as to Bancroft's background since the 1760s. What interested Silas the most was the fact that Franklin, while a colonial agent in London, utilized Bancroft's popularity as his own private secret agent to learn what the inner circles of British government were planning for the American colonies. In turn, Franklin had helped Bancroft's scientific career and involved him in the political intrigues over American western land speculations. Knowing all this, and likely a lot more, Silas did not hesitate to quickly rely on Bancroft as his chief source of information coming out of England. At that point, Bancroft had not yet turned double agent, but this would happen within the next three months. England would know Silas's every move even before Congress knew he was in Paris.

Once settled in his lodgings, at least for the moment, Silas contacted Dubourg, who was delighted to hear from the American firsthand. Silas showed the scientist his credentials and gave him a letter from Franklin with some additional personal papers, which pleased the Frenchman no end. America's first envoy immediately asked Dubourg to arrange a meeting with Vergennes, but Dubourg kept saying it was not wise to meet with the minister at this time since the British ambassador, Lord Stormont, knew from sources in Philadelphia that Deane was due to arrive in France and his arrival at Bordeaux had already been reported to the ambassador.

Actually, Dubourg had had an embarrassing run-in with Vergennes earlier that month for openly shooting off his mouth too much concerning the "secret" aid he was supplying the Americans. Vergennes had told him, "One can connive at certain things, but one cannot authorize them."[8]

Using his friendship for Franklin as a wedge, Silas pushed the reluctant Dubourg to make the arrangements for a meeting with the foreign minister. Two days later, Silas had his audience with Vergennes, which lasted almost three hours. Bancroft did not go with them to Versailles, but waited back in Paris to hear the results of the meeting.

Silas was a bit apprehensive about his lack of knowledge of the French language, but it was an encumbrance he slowly overcame in the ensuing six months. However, it was a problem for both him and Franklin. They never became entirely fluent in the language and gave the French a lot of laughs with their word usage. At reading and writing they became quite adept, but neither man was ever very good at speaking the language.

To the American agent's relief, Conrad Alexandre Gérard, secretary to the king's council and Vergennes' right-hand man, spoke fluent English and acted as interpreter. It was a long productive session as far as Silas was concerned. He did not as yet thoroughly understand the underlying French motives behind their willingness to secretly help the Americans, but he was certain Vergennes had only America's best interests at heart. By the fall of 1777, he would be sorely disappointed and later, in 1780, his disappointment with the French would turn to outright disgust.

The two men talked through Gérard in very formal terms for almost three hours. In fact, the talks went so smoothly to both men's delight that Silas brought up subjects that Franklin had written in his instructions might have to wait for a second or even third meeting.

Through the long session both sides clarified situations, political and private, that needed to be understood. Vergennes made it clear that any open aid by France to the American colonies could eventually cause a war with England. But, he assured Silas that as a private citizen Silas was free to carry on commerce in France. Vergennes quietly pointed out that the French army had adopted new weapons and the old models were still in arsenals. Silas should consider himself under the protection of the French court and, although he could not be officially recognized, he could always reach Vergennes through Gérard. As the long interview ended, Vergennes told Silas in diplomatic language that "the people and their cause is very respectable in the eyes of all disinterested persons."[9] As Silas was leaving Vergennes' office, the minister spoke on a very personal note to Silas. He told the unofficial envoy that Silas, as a private citizen, was also under the protection of the king. If he had any trouble with government officials, he should report it to Vergennes. Also, above all, he should be aware of English spies, for they were everywhere. Of course, Silas already realized French agents were watching his every move. Lastly, Vergennes strongly recommended that he change lodgings as his landlady was well known for her "galantris" at Versailles' court and was considered a possible British spy.[10]

The day Gérard told Silas that two Englishmen by the names of Sir Charles Jenkinson and Sir Hans Stanley had followed him from Bordeaux to Paris to learn what commerce or negotiations might be taking place between the British colonies and France. Silas immediately changed his hotel, and then he learned that Wedderburn, the solicitor who had excoriated Franklin in the Cockpit, had arrived from London, as well as Lord Rockford from Holland, to see what the American agent was doing. As Silas wrote to the Committee of Secret Correspondence, "Not a coffee house or theater or other places of public diversion but swarms with their emissaries."[11]

Alerted by Vergennes that the appearance of Silas Deane as an unofficial envoy of Congress meant chopping ties with Arthur Lee, Beaumarchais immediately wrote the American "secret" agent, hinting in flowery terms how he could supply the colonies with all the arms they needed. This really rattled and puzzled Silas. He knew of Beaumarchais' reputation as a playwright and flamboyant playboy. It didn't match up. So Silas went straight back to Versailles and asked Vergennes personally, in so many terms, if Beaumarchais was just blowing a lot of smoke. To Silas's surprise, the foreign minister said that he could definitely rely on anything Beaumarchais promised to deliver more than Dubourg or Penet.

Silas decided to go for broke and meet with Beaumarchais. To his delight and surprise, the playwright could deliver all his needs and then some. It didn't take Silas long to figure out who was backing Beaumarchais once he realized the scope of the Hortalez Company's operations. Silas wrote back to the Committee of Secret Correspondence on August 2: "Everything he says, writes, or does is in reality the action of the ministry,"[12] Silas went on to point out that, a few months before, Beaumarchais was bankrupt and hiding from his creditors, but at the present he was advancing huge sums. It doesn't leave much to the imagination as to the source of the huge sums.

The pragmatic merchant Deane and the flamboyant entrepreneur Beaumarchais made an excellent team. After a few meetings and discussions, the two men became fast friends. They accumulated enough supplies to fill at least eight or more merchantmen, but it wasn't long before Beaumarchais had spent the original two million livres plus another million livres from his merchant associates, one of whom was Donatien le Rey de Chaumont.

Chaumont was already the main wealthy merchant supplying clothing to the French army. With Vergennes' okay, he gave Beaumarchais credit for

V. Secret American Agent to France, 1776

another one million livres to purchase his clothing to supply Silas's request for uniforms, knowing Silas had only around $7,000 pounds advanced by Congress that was meant for the purchase of "Indian goods." Silas decided to let Beaumarchais handle the clothing credit and used the money he had to purchase, directly from Chaumont, large quantities of gunpowder and saltpeter that were so desperately needed by the Continental Army.

Beaumarchais had written to Arthur Lee saying he had formed his company. Lee rushed over to Paris to find that Silas had replaced him, or at least that is how he looked at it. Arthur tried everything he could think of to split them up, but nothing worked. He then tried to see Vergennes about the source of all the money, but Vergennes had already had it with the "prickly" Englishman and refused to see him. In a fury, Mr. Lee rushed back to London and started his poison pen campaign to his brother and friends in Congress about Beaumarchais and Deane using government money for private gain.

Besides working with Beaumarchais to get the war supplies from the interior of France and Europe secretly to the coastal cities for shipment to America was a task that required all kinds of deception to keep the British guessing. In no time, Silas was up to his ears with dozens of projects, problems and negative situations. To put them in order is difficult because so many were interrelated, criss-crossed and secretive, and all of them full of wartime intrigues. To cover them all in any detail would require several volumes of repetitive information and add very little, if anything, to the big picture of Deane's 1776 mission, which happened in a short, six-month, period.

A few days after Silas reached Paris and was familiarizing himself with the city's layout, he made contact with several businessmen and "water's edge" tradesmen. He learned from them that Freemasonry in France was evolving from groups of businessmen's social-type clubs into a major academic movement of the intellectually elite. The movement was led in Paris by the philosophers and other free thinkers who were challenging the orthodoxies of the church and monarchy.

Less than one month before Silas arrived in Paris, the famous Madame Helvétius, in memory of her philosopher husband Claude-Adrien Helvétius, realized his dream of a Paris Masonic Super Lodge filled with the greatest writers and artists by creating just such a lodge, honoring the muses, called the Lodge of the Nine Sisters.

During the month of August, while Silas was tying his network together, Mason merchants in the largest strongholds of Nantes and Bordeaux warned Silas several times to give the Nine Sisters a wide berth. Both the king, a Mason himself, and the clerics were quite wary of the new renegade lodge. Agent Deane took their advice seriously.

Regardless of what others have believed or written, all through his adult life Silas's motives were always in line with the basic Masonic ideals of the day. Fellowship and civic works were two at which he excelled. Silas had visions for the future of his country, but he was always happy to leave the philosophical side of issues to someone else to argue or discuss. Consequently, when Franklin arrived at the end of the year, it was he who made contact with the intellectual lodge of the Nine Ladies and by 1779 became their "Grand Master." Then, and only then, did Commissioner Deane attend the lodge to see Franklin inducted.

While Silas was working with the merchant Masons from Nantes and Bordeaux, learning their smuggling techniques in aiding America, Penet rushed up to Paris to tell Silas he had to get ships for all the supplies he had contracted for Congress through Franklin. Silas told him flat out to get his own ships and Congress would pay the expense, not Silas. Silas knew from other merchants the firm of Pliarne & Penet could be quite on the shady side and only had the supplies that Dubourg had sent them. Silas was suddenly aware all kinds of "headaches" were beginning to happen.

However, back to the French merchant smuggling techniques. Silas was nothing short of amazed to learn that Vergennes had been backing several leading merchant houses since 1774. It sure made his networking a lot easier. Over a century of rebelling against the British economic rule, merchants, regardless of country or citizenship, had developed a very efficient system of free trade, even though, at times, it could get quite dangerous. Mixing their legitimate commerce with illicit trade, smuggling and false papers kept their system alive and trading with any enemy had become a way of life with the merchant captains. In the West Indies, the French and the Americans had been trading with the British Isles of St. Kitts and the French island of Santo Domingo and Dutch Eustatia. American privateers had been operating in European waters since early 1774, with the merchant community's cooperation. Silas had pushed privateering almost immediately during the First Congress. Silas helped the French merchants set up an efficient system of handling papers that would not embarrass Versailles. A French individual would secretly purchase the prize cheaply away from the docks and inner harbor, thus bypassing the Admiralty Court, then they would change the ship's name, make a few minor appearance alterations to it and paint it. Finally, to create new papers of the transaction making it difficult to trace, it was then sent back out to do some more profiteering for the new owners. Bingham immediately adopted the procedure for operations in the West Indies. The French merchants had been using much the same procedure for a number of years and embellished Silas's procedure with even more specific alterations to make former identification even more difficult.

As Silas put the final touches to network links and locations, he knew he needed additional network security for intelligence gathering as well as arms shipments. Historically, communicating secret information, instructions and plans has always been a specialty of intelligence gathering organizations. In that respect, the American Revolution was no exception. But for Silas, and later Franklin, to coordinate such a vast transoceanic network in the 18th century needed more effective means than clumsy codes, ciphers, invisible ink, mail drops, and the like. Silas knew full well that any agents' mail by normal post channels was opened, read, copied and resealed before the intended recipient ever saw it. Even the overseas correspondence that was officially sent in triplicate during the war got the same treatment.

Therefore, Silas decided to set up a system that followed Franklin's earlier system to spy on members of Parliament in the 1770s using "word of mouth only." Silas insisted on a third, trusted party to "carry" the message — usually a fellow merchant, sea captain or close personal friend, with absolutely no paper trails. Of course, that makes an accurate history of what happened almost impossible, especially if the message is fragmented with "need to know only."

Come the first days of August, 18-hour-day workaholic Deane became aware he had to find some time to catch up on correspondence with other specific individuals, home base and the two Secret Committees. On August 18, per his original instructions, a contact letter went out to Charles W.F. Dumas at The Hague as a person strongly in favor of the American cause and highly knowledgeable concerning current European political affairs. In his first letter to Dumas, Silas told him that the colonies were in dire need of foreign aid and he professed he surely hoped the colonies' commercial expansion would start to occur in the near future. Silas went on to say that he understood the European power politics of the mercantile system, but like so many of his fellow contemporaries in Congress, he feared foreign alliances and preferred that a new nation claiming independence from Great Britain should remain free of any political entanglements and concentrate on free trade. He stated explicitly that "the United Colonies only ask for what nature surely entitles all men to a free and uninterrupted commerce and exchange of the superfluities of one country those of another."[13]

Silas's correspondence with Dumas would continue on an irregular basis and developed into a lifelong friendship event though the two men never met face to face. Moving the clock forward with envoy Deane's correspondence with Dumas to four months later, on December 2, one finds Silas very tired from the horrendous mental, and sometimes physical, traveling stress and strain required, to carry out the three-tier activities of his mission: supply aid, diplomatic arrangements and private trading. Silas just let it all hang out and opened up to Dumas on a personal level. He wrote, "I ever keep in mind the motto, 'de republica nil desperandum.' ... I counted the costs when I entered the list, and balanced private fortune, ease, leisure, the sweets of domestic society, and life itself in vain against the liberties of my country; the latter instantly predominated, and I have nothing to complain of, though much to grieve at, occasioned by the miscarriage or delay of my full power for open and public application."[14] Silas ended his reactions to the various present situations by predicting that America would triumph and become a home for "the sons of men in future ages" living under "unprecedented laws, liberty, and commerce." Then he stated, not knowing what troubles the future had for him, that he would never "despair of my country, for which I shall count it my glory to suffer all things, if it receive any advantage therefrom."[15]

In July and the first week in August, Silas ran headlong into the "two military engineers" requested by Washington a year earlier. He and Beaumarchais had discussed the request, but since it was not in the original instructions, Silas put it on the back burner. Beaumarchais saw all kinds of possibilities with the request and went directly to Vergennes. The foreign minister immediately saw a way to aid the Americans secretly and to get some real French military know-how, more than just engineers to America, without directly involving the king and his ministry. In early 1775, the ministry, with the king's approval, sent a Colonel Tronson du Coudray to the various interior French arsenals to take an inventory of old-style arms that might be shipped to the American colonies if they made an open break with England. Du Coudray made inventories at Strausbourg, Dijon, Metz and Charterville.

When Du Coudray reported back to the ministry, the ministry realized that getting large number of arms to the coast undetected by British spies would be difficult. Beaumarchais was briefed early in 1776 on Du Coudray's findings and the problem of transporting to the major coastal cities of Nantes and Le Harve without English knowledge. When Silas and Beaumarchais completed their contracts for aid to the American colonies, the playwright asked for Silas's help in getting the supplies to the coast. With Beaumarchais' knowledge of the country's geography and Silas's smuggling knowledge, the two agents set up what the CIA now calls "black spots" on the map of France, where there is supposed to be nothing notable except to the originators. In this fashion, mostly at night, arms were barged down the River Seine from such places as Abbeville and Gravelines or carted from Douai, Sedan, and even Mézieres in the north.

Once supplies reached the coast, Silas realized there was no way he could finance ships to take the supplies to America. Beaumarchais said he would get the ships, and load them, too. The next problem was the inspection of what they were sending for quality, etc. Neither man could do it personally because, if they were recognized by the British spies, Vergennes would be in trouble with Ambassador Stormont again. Beaumarchais promptly blew his cover of using the name Durand when he went to see a production of his *Barber of Seville*. Silas refused to use a disguise because fellow merchants worked with one another in trust and a disguise would indicate he might have something to hide. Also, and anyone would have second thoughts about this, he knew that the British ministry and Parliament knew he was in France and why. He could be kidnapped and taken to London to face a charge of treason or assassinated on the spot.

Fortunately, Arthur Lee recommended to Silas that he might wish to see Lee's friend William Carmichael of Maryland, who was on his way home from England. Both Silas and Carmichael were curious, Silas about Lee's motives and Carmichael about Silas's mission. They immediately liked one another and Carmichael agreed to stay on and help Silas any way he could. Silas immediately sent him to the coast to inspect the goods and gave him an account of how the French merchant's aid network was working. Mr. Deane was relieved; at least he could breathe a little easier knowing that the aid supplies would be inspected for their real condition.

On July 26, Beaumarchais wrote Deane a letter that stated a cascade of problems concerning the French military "volunteers" joining the Continental Army. The letter read, "I do not think a large train of artillery as you desire can leave this country without a chief and officers, for among a nation as peaceful as America, all knowledge of the tactics must be unknown, and the proper management of a train of artillery is the most difficult branch of the tactics...."[16] That made it perfectly obvious to Silas that if he wanted the cannons and supplies, he had to take soldiers of fortune as a package. It was an all or nothing deal on the table. Agent Deane strongly suspected the French ministry was behind it.

On August 2 Silas wrote a pleading letter to the Committee of Secret Correspondence expressing his dilemma: "A number of gentlemen of rank and fortune, who have seen service and good character, are desirous of serving the United Colonies and have applied, pray let me have orders on the subject."[17] The committee eventually received the letter but never answered it. Silas was left to his own judgment, which became one of the main reasons for his political downfall. But from that month on through 1777, Silas was known as the American recruiter, until Franklin arrived and inherited the deluge of volunteers as head of the commission.

By September 11, Silas had made a contract with the new adjutant general, du Coudray, who had the reputation of being one of the best officers of artillery in all of Europe. Du Coudray was willing to be general of artillery with the rank of major general. Deane wrote the Secret Committee he hoped "that the terms I have made with him will not be thought exorbitant as he was a principal means of engaging the stores."[18] Silas went on to say, "Considering the importance of having two hundred pieces of brass cannon with every necessary article for twenty-five thousand men provides with an able and experienced general at the head warranted by the Minister of the Court, with a number of fine and spirited young officers in his train and all without advancing one shilling, is too tempting an offer for me to hesitate about, though I owe there is a silence in my instructions."[19]

On August 10, as Silas was wrapping up the deal with du Coudray, news of the Declaration of Independence arrived in London and quickly spread to the continent. But, no official news from Congress arrived in Paris. Weeks, then a month and another month went by, with still no word from Congress.

The appearance of the Declaration of Independence made Silas the sole de facto emissary for a new country. The new emissary was full of questions. Shouldn't he have been the person to announce the declaration to the king of France? Had Congress disbanded? Were all the delegates in jail? Was Washington's army defeated? Perhaps a new emissary was on his way to replace Silas. Whatever was happening, Vergennes was becoming very suspicious of Congress, feeling it probably had decided not to seek aid from France and was talking about reconciliation with England. Silas responded to Vergennes with a memorandum that is one of the best arguments for independent people ever written, but it is still historically ignored. Silas truly saw the revolution as a broad popular uprising, not instigation by a few ambitious wealthy businessmen to seize power. For Silas it was a time of great anxiety and real embarrassment. The European newspapers were publishing the full text of the Declaration of Independence and writing commentaries about it. He was constantly reiterating all the reasons he could think of as to why it had not arrived.

When the Declaration of Independence was adopted on July 4 it was ordered to be proclaimed in each state and read directly to the army. Congress simply forgot that Europe should hear about it along with some positive propaganda. Thankfully, however, on the eighth of July, the Secret Committee of Correspondence did send instructions to Silas to make the act known in France and Europe. The ship was never heard from again. Finally, one month later, on August 7, a second vessel was sent to France. It arrived 38 days later, but the captain forgot to deliver the instructions. After a five-month wait, Silas eventually received the declaration on November 17. Three days later, Silas apologetically made a formal presentation to Vergennes. Agent Deane, in turn, wrote a blistering letter back to the committee that landed on deaf ears — the delegates just didn't get it. Most were too concerned with their personal agendas.

Then, while Silas was struggling with the no-show Declaration of Independence, he had a strange visitor appear in mid–September at his residence in Faubourg St. Germain. The visitor's name was James Atkins. His visit started an episode that is still muddy as to just how deeply Silas got personally involved with a man who has been called "America's first terrorist."

Supposedly, Atkins was a Scotsman who had just returned from America where the British had burned his home, killing his family members. He wanted revenge and he had heard (probably from the Duke of Grafton's announcement in Parliament that appeared in newspapers about Silas's arrival in France) that Silas was an American agent in Paris. The story may or may not be true. Only part of it is known to be the truth. When he finally got by Silas's valet (a bodyguard provided by the French police), he announced that he went under the name "John the Painter" and planned to assassinate King George III and burn down the naval shipyard at Portsmouth. Hopefully, Silas convinced the distraught Scot that it was cowardly to murder the king in cold blood. But, Silas did like the idea of a direct blow to the English pride.

Bancroft had gone back to London, telling Silas that he had private business to handle but that he would keep him informed of what the British were planning. Actually, he went right to Paul Wentworth, England's new secret service ace. Paul Wentworth recognized the advantages of having such a person as Bancroft right at the heart of American intelligence. Secret service Director Eden agreed. Bancroft, not having allegiance to any country (only to money), accepted the position of British spy and mole for 500 annually, which eventually was raised to 1,000, and stayed on the job through the entire war. Theoretically, most icons never knew he was a British spy and shock wracked several diplomatic sources when it was learned from European archives in 1866 that he was a double spy paid by both sides, and on some other occasions even by the French, for specific services.

Of late, there is strong evidence from the CIA-type procedures that Silas, Franklin and Vergennes independently got wise to the fact that Bancroft must be a double agent. They purposefully played Bancroft while he played them, not realizing that these men had other close informants in England who could verify his information; if he said "yes" to a British active, they would know it was "no," etc. Merchants and money men of any nation have very loud voices.

In cipher, and through their agreed secret channel, Silas wrote to Bancroft about the man and the plan. Bancroft was quite apprehensive that the plan might expose him helping the Americans. He returned to Paris in October just in time for the Scot's second visit to Deane's hotel residence. Atkins said he had decided against a plot to kill the king. Outside of a substantial financial advance, just what final arrangement was made among the three men is not clearly known. Anyway, John the Painter left Paris with the American agent's blessing.

Thus in mid-November, armed with a passport, strangely, signed by Vergennes, a book of pyrotechnics and plans for making combustible devices, John the Painter went out on his one-man pyromaniac mission to burn down the Portsmouth Naval Yard. Amazingly, John the Painter succeeded in burning down the great rope walk in the navy yard at Portsmouth. He planted some of his own devices in the bottom of three navy ships, and then set fire to the town of Bristol. The one-man, home-grown American terrorist's attack raised a hysterical alarm throughout England to the point that Parliament immediately suspended the privilege of habeas corpus and enacted several new laws against treason.

Looking for a way to escape the authorities, Atkins headed straight for London and Bancroft's home at Number 4 Downing Street, in close proximity to the Secret Service Headquarters at 17 Downing Street. The sudden appearance of the pyromaniac scared the daylights out of double agent Bancroft. He refused the saboteur admittance and gave him directions to an out-of-the-way coffeehouse where they could meet the next day. Their meeting was cut short by a suspicious individual who kept staring at them. Fortunately, or unfortunately for Bancroft, Atkins was arrested a short time later. The circumstances under which he was captured and arrested are also not entirely clear.

Many members of Parliament soon believed that no one man could have carried out such a mission unless someone had helped plan and finance its execution. Suspicion fell on Bancroft, since his meeting with Atkins was known to the Secret Service and he had failed to report meeting him. A plan had to be devised to get Bancroft off the hook or he would be exposed to both sides as a double agent. Bancroft sent a letter to Silas saying that he was in deep trouble and needed some help to clear his name. Bancroft asked Silas to state he saw Atkins only that one time and refused to help him. Silas took the hint and decided to take the heat for his friend and started writing a series of letters to Bancroft purposefully meant to be intercepted by the British. Silas wrote that he laughed at the ministerial trick of publicly promising Atkins his life if he would confess implicating both Bancroft and Deane. Silas implied that Versailles was getting quite a kick out of it, too. Silas repeated in the letter that he wouldn't be adverse to destroying the king's fleet and arsenal intended to destroy his country. Thus, by repeatedly indirectly claiming innocence of the plot and Atkins' rampage, it would be taken as an admission of guilt as being the person who initiated and financed the mission. As the case dragged on, Silas made an elaborate effort to see that the British blamed only him. Knowing that there was no way of saving John the Painter from the hangman's noose, Silas wrote minute descriptions of the man. While Silas was concerned about saving his American agent from the gallows, Bancroft prayed his duplicity would not be discovered.

Silas's letter campaign worked, largely because the British could not prove that Bancroft had any prior knowledge of John the Painter or his plot. Also in Bancroft's favor was the fact that he turned him away when Atkins came asking for his help.

On a dangerous visit to Atkins in jail that Bancroft thought necessary, Atkins finally confessed to the British authorities that he set the fires to the naval yard at the instigation of Silas Deane and had not intended to include any slurs on such an eminent man as Dr. Bancroft. Immediately the British wanted Silas's head. Silas, using his lawyer background, told London that he had acted as an agent of a foreign, independent country and that the plot was not treason but a legal act of war to weaken a declared enemy.

Unfortunately for Bancroft, he was somewhat distrusted by Wentworth, Eden, North, and especially George III from that period on. Had the British Intelligence Service known the existence of the secret cipher used by Bancroft and Deane during the episode, it would have meant the death of Bancroft for sure. The code number they used in the cipher key for John the Painter was a symbolic zero.

The episode of John the Painter took place over a period of five months. But it's necessary to return to the fallout from the Du Coudray "volunteer" train. From September on, after the word got out that a Monsieur Deane was an American military recruiter, Silas had to deal with a constant and steady stream to his hotel door of professional soldiers and not-so-professional soldiers. They came to offer their services for a large fee and even larger promotion in rank in the Continental Army. It was a situation that would continue for 18 months and beyond, ending only after Franklin reinherited it as head commissioner and the signing of the 1778 Treaty with France. These "soldiers" constituted a parade of mostly phony, arrogant and incompetent young men. Many were the youngest sons of the French nobility who were looking for their place in the sun. It got out of hand when Silas actually signed up some of the youngest sons of the nobility, which could have been seen by the British as a breach of neutrality. King Louis XVI immediately forbad any professional French officers of noble birth from joining any foreign army. However, professionals of lower rank could easily slip by the French ministry's concern for neutrality and either sail for America on their own or head for the American recruiter Deane.

Whatever the specific circumstances for the handling of an individual "volunteer," Silas ended up being charged with sending over to Congress and Washington hundreds of French "officers." Actually and historically, the count is somewhere in the sixties, including de Kalb and Lafayette. Congress never forgave Silas for all the headaches it endured with the uninvited French "officers" that landed by the boatload on the southern colonies' coastline and made

Baron de Kalb introducing Lafayette to Silas Deane (drawn by Alonzo Chappell, lithograph published in 1856).

their way to Philadelphia only to be refused and sent back to France at congressional expense.

Du Coudray turned out to be a bitter disappointment to America's secret agent, let alone Congress and Washington. The du Coudray episode started to go sour when he set sail in the *Amphitrite*, Silas and Beaumarchais' first main loaded arms ship. What had happened a few days before the ship set sail started a chain reaction of events that had Beaumarchais, and then shortly thereafter Silas, ready to jump off the nearest cliff.

Vergennes had been pushed particularly hard in recent days by Ambassador Stormont for violating neutrality laws. As a result, the French ministry placed a restraining order on all ships with illicit cargoes destined for the colonies. Knowing the order would soon be posted in all French cities, Beaumarchais rushed to Le Harve in order to get the *Amphitrite* completely loaded and on its way to America before French authorities could act. The ship left the harbor on December 14 loaded with arms. But Du Coudray was

Lafayette, drawn by Alonzo Chappell from the authentic painting then in the possession of the Johnson Fry & Co., publishers, of New York (print published in 1863).

unhappy with his accommodations and the ship had very inadequate food supplies. He forced the captain to return to the French coast and landed in Port Louis in Brittany on January 5, 1777, where the ship immediately fell under the restraining order.

Silas was sick in bed with a high fever when he heard that the *Amphitrite* had returned. The normally somewhat easygoing (at least outwardly) Connecticut Yankee went absolutely apoplectic. He frantically pleaded with Beaumarchais to yank Vergennes' chain hard — the arms were desperately needed for the American's spring campaign now, not next year. The playwright was on it as only the flamboyant agent could be. He rattled the entire ministry's cage with what could happen if they didn't let the *Amphitrite* sail. Then he spewed off a few of the items that were destined for the Continental Army. There were, besides the known arms and ammo, over 4,000 spades, 300 axes,

> The Delegates of the united States of New hampshire, Massachusetts-bay, Rhode island, Connecticut, New york, New jersey, Pensylvania, Delaware, Maryland, Virginia, North-carolina, South-carolina and Georgia, to all who shall see these presents, send greeting.
>
> Whereas a trade upon equal terms between the subjects of his most Christian Majesty the king of France and the people of these states will be beneficial to both nations Know ye, therefore, that we confiding in the prudence and integrity of Benjamin Franklin one of the delegates in Congress from the state of Pensylvania and president of the convention of the said state & Silas Deane, late a delegate from the state of Connecticut and Arthur Lee, counsellor at Law, have appointed and deputed and by these presents do appoint and depute them the said Benjamin Franklin, Silas Deane and Arthur Lee our commissioners, giving and granting to them the said Benjamin Franklin, Silas Deane and Arthur Lee, or to any two of them, and in case of the death absence or disability of any two, to any one of them full power to communicate treat, agree and conclude with his most Christian Majesty the king of France, or with such person or persons as shall by him be for that purpose authorized, of and upon a true and sincere friendship and a firm, inviolable and universal peace, for the defence protection and safety of the navigation and mutual commerce of the subjects of his most Christian Majesty and the people of the united states, and to do all other things, which may conduce to those desireable ends, and promising in good faith to ratify whatsoever our said commissioners shall transact in the premisses.
>
> Done in Congress at Philadelphia the twenty third day of October in the year of our Lord one thousand seven hundred and seventy six. In testimony whereof the president by order of the said congress hath hereunto subscribed his name and affixed his seal.
>
> Attest Cha Thomson secy.   John Hancock Presid t

Figure XIII. The Three Man Commission to France, signed by John Hancock, then president of the Continental Congress (courtesy Connecticut Historical Society).

Signing the Treaties of Amity and Commerce and of Alliance between France and the United States in 1778. Mural painted by Charles Mills (courtesy Franklin Institute of Boston).

almost 5,000 pickaxes, over 300 blankets, and an endless supply of necessary items that almost landed on another ship with the 130 passengers.

Silas went to Gerard and insisted he be allowed to see Vergennes. Gerard tried to quiet him, but Silas made it plain he had had it with diplomatic fear. Finally, on January 5, the American commission was informed they would shortly receive a loan and the ships would be released. Meanwhile, Beaumarchais and Silas began to round up Du Coudray and his train, who had returned to the capital city to enjoy the Parisian night life along with several other "volunteers" who were originally onboard, and await the release order.

The restraining order situation bitterly disappointed Silas in the diplomatic part of his mission. He was especially disappointed in the behavior of Du Coudray because the "major general" knew of the restraining order. Silas wrote,

> This I must say: He acted an unwise and injudicious part in returning into port; he gave a fresh alarm to the Ministry [French] and occasioned a second counter-order. Indeed, Mons Du Coudray appeared to have solely in view his own ease, safety and involvement. He returned to Paris, without the least ground that I can find for his conduct, and laid his scheme to pass

to America in a ship without artillery, which is absurd, as I engaged this man to assist in procuring and attending in person. His desertion of this charge, with his other conduct, makes me wish that he may not arrive in America at all.[20]

Silas's wish didn't come true and when Du Coudray did arrive in Philadelphia his commission of "major general" from Deane caused an outright uproar in Congress and threats of resignations from several of Washington's generals, including a Deane family friend, General Greene. But, on September 16, 1777, the difficulties were relieved when volunteer "captain" of artillery Du Coudray drowned in the Schuylkill River.

While Silas was desperately up to his ears simultaneously with several related situations of his mission, he became involved in what initially looked like another Du Coudray deal. It was the story of one of the American Revolution's most famous personalities on both sides of the Atlantic—Marie Joseph Paul Yves Roc Gilbert du Motier, Marquis de Lafayette. What is generally not known is the fact that the story of Lafayette's coming to America was a complicated situation of intrigue and deception involving Lafayette, the French ministry, King Louis XVI, and the key figure, Silas Deane himself. There were two other individuals through the entire affair who were kept part of it on a "need to know" basis—De Kalb and Duc De Broglie.

In order to answer so many questions as to the how and why of the Marquis de Lafayette's motives and specific actions it is necessary to go into considerable detail to make any sense of the saga. At age 13, Lafayette had become an orphan literally overnight, a bearer of an ancient name and a millionaire. He soon had two intimate friends, Count Ségur and La Rochefoucauld. They were up on Rousseau's "Social Contract" and all the new theories and discoveries in the field of natural science. When Louis XVI first became king of France, Lafayette, at age 16, married the youngest daughter of the Duc d'Ayen-Noailles.

Given Lafayette's interest in the encyclopedist and propensities toward free thinking, his circle of young friends persuaded him to become a Freemason. Duc d'Ayen had obtained an assignment for Lafayette in his regiment and arranged for him to receive riding lessons with the youngest brother of the king, Comte d'Artois, who was the same age as Lafayette. The actions of the court at Versailles soon made the marquis turn away in disgust because of the unwarranted money-grabbing traits of the French elite. He had no great desire for wealth or possessions.

Duc de Noailles wanted Lafayette to become a fixture at court, but the 17-year-old cavalry captain had other ideas. Taking advantage of a court ball, he deliberately insulted the next in line to the throne, Comte de Provence. The insult got the results Lafayette wanted. He lost his place and standing at court. The duke quickly made arrangements for Lafayette to be recalled to his regiment at Metz, which was still a rough frontier base at full military strength and under the role and command of Duc de Broglie. For his part in the Seven Years' War, the duke was given the baton of a marshal of France.

Silas had described Israel Putnam as fit only for fighting, and the same applied to Duc de Broglie, whose figure was definitely out of place at the court of Versailles. Lafayette's father had died in de Broglie's arms at the Battle of Hastenbech. As a son of a fallen comrade, Lafayette was ordered by the marshal de Broglie to take a place at his table. Lafayette was at the marshal's table when a banquet was given for the Duke of Gloucester, brother of King George III of England. At the banquet, the king's brother blasted George for his handling of the American colonies' revolt. This exposure to the American Revolution immediately fired up Lafayette. Later the Duke of Gloucester was inspecting with de Broglie the fortifications at Metz when a courier brought him mail from England. Opening the envelope he triumphantly read out loud the news of the Declaration of Independence. That did it. Lafayette was hooked on helping the Americans win their "liberty."

Duc De Broglie would have happily sent Lafayette to fight the English — anything to pay back the British for the humiliation of the Seven Years' War. But personally he didn't dare send the 19-year-old on his way. If the kid came to any harm, the Duc de Noailles would hold him responsible for his daughter's widowhood. So he passed Lafayette on to his old friend, deputy quartermaster general "Baron" De Kalb. He knew the Baron was seriously thinking of going to America to fight the British himself.

At the Battle of Rosebach, De Kalb had saved the whole transport under the Duc de Broglie. For such service Captain De Kalb was appointed to the general staff. Later, after the war, the French ministry sent him to America to determine the feelings of the colonies toward Great Britain. He returned to the Metz garrison with extensive knowledge of the New World and the English language. He reported that the Americans were still anti–French. As deputy quartermaster De Kalb was a titular general. However, after years of service his permanent rank was still only lieutenant colonel. By military regulations of the time, if a French officer joined a foreign army he retained the rank he gained. De Kalb wanted to retire a general. For that reason only he asked to go to America and join the Continental Army.

De Broglie hastily sent the two men off to Paris together. De Kalb was savvy enough to realize that by babysitting Lafayette he held a trump card. The Marquis Lafayette was the son-in-law of the Duc de Noailles and part of the official Versailles. If Lafayette publicly announced he was going to America to fight in Washington's army, it would definitely infer that the French court and the king himself favored the American rebels. This kid with the high ideals was a recruit who would be of no small value to the American cause. Try as he might, De Kalb could not convince the Marquis to keep his mouth shut about his plans. Lafayette's two close friends didn't have the money to join him. They went to their fathers for money to make the voyage. The roof went off. The Comte de Maurepas, defacto minister of state, quickly summoned the Marquis to Versailles. On his arrival, Maurepas handed Lafayette a letter de cachet already signed by the king. Now Lafayette could definitely end up in the Bastille. The teenager decided to bide his time and wait for a new opportunity.

Meanwhile, the Duc de Broglie was considering a plan of his own. With his background, he was sure he could do a better job against the British than George Washington could — for a fee and title, of course. For such a glorious recommendation that he wrote for the Baron to the American "recruiter" Monsieur Silas Deane, De Kalb agreed to push de Broglie with Deane to become the ruler of the American Army. Arriving in Paris, De Kalb made arrangements with de Broglie to set up a meeting with Silas on October 30. The American agent accepted De Kalb on November 5 with the title of major general.

Later the same day, the Baron introduced Lafayette to Mr. Deane with De Kalb acting as interpreter. At first, Silas listened to the 19-year-old marquis' zeal, but he recommended against leaving France to fight for American liberty. From that meeting until April 1777, the saga of De Kalb and Lafayette's escapades to win a trip to America was intrigue and deceit at its highest level. The two men, some 40 years apart in age, were pushed together with two entirely different agendas but with the same basic goal of joining the American army.

During that first interview Silas learned much about the men's background that has been previously stated. Lafayette was truly a marquis and son-in-law of the Duc de Noailles, part of the official court of Versailles. Lafayette laid it on hard and strong to Deane as to how connected and wealthy a person he was. Silas immediately saw he had a live one here and he had better play it easy for a while. Silas saw what the Baron saw. If Lafayette sided with the Americans it could easily be construed that the French court and king favored the rebels. This kid would be of great value to the American cause. There was an added advantage. Both men were Freemasons and belonged to the same military lodge, with its enlightened views of Rousseau and Voltaire.

But Silas was aware of the restriction by King Louis XVI that no officer of noble birth could serve in a foreign army. Mr. Deane was not about to openly defy the French king and ministry. He desperately needed Vergennes' trust and aid to continue his work with Beaumarchais.

Somehow the word got back to Vergennes, Maurepas and Sartine about the details of Lafayette's plans. It is not hard to figure out who and how. Gérard and Deane had become good friends with Silas, making frequent weekly visits to Gérard's office to report on the progress of his mission and Beaumarchais' covert aid in war materials. Suspicious of the direction events were going, and knowing he was playing with a stacked deck of secret French approval, Silas decided he had better play the "intelligence end game" and keep the British ambassador off Vergennes' back for violating pervious treaty stipulations.

As plans moved forward the Lafayette escapade became entangled with the du Coudray affair and the loading and holding of the *Amphitrite*. The original plan was for De Kalb and Lafayette to sail with du Coudray. Lafayette had to get away from his father-in-law's anger. Even though Silas was livid about the hold-up of the *Amphitrite* he took the much-needed time to set up a lengthy secret plan with the marquis to leave France regardless of the king's "public" orders.

Knowing the British spies were constantly watching his every move, Silas did two basic things to protect his direct involvement. De Kalb unknowingly helped the cause by writing to Silas stating that many of the supplies on the *Amphitrite* weren't worth the powder to blow it to kingdom come. Silas in turn gave Beaumarchais a very public hard time that got back to the British Secret Service for Stormont to needle Vergennes. Silas's own excuse was that he couldn't inspect the supplies because the British would definitely know they were headed for North American colonies, which, of course, the British already knew and he knew they knew. Beaumarchais was miffed but played along, claiming there were bound to be some inferior pieces in such a large order — all that babble ought to keep the British from figuring out what was really going on.

Second, Silas asked Carmichael to work directly with Lafayette in working out details for his eventual departure but to keep Silas tight in the loop since the overall scheme picked by de Broglie and Baron de Kalb called for a really bold movement to get Lafayette and his ten close comrades on their way. Silas knew what others seemed not to realize. Timing was going to be everything. Lafayette's step-uncle was the French ambassador to the court of St. James. A visit was arranged. In fact, a special audience was set up with King George III. While waiting for details to be arranged Lafayette bought his own ship and boldly named it the *Victoire*. He left it up to De Kalb to work out the details.

As with many Freemasons of the time, the young marquis was very interested in the advancement of science. To the horror of his wife, he deliberately let himself be injected with the new protective inoculations against smallpox. It was now the first week in December. Lafayette feigned sickness and succeeded in obtaining a temporary release from duty, thus avoiding the risk of being charged with desertion. As soon as he received his release from duty certificate, Lafayette met quietly with Silas and signed the contract, which had long been prepared with the title of major general. It stated he would serve Congress without pay. Once the contract was signed, Lafayette headed for his arranged visit to London. In the midst of an enjoyable visit, a pre-arranged message arrived from de Kalb. The *Victoire* was ready for sea. Lafayette made excuses and hurried back to France, stopping in Paris to let Ségur know he was leaving before continuing on to the country seat of the Duc de Broglie. Here he waited three days for the mail packets that would go to Congress. Finally a coach arrived, bringing Silas with the mail packets right to the entrance of the chateau.

On their way, as arranged by Silas, four fresh horses awaited them at each posting station. Arriving at Bordeaux, the two major generals had their baggage and equipment placed on board the *Victoire*, but they were sadly informed that the ship could not depart for at least another day while extra provisions and fresh water were loaded and inspected.

Just as they were getting underway, Comte de Coigny shouted from the dock frantically. The news was devastating to Lafayette. British ambassador Lord Stormont and the Duc de Noailles were furious and an order for Lafayette's arrest, signed by the king, was already on its way to Bordeaux. Knowing he did not want to be cut off from his country forever, Lafayette seemingly gave up his plan and told the Comte de Coigny to find out if the threat was real or simulated in order to quiet Stormont. In any case, Lafayette and de Kalb would remain aboard the *Victoire* and await Coigny's reply at Las Pasajes Harbor in Spain. The ship had no sooner anchored when Lafayette got his answer in writing from Comte de Maurepas expressly forbidding the expedition in his majesty's name. Lafayette decided for the sake of appearances he had better go back to Bordeaux with the two officers sent by Maurepas just in case the king wasn't covering his real agenda enough. What had caused the frenzy was a letter Lafayette wrote to his father-in-law that tipped off the ministry that they had better cover their "real intent."

In Bordeaux the Marquis learned that the king's order to arrest was little more than an invitation to a pleasure trip. His majesty commanded Lafayette to Marseilles at once to await the arrival of his family, who were about to tour Italy. He was assigned to his father-in-law as aide-de-camp. If he didn't go to Marseilles he would be arrested and brought back to Paris and the Bastille. Lafayette took that as a way out. He hired a coach for Marseilles, but on the way he changed into the coach of Vicomte de Maurois hired by Silas to make sure that Lafayette got back to the *Victoire* and sailed for America. The same day, April 17, 1777, Lafayette finally left European shores.

Once the word got out that Lafayette had actually left for America praise and amazement spread throughout Europe like wildfire. Early in the game it was agreed with Silas that Louis XVI and his ministers had to be exonerated from any involvement. In December, after Silas had signed on Lafayette and the ministry was informed, for cover purposes, Silas received a very severe reprimand from Vergennes that supposedly put Silas in the doghouse for several weeks.

On April 2 Silas sent, for the prying eyes of British agents, an apologetic note to Gérard justifying his agreement with Lafayette. He told the foreign minister that the marquis helped espouse the American cause and that Lafayette was a fine specimen of French bravery. Silas also insisted that his new colleague commissioners as of December 1776 had no knowledge of the Lafayette affair, which for once was the truth. It was necessary to protect Franklin from both the English and the French governments. Arthur Lee didn't need protecting; he was already a persona non gratis with both governments.

Three days later, on April 5, to reinforce the fact the he was solely responsible for making Lafayette's dream come true, Silas sent copies of letters he had exchanged with Lafayette while negotiating plans for Lafayette's chance to join Washington's army. Deane's letters cleared the entire French court of any complicity in Lafayette's coup even though the king approved the specific case all along.[21] This made the second time agent Deane took the heat for other individuals — the true mark of a good "secret" agent.

In late October agent Deane received several return correspondences from Bingham that indicated the networking was going to be a big help in keeping in touch with the congressional committee and the conditions concerning the shipment of war supplies and private goods. From the West Indies communications coming and going, if they made it past the British patrols, were taking only about 35–38 days.[22] Privateers were the most dependable source.

Toward the end of November workaholic Deane was becoming quite tired both physically and mentally. Even with the West Indies route of correspondence it seemed Congress had simply abandoned him. He knew from several private sources and privateer captains during the last weeks of October and the first part of November that Franklin and Lee would be joining him to make up a triple man American commission to France, but that was it. When and where his mentor friend would arrive he had no idea or what the commissioner's instructions would be. Silas was definitely not pleased that Arthur Lee would be coming over from England and be around to harass and make life miserable for everybody, including Silas. He just couldn't get to like that guy even though he knew Arthur was a devoted patriot. Silas, with the forgiving personality, probably thought the guy just had "the accent on the wrong syllab-le."

Silas's heavy burden wearing three hats was taking its toll. Keeping up with contracts, political lobbying and the private affairs of William & Morris, along with the Indian goods contract, made life confusing and frustrating, to say the least. In the last weeks of November Silas began to take a hard look at what had been accomplished or was underway. As he did, it bothered him even more when he realized, for the first time, the magnitude and number of situations with which he was charged.

First, he had established a secondary network through his own personal contacts with the London firm of Germany & Geraudut, and also Thomas Walpole, Samuel Wharton, Leicester, Fields and Hammersmith and Thomas Boylston, unfortunately all of whom were known by Stormont to be American sympathizers. Second, the previous six months had changed his outlook about the organization of social classes. Here in France he was fully accepted in elite society without question simply because he was a representative of America, a new and different country.

Third, though he could never accept it, Silas did understand, and was well aware of, European power politics. He realized that the interests of the new United States would have to take a backseat whenever relations between France and England became a little touchy. Neither country was ready for open warfare. They were going to stall until they thought they could win.

Fourth, he knew quickly that French officials and merchants had a tradition that went far beyond receiving a tip. They required specific considerations from foreign representatives and governments. It was more or less a universal and acceptable practice and Silas frequently found it necessary to pay a *douceur*— a sweetener — when doing business in France. Upon his return to France in 1780, Silas himself received a douceur of some 24,000 livres, as an "extraordinary" for his previous services to France, that came directly from the king's private friends.[23]

Fifth, the Caribbean merchants had been around for nearly 50 years and had their own network of friendly collusion among the English, Dutch, French, Spanish and Danish islands. Now, for America, William Bingham on Martinique was in touch with Stephen Ceronio at Cape Francois in Santo Domingo and Van Bibber on the Dutch island of St. Eustatia, known as Statia to Americans. These islands had become responsible for most of the colonies' arms trade by the end of the year 1776.

Sixth, Silas was extremely pleased that he and Beaucharmais had eight shiploads waiting for the hold order to be lifted in order to sail for America and Washington's army.

Seventh, Silas was in a quandary as to how to handle the Tom Morris situation. Robert Morris had written him to watch over Tom, who was coming to take over Deane's commercial agent position. What Robert didn't know was that his stepbrother had a real problem with a bent elbow that was giving Robert's firm a bad name and reputation.

With all his areas of responsibilities, plus his financial worries over the money contracts, Silas was ready for any additional help and encouragement. On December 3, Silas let his guard down and wrote a very revealing letter to his friend John Jay explaining his desperate situation. He told Jay he was "without intelligence, without orders and without remittances, yet boldly plunging into contracts, engagements and negotiations, hourly hoping that something will arrive from America."[24]

That same day Franklin landed in Auray, France. Nobody knew when he would show. Correspondence from America's shores lay at the bottom of the ocean. After sending the news of his arrival to Dubourg (Franklin had no idea where to contact Silas, but he was sure Dubourg would know), Franklin set off for Nantes to collect his luggage. The moment Franklin arrived in Nantes, Penet & Pliarne took charge of the old sage's welcome and took the 2,000 pounds of indigo he brought for the American expenses off his hands for a third of its value. The commissioner never saw the remainder again. Franklin in turn wrote back to Congress to eliminate deals with those two.

Dubourg was exuberant and gave Silas Franklin's letter asking that lodgings be prepared. Word spread through France like wildfire. Maybe the Americans didn't know the old man very well, but he was famous in Europe for all of his scientific achievements. Even before Silas could express his feelings of delight and relief, Vergennes was all over him like a blanket wanting to know why he hadn't been informed earlier. The reason — the arrival of Franklin — could blow all the secret help to America right out the window.

Franklin had arrived in a vessel belonging to a country at war with England that had taken two prizes. French officers were already bragging in Paris coffeehouses and other public places they had the ministry's blessing to join the American army. Worst of all, Silas and Beaumarchais had munitions visibly piled high on the docks of Le Harve, Bordeaux and Nantes just waiting for the holding order to be lifted. Vergennes grabbed his close friend, chief of police Lenoir, and told him to arrest anybody who was being vocal in public about helping the American "insurgents" (he liked that description better than "rebels.") Poor Silas had no real idea yet what Franklin's instructions covered. Unfortunately, it seemed like almost everyone else had a theory as to why Franklin was in France. After enjoying the many accolades and frenzy over his arrival at Nantes, on December 15 Franklin finally began the 300-mile trip to Paris.

Meanwhile, Beaumarchais, on hearing of Franklin's presence at Nantes, left Le Harve in a hurry visibly upset for much the same reasons as Vergennes. He was sure Franklin's popularity would open up the can of worms of his and Silas's covert operations. He got back to Paris on the 16th and wrote to Vergennes and Silas to "lock him [Franklin] up" until they could learn the exact nature of his mission. In spite of Vergennes' and Beaumarchais' apprehensions, Franklin made it as far as Versailles on December 20. Settling in for the night, Franklin sent a courier to Silas announcing their arrival at Versailles and asking what accommodations had been made for the Franklin trio in Paris.

When Silas learned from Dubourg of Franklin's landing in France, he had booked a second-floor apartment at the Hôtel d'Entraques in the rue de l'Université where he occupied a suite on the first floor. Having received Franklin's note from the courier, the next morning Silas headed out to Versailles to pick up Commissioner Franklin and the two boys to bring them to their new quarters in Paris. A new era of change in French and American relations was about to begin. For Silas, life was about to become even more stressful and complicated as Franklin's man in Paris. America's early version of James Bond, 007, was about to enter the pivotal time of his political life, a partnership where one was honored and the other became despised.

Chapter VI

American Commissioner to France, 1776–1778

Arriving back in Paris with Franklin on the 22nd, Silas was not surprised to see dozens of people and carriages lined up outside the hotel. The word was already on the streets, as well as in the ministry, that the old sage was now finally in town. Characters from all levels of society were waiting to see, and they hoped meet, the famous American philosopher and scientist. Franklin's reputation from his previous visits to France had made him beloved by the French people as well as by many savants and members of nobility. He would continue to create and cause quite a stir in French society.

Franklin quickly looked over his new Paris quarters and freshened up a bit. By then Arthur Lee had also arrived at the hotel. After four long months from the time of their appointments, all three commissioners were together in one place. They wasted no time in bringing each other up to speed on important situations and events that had taken place, or were taking place, in their former respective locations on both sides of the Atlantic. It was going to require a week or more for them to get on the same page because there were items that had to be acted upon immediately.

Silas desperately wanted Franklin to meet Jacques Le Ray de Chaumont for a number of reasons, but primarily because this man had given Silas so much financial credit so that America's first foreign agent could purchase directly the much-needed war supply items that Beaumarchais simply could not provide in any quantity. Chaumont was all pro–American and it's estimated that he was their backing for well over 1,000,000 livres. Chaumont had already helped Silas procure thousands of barrels of saltpeter needed for gunpowder and bolts of cloth for Continental Army uniforms. Silas wanted Franklin to know this guy was as about as high-powered as they get. Agent Deane's intelligence contacts and profiteering paid off; he had connections at the French court and all over France, as well as being a personal friend of

Vergennes. This little round-faced man owned a tannery, a flour mill, a saltpeter factory, a glassworks, a textile mill, a limestone quarry, and interests in several other enterprises.

Chaumont lived and owned a spectacular estate in the village of Passy, a short distance from Versailles. Silas had previously arranged with Chaumont to meet Franklin. Late in the morning on the 23rd, Silas and Franklin headed out for Passy as Chaumont's dinner guests. When the two men met it was immediate mutual admiration. They shortly became close friends and remained so until Chaumont's death. In the weeks that followed, Chaumont could be found in the company of either Silas or Franklin or both. He took great pleasure in helping the Americans in any way big or small he could.

That evening when Silas and Franklin got back from Passy, all three commissioners sat down to write their first "official" correspondence. They were notifying the French foreign minister Charles Grenier and Comte de Vergennes that the American commissioners had arrived in Paris and were requesting an audience.

Technically, all commissioners were equivalent in rank, requiring two of the three to agree before any official action could be taken. However, Franklin, due to his age, experience as a colonial agent, and basic speaking knowledge of French, was the agreeable unofficial head of the delegates. Silas was next in line due to his prior association and planning with the two congressional Secret Committees and because he was the only veteran foreign agent of the new United States. Silas also was still working on his French. As he had told Franklin before, he could read and write French and he understood, but speaking in the language definitely kept eluding him. Arthur Lee as the third commissioner was an ardent patriot, highly educated as a medical doctor and a fellow lawyer with Silas. He was a substitute for the original third commissioner. Thomas Jefferson was the first choice of Congress, but he refused the appointment because his wife was ill.

Their first communiqué to Vergennes read as follows:

> Sir: We beg leave to acquaint your Excellency that we are appointed and fully empowered by the Congress of the United States to propose and negotiate a treaty of unity and commerce between France and the United States. The just and generous treatment their trading ships have received by free admission into the ports of the kingdom, and the considerations of respect, has induced Congress to make their first offer to France. We request an audience of your Excellency, where we may have an opportunity of presenting our credentials, and we flatter ourselves that the propositions we are authorized to make are such as will not be found unacceptable.[1]

It was signed B. Franklin, S. Deane, and A. Lee and their signatures remained in that order from then on in any official documents.

The next day was the beginning of the Christmas holidays and was also Silas's 39th birthday. He was hoping to celebrate by getting some free time with Franklin to inform him of the progress that had been made with the Secret Committee of Correspondence's secret aid and intelligence network plan of a coordinated operation both in Europe and the Caribbean Islands. Silas particularly wanted the sage to know he (they) needed more contacts in England for initiations and verifications. Such a conversation would have to take place when Lee was not present. His contacts and friends were known to be on both sides at the same time, depending on internal English politics.

The plan devised back in Philadelphia by Silas, Franklin, John Jay, and Robert Morris had many areas to be considered all at once, including propaganda, covert operations, insulting the British Lion, secret political diplomatic agreements and intrigues. Silas was deeply worried after hearing of the situations. They were more than desperate; they were catastrophic as far as Silas was concerned. There was no excuse; the commissioners had to make some kind of progress with the French ministry — and soon.

While Silas was waiting for a chance to be alone with Franklin, he indulged in putting the final touches on his favorite pastime of formulating a scheme for future action. This time it was raiding the English coast that he had talked to Jay about back in 1775.

In the meantime, Franklin sent his grandson, Temple, to deliver the commissioner's message to Vergennes at Versailles. Receiving the note, Vergennes asked Temple to return the next morning — Christmas Day — for an answer. Temple sent a courier back to his grandfather requesting permission to remain at Versailles overnight as he was so impressed with the place. That was the clue to the commissioners that there would be no audience during the holiday.

Early Christmas Day was spent going over Congress's Model Treaty articles. Both being lawyers, Silas and Arthur had several sticky questions that only Franklin, being the coauthor with John Adams, could attempt to answer. What bothered Silas the most was the fact that there was no mention of a possible political and military alliance, just a commercial trade allowance. To add the need of a political and military alliance would be top priority for all commissioners. Even though none truly wanted such an alliance, they finally realized that if the United States were to survive it was an absolute necessity. The British navy control had to be cancelled out of the picture.

The steady stream of would-be visitors, well wishers, and individuals seeking favors pouring in and around the hotel was endless. The hotel walls grew ears and the door latches grew eyeballs. Keeping any secrets or information from agents, either British or French was almost impossible. After only two nights, Franklin was ready to climb a wall himself and decided to start looking around the next day for better and more private accommodations. A good portion of that day was strictly devoted to exploring adjacent neighborhoods for more suitable quarters. Franklin would continue looking off and on through New Year's Day.

Returning from the initial search for a better place to live, all commissioners took a break and joined a Christmas party for Temple. After the makeshift party, the entire American delegation, to show there were no religious undertones, attended Mass at Notre Dame.

Franklin had brought detailed instructions from Congress for the commissioners. The condition of the Model Treaty, or Plan of 1776, as it is sometimes called, was only a part of the instruction. For the next two days the trio spent considerable time together going over all parts of the instructions. It didn't take long for them to realize, considering current situations, that they were going to have a continual uphill battle to achieve all of the congressional wishes. The articles of the Model Treaty alone were 30 in number.

On Sunday, December 28, after King Louis XVI gave permission to Vergennes to receive the American commissioners, he held a typical diplomatic-style welcome to the commissioner in the south wing of Versailles. Vergennes greeted Franklin as a true friend of France and the French people. He told Silas he admired and appreciated his prudence and cooperation over the past six months. Arthur Lee he congratulated on his zealous work in London. Vergennes found it hard, but held back his anger and disgust at the unsolicited letters telling him how to handle the American cause. Silas was the accredited agent of the United States, not him.

Vergennes' first point during the audience was the fact the Americans should definitely avoid open publicity that might get British ambassador Robert Murray Stormont agitated. Then, almost in the same breath, he told the commissioners that French ports were open to them, but they should keep in constant touch secretly with him through his "secretary" Gérard.

After their meeting, Vergennes was left rather bewildered. The Americans had asked for nothing even though he warned them to watch their step dealing with Dubourg and Beaumarchais, insisting the French ministry had no deal with either man, which was to be Vergennes' official stance any time Stormont appeared at his door.

On Monday, after staying overnight at Versailles, the commissioners requested a meeting with Conde de Aramada, the Spanish ambassador to France. Aramada agreed to meet, but suggested, for obvious reasons, that they call after dark that evening. It was tough going for all the men trying to understand one another. Aramada reported that Franklin's speaking French was very limited, and Deane's even more so; Lee could speak it not at all. The commissioners did make it clear that they wanted to know if they could "use"

Spanish ports as safe harbor allowing them to sell captured cargoes. The ambassador reminded them that under the current treaty terms with England it was impossible. Like Vergennes, Aramada remained puzzled. It was well known the Americans were in tough shape. Why weren't they asking for aid and protection?

After Vergennes' December 28 meeting with the Americans, he went back to the king, who kept asking just how they were going to help the Americans and still not cause an early war. France had already decided in May of 1776 that a war with England was inevitable but realized that both sides needed to prepare. It was decided, for the present, that secret financial aid was still the way to go, to the surprise and delight of the commissioners. Then on January 3, Vergennes notified them they had been granted a subsidy of 2,000,000 livres forthcoming that would be managed through the French ministry's friend and confidential banker, Ferdinand Grand, and his brother and partner in Amsterdam, George Grand. The best part of that news was the fact there was only a vague reference to any repayment schedule.

The news of the subsidy immediately encouraged the commissioners to request another audience and make a bold request of the foreign minister. On January 5, in an official memorial, the commissioners submitted the following:

> Sir, The Congress, the better to defend their coasts, protect their trade and drive off the enemy, have instructed us to apply to France for eight ships of the line, completely manned, the expense of which they will undertake to pay. As other princes of Europe are lending or hiring their troops to Britain against America, it is apprehended that France may, if she thinks fit, afford our independent States the same kind of aid, without giving England any first cause of complaint. But if England should on that account declare war, we conceive that by the united force of France, Spain and America, she will lose all her possessions in the West Indies, much the greatest part of that commerce which has rendered her so opulent, and be reduced to that state of weakness and humiliation which she has, by her perfidy, her insolence and her cruelty, both in the east and in the west, so justly merited.[2]

In the same memorial the commissioners went on to request that, as Congress had stated in its instructions, 20,000 muskets and bayonets, etc., be shipped under French convoy protection. They pointed out that this was absolutely necessary since Mr. Deane's private purchase of these materials had not yet been granted an export license. The memorial ended by offering both France and Spain America's "amity and commerce" and stating that in time this commerce would be immense and "if neglected, may never again return; and we cannot help suggesting that a considerable delay may be attended with fatal consequences."[3] Without question, that phrase was a deep diplomatic threat, like a bomb waiting to explode. It definitely let the monarchs know that it was a real possibility that America could rejoin England and take on the Bourbon kings of France and Spain.

The memorial caught Vergennes a little off guard, but he didn't have to wonder what the Americans were planning anymore. The day before, he had said to ambassador Aramada he wondered if the Americans "might be hiding something in their pocket"[4] and he wasn't about to dig in those pockets to find out.

For more than two centuries the French have used a political diplomatic technique when a communiqué from a foreign country does not please the Foreign Ministry: it simply doesn't answer. But in this case, within a few days an answer in a strong negative fashion was given. Unfortunately, no exact record of the reply seems to still exist, yet there is a letter dated January 15 from Franklin to Gerard for Vergennes and delivered by Silas protesting that they didn't mean to irritate the king and apologizing all profusely for offending his majesty. This was really "assuming the position," but Franklin knew he had to get Vergennes and the king to aid and recognize the new republic.

Silas must have chuckled a bit to himself. He had been on Vergennes' wrong side before. He knew that, as with Mother Nature, "you don't mess with Foreign Minister Vergennes." Silas told Franklin to slow it down and explained that Vergennes always moved slowly and with deliberate determination and to make sure to be candid and honest but not too forthright. Silas had learned the hard way that when Stormont protested his own and Beaumarchais' activities with threats of war, Vergennes simply gave Antone Sartine, minister of the navy, the high sign to refuse any export permits blocking ships in port, especially at Le Harve. When Vergennes felt Stormont had cooled down he would tell Sartine to slowly restore export permits. Franklin, up to the strong negative response to the memorial, had not been aware how duplicitous Vergennes could be. Silas could easily see that the foreign minister's policy of "stop and go" actions weren't about to cease for some time to come. France was not ready for a war with the British Empire.

January was sliding by rapidly and the commissioners realized they had to get their actions and plans in high gear if they were to keep on top of all the "breaking news" in European politics and situations across the Atlantic. Franklin wrote Congress on January 17 that the potential contracts with the Farmer's General initiated previously by him through Dubourg were beginning to take shape in negotiating purchases of Maryland and Virginia tobacco below the going market prices. For Congress to understand its existence, Franklin explained that the Farmer's General was the official governmental tax agency over all commercial and financial concerns.

The commissioners and the network of agents, both American and foreign, were immediately busy all over Europe bargaining with American tobacco, and other agrarian products, in exchange for gunpowder and a myriad of war supplies. Dumas reported the Dutch gunpowder industry was the biggest in Europe, but Holland was diplomatically an ally of Great Britain. That, however, didn't stop Dutch merchants from turning big profits in gunpowder, as it doubled in price when it reached St. Estatia in the West Indies.

After much earlier prodding and persuading of his Masonic merchant brothers by Silas, the merchants on their own were becoming much more active in shipping all types of contraband and general merchandise to the United States via the Caribbean islands. Six months into 1777, Carmichael reported back to Silas from the French coast that Le Harve had some 117 vessels in American trade with Bordeaux only a dozen or so behind. Nantes, however, continued to be the leader, with well over 200 vessels going back and forth across the Atlantic. Merchants now from several foreign countries were becoming major sources of covert operations and undercover work for the "American at Paris."

Regardless of all the political waffling with the French ministry, Silas felt very fortunate in having congressional agent Bingham on board at Martinique. He was doing an incredible job of coordinating shipments up the American coastline with supplies for the Continental Army. Bingham was also coordinating the shipping of supplies for America in and out of other major island ports.

One big plus for the American privateers was the fact that they could bring in hundreds of captured ships to Martinique instead of sending them back to an American port with prize crews. It saved time, men and the risk of recapture by the British warships. For Silas, there was also an added network benefit of receiving the latest American intelligence by ship captains sailing back and forth from Europe, and the point (lost on many at the time) that it was very easy to "trade with the enemy" in the West Indies for needed supplies not readily available elsewhere.

Unfortunately for the American commissioners arriving in Paris in late December 1776, it could not have been at a worse time. The news of Washington's continuous defeats in Long Island, New York and the Jerseys turned the entire French ministry tepid toward additional aid to the insurgents until they could show some promise of success in making the new United States truly independent.

Seeing the downhill trend of all activities to help America, Franklin and Deane decided on only one major theme with detailed planned areas. Insult the British while operating on French soil to cause an outbreak of war or a French decision to form a military alliance with the United States or both. "How" was the big question. The pragmatic duo decided it would have to be basically a "water borne" approach, with Silas in full charge while Franklin put his full attention on the court — and the ladies. The third man out, Arthur Lee decided he wanted to see if he could make some headway in obtaining a loan from Spain. He had no intention of continuing the third man theme.

Now for some action. Silas was determined to "hit the British on their home court." Before leaving America Franklin and Morris had drafted instructions for Captain Wickes after he had delivered Franklin to France. Wickes' instructions were to cruise the British waters and bring prizes into a French port. This became a deliberate policy of Admiral Franklin and Commodore Deane and the crux of their scheme to build a navy in order to harass the British maritime and coastal towns while operating out of the French seaports of L'Orient, Nantes, Le Harve and Bordeaux. It was an 18th century version of psychological warfare. By continuously being humiliated, England might just throw caution to the wind and declare war on France.

In Wickes' instructions he was told to capture the royal mail packet to Lisbon. On January 24, the *Reprisal* sailed out of Nantes. In the English channel, Wickes took four vessels and sent them back to L'Orient. Then, as instructed, he captured the royal packet *Swallow* running between Falmouth and Lisbon, but not without a fight that took a seaman's life.

Half of the prize money was supposed to go to the *Reprisal* crew and half to Congress. But Tom Morris, half-brother of Robert Morris, was the newly appointed congressional commercial agent to France and had hooked up with a shady pair of French merchants, Penet and Plarne. Hearing of Wickes' prizes, they raced overland from Nantes to L'Orient, sold the prizes at one-fifth their value, pocketed the money and beat it back to Nantes. They claimed they represented the Commercial Committee, formerly called the Secret Committee of Commerce/Trade, and all congressional funds should come through them.

In spite of the stealing of prize money, the commission had, earlier in the month, sent correspondence to the newly renamed Committee of Foreign Affairs, formerly the Secret Correspondence Committee, that fitting American vessels in French ports was winked at by the French ministry, but the bringing in of prizes by a ship fitted out in a French port was contrary to all current treaties among and between England, France and Spain. Doing so could possibly cause an immediate war between France and England. Of course, that was Deane's, Franklin's and Robert Morris's goal.

The commissioners got the expected results from Wickes' raid with the *Reprisal*. Stormont stormed out to Versailles and protested everything to Vergennes, demanding the ships be returned immediately. Vergennes simply implied that as soon as he heard about the episode he sent out an order preventing Wickes from bringing his prizes into a French port. The minister also swore to Stormont that he had seen Franklin only once since he arrived in

Paris, at which time he read Franklin clauses of the Treaty of Utrecht of 1763 (and also read him the riot act). Stormont knew he was lying, but you don't call a foreign minister a liar in diplomatic circles.

Silas had spoken out hard and strong that he should be the only commissioner to continue handling all commercial material and shipping transactions since he was the first American agent in France and he was also the one with the most commercial experience and understanding. Franklin was more than happy to oblige. Arthur, at this juncture, didn't quite dare cross Silas openly. He knew the power that Silas had attained. Franklin was quite peeved about his longtime dear friend Dubourg being replaced by Beaumarchais whom he understood to be more than just a shady character. Silas had also explained to Franklin that Dubourg had a "big mouth" and Vergennes had told him to cool it more than once. Silas could handle Beaumarchais, Franklin had more important issues to worry about. It would take over 11 months for Beaumarchais to get Franklin to even acknowledge Beaumarchais' personal importance to the American cause.

After Lee left to prepare for his mission to Spain, Franklin and Deane sat down to plan their mission actions in detail. First, Silas reminded his chief of station that he had been pushing Congress since 1775 to start issuing privateering commissions in its name. Actually, Congress approved 50 commissions in December of 1776, but Silas did not receive them until April. In the meantime, American privateers from the various states were infesting British waters and doing very well with prizes brought to the West Indies island ports, especially to Bingham's agency in Martinique.

Just before Wickes made his successful cruise against the British he had sent his cousin, Samuel Nicholson, to Franklin with a recommendation that he be given command of a war vessel. Nicholson was a friend of Carmichael and both men were friends of a Captain Joseph Hynson. Coincidentally, Hynson was a stepbrother of Franklin's friend Captain Lambert Wickes.

Both Franklin and Silas understood that if they were to continue harassing and insulting the British in their home territory, they were going to need more ships, crews and skilled captains to create the Deane/Franklin navy. Previously Silas had befriended several rogue privateer captains and American commercial agents in French ports. They decided to add all three men to their naval venture. Nicholson was sent to the north coast to buy a cutter and bring it to a French merchant friend of Silas's at Le Harve. For the purchase of the cutter, Nicholson was given a letter of credit from the commissioner's banker Ferdinand Grand. Hynson was sent secretly to Nantes to await orders from Deane. Unfortunately, and completely unbeknownst to the entire American delegation, Hynson would become a turncoat for money. He would pull off the most astounding feat in all of the American Revolution's European theater through 1778. It was then January 1777 and Hynson's betrayal would not be discovered for another four months.

Although they often differed in their approach to a situation, the old chief of station and America's first James Bond 007 secret agent worked out their initial approaches to Deane's navy and Franklin agreed that Silas should handle all general and detailed aspects of their future strategy but should keep him informed and updated. Next the duo moved into several serious problems that faced them and started initiating plans to deal with them.

Franklin told Silas that the members of Congress were extremely upset with him for commissioning so many fame and fortune hunters for the Continental Army. They were especially angry over the recommended high ranks bestowed upon them. After only one month of being deluged by hordes of individuals Franklin now knew firsthand what Silas had been up against. What bothered Franklin the most was the pressure he received from friends and people in high places wanting some relative or friend to be given a specific position. One of his first visitors had been Broglie pleading his case to replace Washington, which was to get Silas into even more trouble with congressional members. The sage decided he would relieve Silas of the "volunteer" problem by simply but firmly refusing them, but he soon found that even the most unknown and unqualified had a lot of juice from official governmental backing. Franklin even devised a letter of introduction for them which said he didn't know the person and didn't recommend him for anything. It didn't work. They kept coming.

Next the pair looked at each other with a very big question mark on their faces. How could they at least partially neutralize the legion of British agents and spies? They were like flies, they were everywhere. The two commissioners settled on a simple three-pronged policy. When any project needed discussion between them it would be by word of mouth only — nothing would be written down that could give away an overall scheme. The second was the use of very open propaganda, which was Franklin's forte, and the third was to openly deceive (lie) using the phrase "he didn't know he didn't know." As to secret writing and invisible ink, they were time consuming and a general nuisance, but they would use them in official correspondence with Congress, in triplicate no less. Unfortunately, it was still early 1777 and the British naval blockade was extremely effective. Congress didn't even know that Franklin was in France.

The last area that needed help badly was personal finance. How could they produce some personal funds? Congress forgot to allow for expenses and had little or no money most of time. North American land speculation had been part of the two men's being from a very young age, Franklin at 22 and Silas at 15. They would work well with their prewar contacts in England to get the land speculations back on track. Franklin would renew his English financial contacts concerning Vandalia, and Silas would woo the Ohio Company. Silas decided he wanted to check out the English stock market. Of course, all this was consorting with the enemy, but they reasoned this would be money taken away from the enemy. Franklin also knew that if Bancroft ever got out of London he could help. He was always up to his ears in speculation and stockjobbing.

Franklin had one other item that needed reiterating. He reluctantly told Silas it was absolutely necessary that Silas remain Franklin's "point man in Paris." Primarily because of his age Franklin couldn't continually make the 14- or 15-mile round trip to Versailles, to keep Vergennes in the loop, when he had so many painful attacks of gout that kept him from walking any distance. Franklin was wise enough to be cognizant of the fact that the French ministry admired and trusted Monsieur Deane and they had already distrusted Lee for his previous actions and English government contacts. As for himself, Franklin told Silas he didn't think the French Ministry had figured him out yet, but they would in time and he needed that time to stir the savants and nobility to more pro–American influence over the king and his ministers. Silas agreed to the extra duty of making the mission's trips to Versailles. It would keep him closer to diplomatic moves and Vergennes' reactions. January had come and gone. February would be full of individual failures, but there would be an occasional step forward.

Carmichael returned from Bordeaux and gave Silas a full report on exactly what had happened with the *Amphitrite* affair with DuCordray. That situation, which Carmichael investigated for Silas, openly soured him toward the French. It made him a target of the British to turn spy for England, but it didn't work. Carmichael preferred criticizing Franklin and Deane for not being more on the ball dealing with the French.

Feeling better after working out a basic approach to the mission with Silas, Franklin told his fellow commissioner that he was going to back off the French ministry for a while. He said he needed to enjoy some social life and began to go out every night, regardless of his health.

Later, Gérard told Silas that Stormont was really shook up over Franklin's success with European diplomats and secretly he said Captain Wickes' successful voyages didn't help either. The French ministry was also very impressed with Franklin's visitors. Paris chief of police Jeane Charles Lenoir informed Vergennes' office of everyone who came through Franklin's door. They included the Russian minister to The Hague, and a Freemason, Prince Gallitzer, and the minister of Denmark, Baron Blume.

One morning in February, with Silas's knowledge, Franklin decided to personally contact Lord Stormont. He wrote the English ambassador a letter asking about the possibility of a prisoner exchange. Stormont returned the envelope, theoretically unopened, and wrote Franklin separately that the king did not recognize or deal with the rebels. The two commissioners were not surprised at the reply, but from then on they continued to try for the release of American prisoners from Old Mill Prison at Plymouth, Fortin Prison at Portsmouth, and prison ships. The two pragmatists decided they would use their network to organize an underground organization to aid the prisoners, most of whom were seamen, in making an escape and then finding new work for them. In a short time, the organization was up and running and remained so in various forms throughout the war.

Arthur Lee finally made it to the Spanish border. He had made an extended stop in Nantes. His purpose was to, it was hoped, find wrong-doing by Silas and his "subagents." Actually he was checking out the mess made by dipsomaniac Tom Morris' agency and the Penet & Plarne pair. Arthur wanted to get his brother William over from England to take over control of the commercial agency. He wrote his brother Richard Henry Lee, now chairman of the Committee of Foreign Affairs, about his plans. It became a reality in a few short months and started a whole new episode of internal controversy among the American representatives.

While America's dynamic duo were occupied with the innumerable operational problems of their mission, they did not altogether realize how high the tides of war were running against them. They were often puzzled by and didn't fully understand the flamboyant society of Versailles and its foibles. Nor did they comprehend how much they were at the mercy of any kind of intrigue from both friend and foe. With their quasially France as an example, Silas's early landlady was actually the wife of the minister of state, Comte de Maurepas. Through her the entire French ministry was unofficially informed of the everyday moves made by the American secret envoy Deane. Consequently, later, when the three men got underway, Silas, being the most openly liked and active American involved with the French ministry, became the main target by the British to discredit.

Paid enemy and friendly informants were so plentiful in and around Paris that the commissioners had to find their own way around conflicting information to interpret what came back to them through their own intelligence network. Fortunately, Beaumarchais was very close, along with Dubourg and Dumas, to the original sources both English and French.

By February, Silas had as many as six or more ship captains staying at his suite of rooms in the Hôtel d'Hamburg. It had become commission center for launching covert plans, espionage projects, and all kinds of other double-dealing means of getting aid to America.

A William Hodges, of Philadelphia, arrived in early February with orders from Congress to buy two cutters to be used as packets carrying dispatches between the American commissioners and Congress. When Hodges located the cutters, Silas quickly made him a deal to become part of the cruising projects of Admiral Franklin's fleet. Silas then arranged through, and with, Chaumont for a commercial monthly packet service. The packet service turned out to be a dismal failure due to the information Bancroft sent to Eden. The packet was destroyed on its first trip. A packet service was never again tried by the Americans.

All during February Bancroft, still in London, kept sending Silas his "traditional" scare letters about British spring campaign plans to split off New England from the other colonies. By this time Silas could easily double check on Bancroft's information with the intelligence network members in England. What really bothered Silas, and made him a little suspicious, was the information coming back that the British were now seriously looking for the person, or persons, behind the John the Painter rampage. The English authorities were especially concerned about the passport in John's name signed by Vergennes. The Americans' goal was to take the pressure off the ministry and Bancroft, and this was the point where Silas and Bancroft decided on the letter campaign (aimed at British eyes) to Bancroft claiming all credit for the episode. It worked, although Silas had hoped the passport that Vergennes signed on Silas's recommendation might have caused a "little more trouble" for the French ministry.

When March rolled around it was time for Franklin and his entourage to move to the village of Passy. At that time Passy was a small village about three miles from the outskirts of Paris. It was a beautiful collection of villas and chateaus located on the edge of the Bois de Boulogne. One of the finest estates was owned by Jacques-Donatien Leray de Chaumont.

After two months Chaumont had finally persuaded Franklin, with considerable encouragement from Silas, to move to one of his villas. Vergennes more than once also had strongly suggested the move, realizing how much attention Franklin was receiving in Paris. But actually, it was more of Chaumont's personal strong sympathy for the Americans and the thought of even bigger contracts with Silas that pushed the move forward. He offered Franklin one of the villas at free rent and board. In the commissioner's instructions Congress showed its utter ignorance of specific real world situations. The trio was told to "establish a residence in the French capital that was consistent with their dignity as public representatives."[5] Congress had no idea of the costs of rent, transportation, food and personal expenses. Two years later, in 1779, Congress finally voted their emissaries the 18th century equivalent of $13,000 — and that was less than half a year's rent. Another point that irked all American agents was the fact that costs were expected to be paid by them with the hope that someday they would be reimbursed. Where they got the initial money was *their* problem.

When Franklin moved to Valentois at Passy, he made it a point to ask Silas to join him. Silas responded he would be happy to shortly, but first he had to move his Hotel d'Hambourg operation to new, larger quarters preferably in the center of the city where he could entertain waiting ship captains and their mistresses, various merchants, and political intrigues. Silas's d'Hambourg center had become the American base for espionage and double-dealing — secretly, of course.

During all the time that the commissioners were together in France they took a lot of flack from Lee, Izard and Carmichael for Deane's own "loose tongue," which was noticed often by British agents, especially in coffeehouses, and also by supposed "friendly visitors" at the espionage center. He has been charged for over two centuries with inadvertently giving crucial intelligence to the enemy, backed up by the following quote from a British military spy, one Lieutenant Colonel Edward Smith, assigned to watch and get Silas's confidence within weeks after the American agent arrived in Paris. Smith wrote to the British Secret Service explaining the "profiles of Franklin and then Deane": "The latter appears to be the more active and efficient man, but less circumspect and secret, his discretion not being always proof against the natural warmth of his temper being weakened down by his own ideas of the importance of his present employment."[6]

What has not seemed to be realized by historians is that the information blurted out by both Franklin and Silas was part of the procedure they settled on early in 1777 to confuse and mislead the enemy. It is an age-old intelligence ploy. The action always caused considerable inconvenience for the enemy to check out the information, never knowing for sure if it was true or false.

The story behind the double spy Bancroft was much the same situation except he was a personal friend of both Franklin and Deane. However, neither man believed in coincidence. They either were sure or at least had a strong suspicion of "Edward Edwards." At any rate, they both deliberately used Bancroft and he never seemed to catch on. When Silas needed to gently rattle Vergennes' cage, he set up a real crisis situation that would then be leaked by Bancroft through the Secret Service and Stormont. When Franklin wanted to check out intelligence coming out of London he would send Bancroft on a "mission."

Chaumont had installed Franklin and his family in a two-story, sumptuous, neoclassical garden pavilion on the grounds of the Hotel Valentois that led to formal terraced gardens lined with chestnut and acacia trees. Silas joined Franklin in mid–April after he had signed a one-year lease on a luxurious suite in the center of Paris overlooking the new Place Louis XV. Silas fully realized that he was going to have to network individuals as well as war goods. During that year commissioner Deane would have the sole responsibility of placing, and entertaining, individuals of all levels of society and background in the name of the Americans' cause, including "likeable" spies. At times such a group of individuals would even include Beaumarchais, Grand, Gerard, Bancroft, Carmichael, Nicholson, Hynson and Wickes. They would have dinner in Deane's suite and spend the rest of the evening partaking in a variety of night life activities, which abounded in Paris.

Franklin and Silas, when he was not in Paris, lived a very lavish lifestyle at Valentois. Chaumont supplied servants and stocked the wine cellar with a mix of red and white Bordeauxs, champagnes and sherries. There were always at least 1,000 bottles on hand. In the food department the duo, and their family and friends were also eating very well. Vast quantities of strawberries, cream, Roquefort and Parmesan cheese, leeks, duck, rabbit, chicken, eggs, pancakes, apples, turkey, plum pudding, and oysters were available and consumed, but not necessarily in the above order.

Franklin and Silas wholeheartedly agreed on the philosophy, and always gave it in explanation: both politicians and merchants have always known a little luxury will often spur individuals on to do more energetic work. Now in his 70s, Franklin definitely felt he deserved such luxury.

It must be understood that the trips Silas was taking so often to Vergennes's office at Versailles were for the purpose of explaining to the foreign minister, through Gerard, what activities the commissioners were considering, not for Vergennes' permission, but to give him a head's up. While Silas used a personal approach as to his dealings concerning military aid, privateering and the "Deane navy" activities, Franklin was using a different approach with the diplomatic and political activists of the French society. He utilized his personal fame to work the French socially elite. He made visits to the general assembly and royal societies dedicated to science, philosophy and the arts. But first on his approach was the many famous salons. His working in this fashion really made Vergennes wonder just what Franklin did hope to accomplish.

For the commissioners, the village of Passy turned out to be a virtual Who's Who of French governmental and military officials as well as several savants. The residence of Ferdinand Grand at Passy truly made him the immediate and most important person to the American commissioners. From the very first decision to help the Americans, King Louis XVI's monies assigned to the American commissioners went entirely through the hands of Monsieur Grand, a very precise and powerful banker with an equally powerful banker brother in Amsterdam. His estate was conveniently located to the rear of the terraced gardens of Valentois. In addition, Deane, and then Franklin, learned that Ferdinand Grand was a close friend of both Vergennes and Chaumont. Shortly after their official arrival, the commissioners left the large expenses, disbursements and calculations to Grand. Silas, because of the minutia he had to deal with in cash, carefully kept all his own personal records of disbursements both public and private. They were in letter books, ledgers and "project diaries." Most still exist and can be found spread all over the map in federal government agencies and the Library of Congress; the New York and Connecticut historical societies' collections and various university libraries. A few known pieces of Deane's correspondence also still remain in private family collections, published and unpublished.

Franklin started out doing much the same with all official commission correspondence and personal records, but he gave up. They became such a mess that he asked his grand nephew, Jonathan Williams, to make a special trip up from Nantes to try and straighten out the official records, but to no avail. Arthur Lee, back in Congress in 1782, messed around with what papers were in Congress, but only with the basic purpose of hammering Deane's and Franklin's reputation concerning money. At last report, Yale University is still collecting "Franklin papers" from all over the world for publication.

At the end of April, Franklin had had it with volunteers and wrote Congress asking whether he should encourage more applications. Franklin did not know that Congress had written him previously to cease and desist. But the rampage of incompetence continued to roll on. In fact, by August, Washington was writing directly to Franklin asking to spare him the need to continually refuse applicants requesting Continental Army ranks.

There were, however, a few notable exceptions to the applicant roster out of the over 400 that Franklin is known to have "signed for," with or without recommendation, not Silas, as is usually claimed in history books. Two applicants stand out over several other good "French connections." They were Gladimas Polaski, whom Vergennes personally vouched for, and Baron von Steuben, by Saint Germain. According to both Silas and Franklin, records indicate the recruiting story of Von Steuben happened in an unconventional way.

A few days after Franklin had finally received his cease and desist orders regarding sending volunteers to Congress, he and Silas were taking a break from their multitude of responsibilities when an unexpected carriage drove up. Franklin cringed with the thought of being nice but firm in another refusal. But, Silas's voice in the entranceway seemed to indicate he knew this individual. Entering the room, Silas introduced Franklin to Baron Friedrich Wilhelm von Steuben. Silas said that Beaumarchais had told him of this man's abilities and thought he would be of some real service to the American cause.

Von Steuben immediately handed Silas a letter, which he in turn promptly handed to Franklin. The letter had the seal of the French War Ministry. It seemed to the commissioners that this man in a Prussian uniform must have certainly impressed minister Count Saint Germain. Silas alerted Franklin that he had been told previously that the Baron spoke no English, upon which all three men switched to their limited mastery of French. In French the Baron said he sought service in the American Army and that he brought a salute from King Frederick of Prussia for their cause. He asked only to serve.

Reading further in the letter Franklin was very impressed with the baron's experience, but surprised he held only the permanent rank of captain. In order for the matter to be noticed in Congress, Franklin upgraded the letter of recommendation to lieutenant general. The rest is history. Von Steuben turned the Continental Army into the finest modern fighting machine of the day.

Last, there was good shipping news. Carmichael informed Silas that the *Amphitrite*, with good old Coudray aboard, had, with Beaumarchais constantly complaining to Vergennes, received its export license and sailed for Santo Domingo — supposedly.

In a kind of domino effect, several of the other vessels received their export licenses and were already at sea. They were *LeMercure, La Concorde, L'Amelie, Le Marquis de Chalotias* and *La Seine*. There were also two Bermudian ships almost ready to sail. At Nantes Jonathan Williams was ready to send out a chartered ship. Beaumarchais asked if he could name it Comte de Vergennes. Vergennes gave a nod.

Beaumarchais had heard rumors out of London that mail was arriving in France without being blockaded. He learned that the British had been defeated in major battles. The rumors were a little off the mark and actually referred to Trenton and Princeton months earlier. But to Vergennes the news reaffirmed his risking Stormont's tirade allowing by Beaumarchais ships to sail with Silas's cargoes.

The first day of spring arrived in Paris with spies outnumbering all diplomats. The commissioners knew that Vergennes kept his awareness sharp and clear. Stormont was always waiting for a chance to embarrass Vergennes over "secretly" aiding the Americans. After months of the awareness of being continuously watched by both sides, Silas and Franklin treated the spy agents with more or less contempt. They entrusted the written word only to close friends or tough sea captains. They literally felt there was little point in worrying about shipping information leaking from Paris when Le Harve, L'Orient, Cherbourg, Nantes and Bordeaux were crawling with spies. There was the fact that Vergennes and Sartine constantly changed the orders of local authorities, and seamen were bribed by spies, and ship captains were continually changing their route and sailing date and time. The bottom line was they relied primarily on the captain's seamanship and luck to get through the British blockade lurking just beyond the French coast.

Back during mid–March, a bundle of dispatches dated December 21 through 30, arrived from Congress after almost a three-month delay. They contained a whole new series of orders and instructions to the commissioners. The dispatches disclosed the fact that Congress at that time didn't know that Franklin had arrived in Paris and that Thomas Morris had been appointed the new representative of the Secret Committee of Commerce, Congress asking that the commissioners work closely with him. In the dispatches there were four other main items that rattled the commissioners a bit. First, as an inducement to France for more military assistance, they were to offer aid for additional French territorial acquisitions of Newfoundland and British West Indies. Second, Congress had lost the original commission's instructions and asked for a copy to be sent to them. With childlike ignorance, Congress chastised Silas for corresponding with Bingham at Martinique without using his invisible ink. Congress felt Bingham was far too young to shoulder and handle such sensitive material adequately.

Last, Congress notified the commission that it was appointing new commissioners to Vienna, Russia, Spain and the Grand Duchy of Tuscany. For Franklin and Silas it would not take a genius to figure out what future confusion for Europe concerning America's cause would result.

The reaction to the dispatches by the commissioners was immediate but not the same. As chief commissioner, Franklin sent off memorials to Vergennes explaining all the proposals of Congress. Franklin added that if France could not supply the additional aid he would like to know what King Louis XVI would think of Americans making a peace offer to England or perhaps they should just continue the war. Franklin knew that the last thing Vergennes wanted was the Americans and British ganging up on France.

A week later Vergennes informed Silas and Franklin that the first half million installment of the two million livres previously requested would be raised from private bankers since the French treasury was being depleted by preparations for a possible war.

Meanwhile, Silas had gone directly to Vergernnes's office, and in a straightforward manner told Gerard that if a new loan was not forthcoming the Americans would have little choice but to start reconciliation procedures with England. Vergennes knew Silas well enough to know he wasn't kidding. Surprisingly enough, a new two million livres loan was shortly approved. Vergennes now definitely needed Silas as a friend of France to help Franklin keep working the enthusiasm of the nobility and savants toward an open alliance.

That same week in April, Silas told Gerard that an American captain had arrived from Baltimore reporting that Washington had been consolidating his army for a large spring campaign and Congress was hopeful for additional financial aid. Silas also thanked Vergennes for agreeing that his actions in the Lafayette affair were greatly appreciated.

Unfortunately, Arthur Lee was back in town in a bad humor after the halfway failure of the Spanish junket. He was going out of his way to be obnoxious and against the fact that Silas had moved into Valentois while he was gone. As an example of what Silas and the French merchants had to endure, the story of the Army's winter coats became famous among the French merchants. Silas, as always, wanted the coats to be at least six inches longer because a typical American male was much taller than the average French soldier. Arthur objected so much because of the extra costs that Chaumont said he would swallow the difference. That was the last time Chaumont would do similar business with Lee present.

Although nothing was expected to come of it, Franklin okayed Arthur Lee's desire to go to Prussia to seek possible aid. It would keep Lee busy and give Silas a break from continuous harassment. Franklin was not immune from Lee's nasty disposition. Franklin complained to Silas: "I bear all his rebukes with patience for the good of the service, but it goes a little hard on me."[7]

One evening while Silas was entertaining a motley collection of sea captains at dinner in his rented suite on the Place Louis XV, Captain Henry Johnson of the Continental Navy brig *Lexington* arrived with Deane's long-awaited blank privateering commissions from Congress. Knowing that the commissioners could use the commissions as they saw fit, Silas was ready to roll. He had waiting American sea captains in every major port just hoping for a chance to make privateering sorties. All he needed now was more ships for his navy. As for Captain Johnson, his brig was going to be ideal for the planned raids in May and June.

Another ship captained by Thomas Bell that Silas could get for "Admiral" Franklin's fleet was one sent over by Morris for ongoing privateering. Robert Morris wanted Deane and his half-brother Thomas Morris to invest in the venture. Beaumarchais loaned Silas the money. It was decided that Bell would operate in the Mediterranean. For extending the plan, one of Beaumarchais' merchant agents in Genoa bought another needed vessel for privateering in a very slippery deal. The local government authorities got wise and made the agent return the ship to its rightful owner, thus ending Silas's attempt at private privateering speculation.

It took quite a few months, but Silas and Franklin finally became aware of Gustavus Conyngham, the famous captain of the *Charming Peggy* lost to the British at the Nieuport Canal in 1776. Conyngham had stayed on at Dunkirk. William Hodges arrived there with the cutter he had purchased at

Dover named *Surprize*, which was half-owned by the commissioners and half by Hodges. While the cutter was being fitted out, Hodges sent Conyngham to Paris to receive a privateering commission from Deane and Franklin and then back to Dunkirk to await orders.

The spring raiding plans were now in full gear. Conyngham would operate out of Dunkirk with the *Surprize*. Wickes, Johnson and Nicholson would sail in trio in the Irish Sea attempting to intercept the linen fleet. Nicholson was given a privateering commission and captained the cutter Hyson had purchased earlier in England and named the *Dolphin*.

After Silas had made the final arrangements during the last week in April, he realized that he desperately needed a diversion to keep the British navy in home waters. Silas suggested to Vergennes what was, to say the least, a bold plan. He asked if the French navy detachment at Brest be ordered to sail out as if it was going to America.

Because the latest news from America via American ship captains was rather frightening to the commissioners, Silas wrote to Gérard that he now foresaw that the United States would be absolutely ruined in the coming campaign unless some relief could come from some source. He requested again at least a small diversion of some kind. Perhaps letting a few French naval ships sail directly to the New York harbor.

Launching the spring raids, Silas sent Carmichael up to Dunkirk to deliver verbal instructions to Conyngham personally for the first cruise. He was to capture the mail packet to Holland and then cruise the North Sea. The exact verbal instructions will never be known, but on May 3 Conyngham captured the *Prince of Orange*, the mail packet that ran between Harwich and Helvoetslurs. Finding a goodly number of revealing letters on board, Conyngham decided he had better head back to Dunkirk and captured a brig on the way. Hodges grabbed the mail pouches and personally delivered them to Franklin.

Hodges arrived in Paris just shortly before the roof went off between Vergennes and Stormont. Vergennes had been caught allowing a raid on a British ship by an American vessel fitted out in the French port of Dunkirk. There was nothing that Vergennes could do but return the *Prince of Orange* and the brig. Then he had Sartine send two French sloops of war to Dunkirk to cart the master of the *Surprize* and his entire crew off to the local jail.

Silas became quite worried since there was talk in London of having Conyngham turned over to the British for hanging as a pirate. He wrote directly to Vergennes several times stating that the "unhappy affair at Dunkirk would be most fortunate for our Enemies, if Captain Cunningham & his crew are to be treated as Pirates."[8]

Sitting in jail, Conyngham was itching for another cruise. Conyngham's cousin, David, and Hodges found another cutter named the *Revenge*. David Conyngham and Hodges financed half and the commissioners the other half. The *Revenge* had 14 six-pounders and 22 swivels with a crew of more than a hundred.

Knowing that they were way beyond their instructions in creating an American navy in European waters, Franklin and Deane both wrote Congress asking for, and suggesting, ways to cripple English trade. They didn't mention "another navy" for the European theater of the Revolution. The letter that Silas wrote is now famous in Jay's papers, but it was first located in the H*artford Courant* building in 1961. In it was Silas's familiar plan that he agitated the Secret Committee for two years earlier, the main theme being to burn and plunder Liverpool and Glasgow and panic the English countryside.[9]

On the 28th of May, the trio captains, with Wickes acting as commodore, headed for the North Sea. Silas's instructions were to send their prizes into any French or Spanish port but to disguise them as American ships from whatever point seemed likely according to the cargo they carried. The hope was that this would prevent the vessels from being confiscated and there would be prize money for the crews.

Entering the Irish Channel from the north, since contrary winds blocked them from the south, the commissioners found several small merchant vessels going to nearby ports. Nine ships were captured in rapid succession. Five were sent to French ports and four were scuttled. During the cruise the commissioners took several other ships. There was a grand total of eight prizes, with 10 other vessels destroyed, scuttled, or sent back to England with "prisoners."

The captains found the southern end of the Irish Sea crawling with British warships, but with skill and luck they were able to outdistance them until they were almost back to the French coast, when a ship of the line appeared on the horizon mounting 74 guns. It was the somewhat famous *Beauford*.

Wickes signaled the *Lexington* and the *Dolphin* with their prizes to separate and take off. Wickes then took on the *Beauford* alone. The chase started about noon and lasted into the early evening when the ship of the line got close enough to try for a broadside but missed. Wickes dumped everything he had overboard, but couldn't quite shake off the *Beauford*. In desperation he ordered several structural full beams be sawn through to give his ship more resilience and made a fast dash for the rocky coast of France where the *Beauford* could not go. Staying close to the shore, Wickes sailed all night for St. Malo. By noon, both the *Reprisal* and *Dolphin* were safe in St. Malo. The *Lexington* made land at Morlax. Hearing the great news the commissioners sent Jonathan Williams to take charge of the prizes. But it was too late. Tom Morris and company grabbed the winnings for themselves again.

The three successful cruise ships caused more than a little concern in the British Isles plus another gigantic jump in shipping insurance rates. Best of all, as far as Silas and Franklin were concerned, was the fact that Stormont told Vergennes, "Peace, however earnestly wished, cannot be maintained unless effectual stop is put to our just causes of complaint.... The Honour of this Country ... will not submit to such open violation.... The necessary consequence must be a war, which is the object they have in view and they are not delicate in the choice of means that may bring about an end so much desired by them."[10] Stormont knew exactly what the Americans were doing.

On July 8, Stormont told Vergennes he knew the *Revenge* was secretly being outfitted for another cruise. That did it. Vergennes promised the *Revenge* would be sold. As for the two captains' crews, Stormont demanded that they leave France immediately as he knew the British warships would pick them off as soon as they left port to the open sea. Vergennes found a way to placate Stormont temporarily. The captains and ships were put under arrest and forbidden to leave port without permission.

Hodges got the orders to sell *Revenge*. Carmichael was then in Dunkirk and arranged one of those extralegal rights of "changing the property" with the promise the *Revenge* would not privateer. Conyngham and his crew were finally released from prison. The *Revenge* was almost ready and the British were waiting for her. Carmichael also arranged "friendly ownership" of the *Surprize* and sent her down to Nantes to join the rest of the privateer fleet.

On July 16 the *Revenge* left port unarmed, but that night small boats brought out to her cannons and French seamen. Carmichael had given Conyngham Silas's written instructions not to attack the enemy "but if attacked at Liberty to retaliate."[11] Conyngham later wrote that his verbal instructions could not be put to paper. Though he was chased the moment he was in the open sea, Captain Conyngham managed to out-sail the British navy again and headed in a northeasterly direction. For two months the *Revenge* raided in the North and Baltic seas and sailed around England and Ireland. Not daring to return to France, Conyngham made it safely to Cape Ferrol in Spain.

Silas wrote to Morris: "Our last accounts are, that they have taken and destroyed about twenty sail and had appeared off the towns of Lynn, and threatened to burn it unless ransomed."[12] Conyngham had become the terror of all the eastern coast of England, and was called by the natives the "Dunkirk Pirate."

As an overall result, Stormont hit Vergennes with threats only a step removed from open warfare. If Conyngham was not punished, Stormont would resign, breaking off all diplomatic relations with France. There was a very frightening "also": the British navy was given orders to seize the French fishing fleet returning from the Grand Banks off Newfoundland. The foreign minister had to buy time and it had to be at the expense of the Americans, who had violated their promise to conform to the treaty with England. Vergennes told Deane, with "Admiral" Franklin present, that all privateers were being held in port until the king could be sure they would return directly to America and all prizes were returned.

The commissioners replied they had not meant to offend his majesty. They had ordered Wickes, Nicholson and Johnson to leave for America as soon as the vessels were repaired. Also the royal orders would be given "to our friends residing in your ports."[13] Deane and Franklin both informed Vergennes that they were sure Congress would strictly abide by the king's orders in the future.

Having taken such action, Vergennes worried that a reunion of England and America might now occur. He urged Louis XVI for a closer alliance, as secret aid was no longer sufficient, and war with Great Britain in any case was inevitable. Unknown to the American commissioners on July 23, the king hesitantly gave his consent to an alliance with the new United States on the condition that Spain would also consent to an American alliance. Three days later, on July 26, an official memorial was sent to the French ambassador in Madrid. Charles III absolutely refused to go along with an American alliance, leaving Louis XVI helpless. The French were still not ready to start a war with England alone.

While Vergennes was waiting to hear from Spain, he had to placate the English. So on April 11, William Hodges, then in Paris, was arrested in his hotel. He was immediately taken to the Bastille. A search was half-heartedly made to find Hodges' partner Richard Allen although Vergennes knew he had already joined Conyngham.

The commissioners wrote a formal request to Vergennes for Hodges' release, stating young Mr. Hodges was "a person of character connected with the best houses in our country, and employed here by a committee of Congress to purchase goods."[14] Deane and Franklin leaned hard on both Chaumont and their banker Ferdinand Grand to intercede. Unfortunately, Hodges had promised that the *Revenge* would not privateer when he "changed ownership." Vergennes used this point to keep Hodges in the Bastille. Though Grand in no uncertain terms told the commissioners "in France and Europe it is a very serious fault to tell the King a falsehood."[15] Vergennes did not release Hodges until the last ship of the French fishing fleet was safely in port. While Vergennes was punishing Deane and Franklin for their political indiscretions, Arthur Lee returned from Prussia with another diplomatic failure and his commission affairs papers stolen by the British. The theft was devastating for the commissioners secrets, resulting in the building of the special frigate in Amsterdam having to be sold to King Louis XVI.

Arthur's brother, William, finally arrived in Paris from London during the month of June with his entire family complaining loudly for the great sacrifice he was making. William never got to carry out his commission to Berlin and Vienna. He was pointedly told he would not be acknowledged. The same situation resulted for his friend Ralph Izard, who had been commissioned to the Court of Tuscany. Both men waited impatiently for Arthur to return to Paris from Prussia with expected grand success. Angered by Arthur's failure, and their own, to grab the spotlight, the three men set to work planning what they had really been sent to France to do — take over and bounce out Deane and Franklin.

The original New Englander duo were well aware of the animosity of the Lee clan and vaguely knew of their Adams/Lee Bloc in Congress. What they never fully realized, until it was too late, was the true power of the Lees and their allies. To the Lees, the pragmatic pair were considered just plain hardscrabble New England bumpkins. It was no compliment. Although both men were now part of the colonial elite, they would never be considered part of the original colonial elite, with founding family names of English gentlemen. In the eyes of the old families, Silas and Franklin were just bootstrap elites without the proper polish.

The Lees and Izard settled on commencing with their all-out effort to supplant the duo in power by targeting Silas first and openly harassing Franklin about ignoring their input for the American commission and the lack of regard for administrative procedures, especially since Congress had conveniently forgotten to provide living expenses for William and Izard.

William wrote to his brother Lightfoot Lee, in Congress known as Frank: "You can't at this time be unacquainted with the faithless principle, the low dirty intrigue, the selfish views & the wicked arts of a certain race of Men, &, believe me, a full crop of these qualities you sent in the first instance from Philadelphia to Paris."[16] Continuing their expose, Arthur wrote Sam Adams two months later that the court of France "is the great wheel that moves them all."[17] At the same time, Arthur wrote to Richard Henry Lee: "My idea of adapting characters and places is this: Dr. Franklin to Vienna, as the most respectable and quiet; Mr. Deane to Holland; and the alderman to Berlin.... France remains the center of political activity, and here, therefore, I should choose to be employed."[18] Lee further explained just how he could get rid of the New England duo by creating the impression of tremendous scandal involving the use of public money for private purpose both by Franklin and Deane.

While the Virginia brothers were refining their plots, Vergennes was getting ready to throw in the towel on the Americans. All the bad news coming from America and the intense threat of immediate war with England made the Foreign Minister very jittery and anxious. In fact, in August he and Sartine officially closed all French ports to privateers and their prizes. However, he did expect Silas to be very discreet in finding a way of getting around the latest official orders.

The summer months of 1777 turned into a chain of one episode or situation after another that constantly kept "the rabbit's tail short." Regardless of this state of affairs, Silas always made his main focus getting ample supplies to Washington's army and giving the British heartburn. From day one, Silas was troubled with a situation he just physically could not attend to personally. That was the need for America to court the friendship of Holland on a more one-on-one basis started by Franklin in 1774. At last, in early June, Silas just took the time from other pressing duties to write Alexander Dumas at The Hague a very personal and philosophical letter, creating a lasting friendship although the men never got a chance to meet personally. Up to this point, Silas had given Carmichael all communications with Dumas to carry out, which also made these two men friends.

In this letter Silas expressed several political and economic opinions, but two of them indicate how deeply and convincingly he felt the future of America would be regardless of the Revolution's outcome. They showed his thinking to be clear and bold and, what has rattled 19th and 20th century historians, frightfully close to modern-day political and economic principles. In summary he wrote Dumas: "It is my ultimate and early wish that America may forever be as unconnected with the politics or interests of Europe as it is by nature situated distant from it, and that the friendly ties arising from free, friendly, and independent commerce may be the only ties between us."[19] Silas claimed he did not understand the "balance of power concept," and he wanted relations with the rest of the globe on a simple commercial basis; at the same time, he realized from his study of history that the historical process brought on a continuous decrease in independent states and countries. He foresaw the unification of Europe, with Great Britain forming alliances with Russia and America. He wrote, "Great Britain, America and Russia united will command not merely Europe, but the whole world united."[20]

While Silas and Franklin were tending one situation after another, a serious internal problem that had been brewing for well over a year came to a head. The situations at Nantes had become increasingly tangled. Franklin, with Silas's request, gave Jonathan Williams, Franklin's grandnephew, the authority to take charge of all cargoes arriving for the commissioners in order to keep Tom Morris's hands off them. Silas's warnings that Tom was unfit had not been received by Robert Morris, but he had received word from one of his European Willing & Morris Co. agents that his half-brother Tom was in deep trouble. To check out the situation, Robert asked a trusted agent friend, John Ross, to come down from Hambourg to Nantes.

Ross found an outright mess at Nantes. When William Lee arrived to be a joint commercial agent with Tom Morris he found Ross guarding Robert Morris's interests and Jonathan Williams holding authority over the commissioners' cargoes, all of which was quite legal and proper. Since Franklin and Deane had written Congress asking for Tom's dismissal, with Ross and Williams agreeing, William Lee saw no point in staying at Nantes and headed back to Paris to make life miserable for the two pragmatic commissioners, targeting Silas especially about what had happened to Indian goods money. At the same time, Robert Morris's wrath came down on Silas like a bomb burst because Morris first heard about Tom on the floor of Congress. Robert suffered deep public disgrace and embarrassment. Only months later did he finally receive Silas's first letter. Morris blamed Deane and Franklin and blasted their characters, having expected the two would be Tom's babysitters. In a rage, Morris wrote to his brother that he stood behind him. Tom went roaring up to Paris and tried to face down both men. Silas wrote another letter to Robert giving the details of what had happened at Nantes and enclosed letters from Ross, Carmichael and several leading French merchants. Eventually Morris apologized to Deane, Franklin and Congress. But the harm was done; Silas never trusted Robert Morris again.

As Vergennes had feared, Stormont gave him an ultimatum on August 19. The three cruise ships, unarmed and without convoy, must leave France immediately. Vergennes said the ships were in the process of being sold to French merchants, which for the moment tied Stormont's hands. An agent of King George III, one Nathaniel Parker IV, a friend of minister of state Maurepas, told the minister that the British Privy Council would surely declare war unless France agreed to make the ships leave and all prizes were returned. This time Stormont's demands gave the French ministry a real scare.

The French ministry agreed that peace was necessary to France and Spain, but national honor was more important. Yet, some compromise had to be worked out. It was finally agreed the three ships had to leave, along with the Connecticut privateer General Mifflin, and the *Reprisal* had to be unarmed. The ministry's decision didn't reach Passy for three days. Silas and Franklin realized all too well that the ultimatum had been a successful ruse by Minister North and the British Secret Service, but they followed through with Sartine's orders since the Americans were already left with little hope of success for their mission. Deane, with Franklin's agreement, decided that only the two navy ships would leave. The *Reprisal* and *Lexington* sailed out to the open sea on September 16. The *Dolphin* was in such bad condition she was left to rot in port.

Off Ushant on September 19, the British cutter *Aliet* caught up with the *Lexington*. After a four-hour battle, the *Lexington* was forced to strike its colors. One week later Captain Johnson and his crew arrived at Old Mill Prison in Plymouth. Captain Wickes, after brilliant naval service, fell victim to the sea in a violent storm off Newfoundland, losing every man aboard except the cook.

One morning in September Silas opened a newly arrived edition of the *Connecticut Gazette* and read a notice of his wife's death "after a long indisposition." A short time after the initial shock and grief, Silas wrote to Dumas that the news of his wife's death came during a time of "public distress and calamities," which didn't actually displace his sorrow but at least distracted him enough to soften his suffering awareness.[21]

With the news of his wife's death riding heavily on him, Silas kept busy at every detail of his mission duties. On the verge of outright depression, he deliberated over his personal future. He wanted his son Jesse to come to France for an education, like his grandson, Benny Bache, and asked his brother Barnabus to see if Washington could arrange a safe route. Perhaps Barnabus could arrange passage out of New York to London on an English ship. It would be easy to get Jesse from there to Paris. Another family situation was getting underway. Simeon Deane was starting a tobacco business in Virginia and had just arrived in Paris to set up connections. Silas planned to move heaven and earth to make the venture successful.

Even with the catastrophe setback with their "navy," Silas, and also Franklin, had no intentions of stopping the privateers. The "Dunkirk Pirate" continued privateering near Spain. The commissioners supported a merchant at Corinna as an agent for any American vessels cruising near the port of Galacia. Silas instructed Conyngham to send his prizes to Gardoqui in Bilbao.

For a while the privateers obeyed the French orders — no French ports — as Vergennes knew they would, Silas set up a new procedure to bring in prizes to French ports if the captains felt it was absolutely necessary. On October 10, Silas wrote to the Delaps at Bordeaux and to other French merchant homes to tell their "pilots" bringing in prizes to show American colors, hide prisoners, and declare for Boston or other American ports depending on the prize cargoes. Silas added in his "instructions" that actually it probably would be better to send prizes to Bilbao.

Silas was handling the British harassment plan at a low key while Franklin kept shaking up the spies. The old sage confused and quite concerned them. One evening in late September, Franklin made a social trip to Versailles. As he left Valentois he off-handedly said rather loudly and with gestures, "I'm off to see the queen." A couple of days later, Stormont had a dispatch sent by Bancroft relaying the quote that Franklin went to visit with the queen at her desire. To the British this was scary. Marie Antoinette was not known to be particularly fond of the American cause. Did this mean that Franklin was making better progress with the French than had been expected?

In the same dispatch, Bancroft had told Wentworth that he was also having increasing difficulties getting real inside information. Anything sensitive seemed to be handled only verbally, and in private, among Silas, Franklin, Chaumont, Gérard, and even Vergennes. They had ceased writing down memos concerning their various conversations.

From the time Hynson signed up with the commissioners, his main goal was to make a lot of money. Mentally he was rather a dim bulb, but he had a gregarious personality. Unknown to Silas or Franklin, he quickly negotiated with the British Secret Service for a pension if he would deliver dispatches from the Americans bound for Congress. In mid–October, after the failure of the first attempt, Hynson got his real chance. His new buddy, a Captain Folger, relative of Franklin, was selected by Silas to take five packets of mail on a French vessel for America along with dispatches from the commissioners to Congress. The dispatches for Congress contained the official correspondence with the French ministry over the past eight months. Hynson acted quickly and created a trivial diversion for Folger to keep him out of the building for fifteen or twenty minutes. He then searched through the packets to find the one marked dispatches. Removing the dispatches, Hynson substituted blank paper and resealed the packet and beat it to England and the Secret Service office. Not until Folger arrived at Philadelphia was the theft discovered. The entire story was not clear until Silas returned to Philadelphia in 1778.

Hynson, returning to England, made Silas very suspicious, but knowing nothing of Hynsons's treachery, Silas wrote Jonathan Williams at Nantes: "This wrong-headed conceited fool has at last turned out one of the most ungrateful of Traitors ... and fled into England."[22] In London, Hynson had the gall to write Deane and offer to send British information to him for a price. Silas's reply is well worth recording:

> Sir, I do not write to reproach you for the ungrateful and treacherous part you have acted, I leave this to your own Reflections; but as you have had the assurance to write to me, & to propose the betraying your new Patrons in the manner you have wickedly, but in vain, attempted to betray your former, & with them your Country, I must tell you that no Letters from you will hereafter be recd by
> Silas Deane[23]

By the end of September and the first week of October Franklin and his faithful point man were short on operating cash again. Congress had just sent over a pile of bills they had made they hoped would be paid up by a new French loan. The two working commissioners were obligated to plead with Vergennes for further French livres. When they had finished their all-too-common plea memorial and placed it in Vergennes' desk, the foreign minister quietly said he already had a complete summary of their request and the letter from Congress asking for aid. Stormont had delivered it the day before. Needless to say, the commissioners returned to Valentois in a very quiet, pensive and embarrassed mood.

Both Silas and Franklin had been suspicious of Bancroft ever since he had come to Passy after getting out of jail, having been charged as an American agent. The plan was to ignore it and wait for validation. Something was missing, but they just didn't know what yet. This time the leak from Passy was too fast and accurate to be from just anyone — it was too close to the original source. Franklin's explanation of who didn't matter to him. He was more concerned that Vergennes kept using leaks as an excuse not to help the Americans — leaks were always part of the diplomatic end games. Being more on the "inside" than anyone else, Silas had had it with Vergennes' waffling. He knew the eventual outcome, having talked with Gérard about a very recent decision made at a ministry meeting with the king. Silas did point out, however, that the leak could possibly have come from some of their close Amsterdam sources. Lee blamed the secretaries and worried that money already promised would be cut off if they didn't stop the leaks of information.

A month went by after the embarrassing meeting with Vergennes and the commissioners still had heard nothing concerning their financial request. The American trio asked Grand to intercede for them. Grand came back the next day and told them Vergennes hadn't even take the request to the king yet. He thought it far too much. Grand did say that all previous monies and installments to come were to be considered gifts. Arthur Lee jumped on that right away and started another letter campaign that the Hortalez & Co. monies were also gifts. Gerard was to settle that matter over a year later when he was ambassador to the United States. Meanwhile, Silas and Franklin were literally getting ready to quit and go home.

The months of October and November were a very personal time for Silas. He was quite fed up with the French ministry's politics. The commissioner's coffers were almost nonexistent as they waited for the next scheduled payment from France to Monsieur Grand. Silas's interest in any diplomacy was fast reaching its lowest ebb. For Silas, several issues had to be worked out for his son's future, and his own. At the top of the list were the personal economic considerations after the war ended.

Gray November came and went. Silas was becoming more certain that an inept Congress and the continuous game of tick-tack-toe diplomacy with France were greater evils than anything that England might have to offer. He was seriously considering the need for a possible reconciliation with England.

At the end of November, with the three commissioners differing widely in their opinions as to what to do next, they decided on a very official powwow to discuss their future actions and reactions. Silas was for giving the French a single ultimatum: either support the Americans or they reconcile with England. Franklin was afraid that such an ultimatum might anger the French ministry enough to abandon them altogether. Lee was primarily concerned about losing the existing French "gifts." Silas was outvoted, but an ultimatum was definitely still considered a choice.

On a very personal level, what bothered Franklin and Silas was the treatment of American prisoners by the British. To both men the first priority in war was the conditions for the "fighting man." Over the months, Franklin and Silas devised an 18th century version of an underground escape system from English prisons and aid for men on prison ships. Silas, with some assistance from Franklin, kept close track of captured vessels and the whereabouts of their captains and crews, through the efforts of Jonathan Williams, Carmichael, and many friendly merchants in various French ports. An elaborate network had been arranged to get money to the officers in prison and get them in touch with English sympathizers who once the officers escaped from prison, could smuggle them across to Holland or northern France. In each port, Silas had set up designated agents who would find them work until a ship became available. One of the most successful escapes was that of Captain Johnson of the *Lexington* and several of his crew in January of 1778. They returned to France where Silas already had a special assignment and a vessel available.

As the last days of November slipped by, it seemed to the commissioners that the work and purpose of their mission would result in complete failure. But, while they were licking their political and economic wounds, and generally feeling sorry for themselves, a ship sailing from Charlestown six days after Burgoyne's surrender at Saratoga arrived at Nantes on November 27. The news did reach Passy on October 30. Then, on October 31, Jonathan Loring Austen, secretary of the Massachusetts Board of War was hurriedly sent to France in the brigantine packet *Perol*. Austen rode into the courtyard at Valentois, Passy at 11:30 A.M. on the morning of December 4. Austen found the commissioners and Beaumarchais had already heard the news but no details. Franklin worried about his family and asked if Philadelphia had actually been taken by Howe. Austen answered yes, but General Burgoyne and his entire army were prisoners of war, and he handed Franklin the correspondence with all the known details of the American victory. Silas breathed relief, saying a "cordial to the dying," better days are here.

After receiving Washington's official dispatches from Austen, the three commissioners quickly sat down and composed letters to Versailles and Madrid announcing Burgoyne's defeat at Saratoga. The very same day, a messenger knocked at Vergennes's door in the late afternoon with a letter from Franklin, Chief American Commissioner. It read:

> We have the Honour to inform your Excellency that we have just received an Express from Boston, in 30 days, with Advice of the total Reduction of Force under General Burgoyne, himself and his whole Army having surrendered themselves Prisoners. General Gates was about to send reinforcements to Gen. Washington, who was near Philadelphia with his Army. General Howe was in Possession of the City, but, having no Communication with his Fleet, it was hoped he would soon be reduced to submit to the same terms with Burgoyne, whose Capitulation we enclose; and shall send your Excellency further Particulars of the State of Affairs in America, as soon as we collect them from the Papers.[24]

To say the least, Vergennes was elated. The Americans had confirmed his judgment and probably saved his job and career. The foreign minister quickly wrote back an official congratulatory note.

On December 8, after receiving Vergennes' congratulations, the commissioners sent him a very aggressive note reminding him that it had been well over a year since they first gave him a copy of the "model treaty." In the same correspondence, the trio also thanked the king for granting the December subsidy of three million livres with the expectation of the same from Madrid. The subsidy was Vergennes' signal to the Americans that negotiations would start to move forward. The victory at Saratoga had produced a triumph for the foreign minister personally, and for the Court of Versailles.

The next two months would be full of intrigue, accusations, threats, compromises and bitter considerations and everyone worked toward finalizing a Franco-American alliance. As much as modern history texts give most credit to Benjamin Franklin as head of the three-man commission, it would be Silas Deane who became far more than Franklin's point man; he became the key man because he was the only real insider with French ministry contacts.

CHAPTER VII

Franco-American Treaties at Last, 1778

On December 10, the commissioners received a message from Vergennes requesting a meeting on the morning of December 12. The French foreign minister asked for very tight security and the utmost secrecy. He told them to come in a private coach to the east wing of the palace.

Once the commissioners arrived at Versailles, Gerard's servant led them to Vergennes' country home in a wooded area just outside of town where Gerard and Vergennes were waiting for the Americans. Vergennes was very effusive and applauded all American triumphs, after which he pushed Franklin for a prediction as to the outcome of the war. All the commissioners chimed in that America would be victorious and the British would tire of fighting.

Vergennes went to his dispatch case and pulled out the "Plan of '76" or "Model Treaty," stating he was happy to see the Americans had not added up any new demands during the year. He assured the trio the king would be happy to go over the proposals and repeated to the commissioners that for France to enter into a commerce treaty with America was tantamount to declaring war on England. Therefore, it was imperative that the Americans negotiate in good faith. He promised that France would take no advantage of them and would demand nothing that was not in the best interests of the United States. Vergennes did object, however, to the twelfth article granting equality of tariffs between West Indies and French products, or the monopoly of trade in the islands. All in all, Vergennes did fully realize that whoever was first to recognize American independence would be first to benefit from the fruits of war, meaning that England had to be blocked at every turn from coming up with an argument with the Americans for reconciliation.

As soon as the news of Saratoga reached London the British secret agents began lining up to head for Paris as peace emissaries and get a crack at sounding out the American commissioners on peace terms. The British Secret Service ace Paul Wentworth arrived in Paris on the same day that the commissioners had met in the woods beyond Versailles with Gerard and Vergennes. It was Friday morning and Wentworth immediately fired off a note specifically to Silas saying, "A gentlemen who has some acquaintance with Mr. Deane wishes to improve it."[1] The note suggested a meeting at noon in the Luxembourg Gallery or at the "Bathing Machine on the River" (one of Franklin's favorite haunts).

When Silas returned from the December 12 meeting with Gerard and Vergennes, he answered Wentworth with a tersely written reply saying he would find Mr. Deane at his lodgings the next morning or at Passy on Saturday evening. A bit hesitant, Wentworth waited over the weekend, until Monday the 15th, before sending another epistle to Silas. This time he gave Silas his hotel address and stated he was returning to London soon. If he could be of any use in promoting peace, Mr. Wentworth would be happy to provide conditions and ideas.

This was interesting. Franklin and Silas were being approached directly. So — Wentworth was "the something missing" when "dealing" with Bancroft. Anyway, the two years of the rattling hinges approach to diplomacy finally was getting overt results. From then on as number two man, Silas did not hesitate to keep Franklin in the loop right down to the first details of his actions. Franklin had had dealings with Wentworth previously during his years in London. At one time he even stayed a short while at the Englishman's home. Silas knew of Wentworth through previous personal financial dealings through Bancroft's stockjobbing "friends" on the London market. Neither man as yet knew that Wentworth was Eden's top agent. But, it would not be long before they would have very strong suspicions along with Vergennes.

After a quick consultation the pair of commissioners decided that the best strategy in dealing with British feelers was to keep Vergennes informed of any conditions and offers, but to hedge a little in the details. After the decision, Silas arranged to meet Wentworth for dinner on Wednesday, the 17th.

The initial personal contact with Silas rather than with Franklin by a British agent was no accident. Both Great Britain and France had good reasons for working more closely with Silas than with the old sage. Franklin was consistently inconsistent. Consequently, neither ministry completely trusted the old colonial, even with his widespread fame. Both sides were impressed with Deane's apparent frank and straightforward approach to issues and situations. British agents kept sending back reports that America's first European agent was publicly saying he was ready to throw in the towel from dealing with the French indecisiveness. On the other hand, Franklin was particularly quiet and nonpolitical and that really baffled both sides. Of course, unknown to anyone except themselves, the New England pair had decided on such a strategy to cause confusion.

There was good but very confused reasoning as to why Silas was sought out to be approached first for possible peace or conciliatory negotiations. For months now, Franklin had been playing the fox in the henhouse, keeping both the French and British ministries off balance with the untraditional style of diplomatic actions. At one time, Stormont wrote Lord Weymouth that "whatever Franklin's talents, I am persuaded that he is a less dangerous instrument than Deane."[2]

Silas, although known to be an accomplished schemer and a strong American patriot, seemed on the surface to both monarchs to be honest in his governmental dealings on both sides of the channel. The British liked the way Deane had taken the heat off Bancroft in the John the Painter affair and his occasional trumpeting in Parisian coffeehouses that it was "time to dump the French and start reconciliation talks with England."

The French liked and trusted Silas for his cooperation and patience with the "Simon says" French ministry dealing with Beaumarchais and his Hortalez front. They especially liked his amazing intrigues in getting Lafayette to America. In fact, on the last day of 1776, concerning French aid, Silas wrote that it "would be equated only by the endless gratitude of the numberless millions rising into existence in a new and extensive world."[3] All Europe was watching and well aware that England and France had a tiger by the tail dealing with the Americans. At that moment it was the most crucial political game in Europe.

From December 12 through 18 the saga of meetings between Silas and Wentworth came from three original sources. They play like a bad soap opera. Each man tried to set up the other in case their meetings fell apart and became distastefully known at the top on both sides.

For Silas, the meetings were a chance to speed up the official diplomatic process. He was sick of constant political intrigues and schemes. This was a chance for him to get out of the political and diplomatic world and get back to being a successful merchant, maybe even an international one. Anyway, this wily Englishman was going to get an earful of Yankee braggadocio Deane-style about his part in the Revolution and those brave soldiers/patriots who fought with inadequate weapons and supplies. Silas figured it would be worth hearing out Wentworth in case he might come up with something new. So Silas proceeded to play the old game of "what do you have that I want."

At their first meeting Silas learned just how far the British might go without throwing in independence. It included all the standard spoils for which England was noted, plus the forgiveness of all patriots. When Vergennes heard that offer he got so nervous about the true identity of this Mr. Paul

Wentworth that he had the man shadowed everywhere he went. Wentworth realized he was being followed and became so shook up (he hated being considered a spy) he went to Stormont, who arranged for Wentworth to actually have dinner with Vergennes and the ministries. Vergennes, in the meantime, had a mutual friend with Wentworth, a well-known informant for both sides, Jeane-Loris Favier, to check out what Wentworth was really doing in Paris.

After their first meeting, Silas was quite hopeful for initial negotiations. Silas felt it was time to talk with Lee man-to-man on a private basis. Because the countries across the channel from each other did not trust one Dr. Arthur Lee, the French ministry made it a point to keep Silas and Franklin up to date in most of Lee's questionable activities and letters to America. Silas wrote a straightforward letter asking for a meeting. He wrote that in the public interest he invited Arthur to tell him frankly the "grounds for all his uneasiness." Silas said this way was "certainly a more honorable and just way, between equals at least, than Private insinuation and threatening Billets or Complaining ones."[4] Lee never acknowledged or answered the letters.

When Favier and Wentworth got together, Favier told him flat-out he had been nuts to contact Deane so openly. Then the Englishmen dropped a bomb, showing how much the British trusted Silas as a result of the New Englander's game of charades. He gave Favier the story that he was sending money to his family in America through agent Silas at Passy. Further, he told the double friend that he was quite ticked off with him for refusing a stock scheme because Deane was already hooked up with a group of men dealing in the stock market. Silas told Wentworth he was utilizing the British market primarily to make some money for personal expenses and replace the absence of a salary that Congress conveniently forgot to allow its agents and commissioners. Silas probably told Wentworth that gem because by December 1777 he had spent 4,000 of his own cash he had brought over with him in 1776.

Later in the supposed secret negotiations, Wentworth dropped another bomb that fairly well verified Silas's and Franklin's suspicions that Bancroft was a double spy. Obviously it was knowledge they felt necessary to keep to themselves because Bancroft was much more valuable to them in order to see that an alliance with France became a reality. Wentworth had stated in so many words to Silas that if he needed more assurance to check with Bancroft.

Even though Silas and Wentworth were both Freemasons and shared the same basic ideals, on a personal level Wentworth had a hard time dealing with Deane's "republican pride" and his irritating habit of quoting statements from history when appropriate situations arose. It was a hobby Silas had started while at Yale.

One of the concepts offered by Wentworth did make Silas sit up and take notice. It was a 1778 version of the modern-day Congress's 2009 stimulus package. The British ministry was willing to finance improvements and updating of American commercial and agricultural methods. Now the Yankee merchant was in his element. For the second time Wentworth said "check with Bancroft." Wentworth had previously asked Bancroft to explore the nature of a possible new approach for the colonial commerce and agriculture. That statement, plus the fact that Wentworth had laid out his plan for reconciliation and that Deane was told he should ask Bancroft about the basics of the plan which the double spy had said (way back in 1763) should be widened much further, more than verified to Deane and Franklin that Bancroft was definitely playing both sides.

Silas kept meeting with Wentworth. On the morning of December 15, the English spy ace picked up Silas at the Café St. Honoré where he was having breakfast with Franklin and Lee. For some unknown reason, it wasn't until the 18th that Lee paid any attention to Silas and Wentworth when Izard chided Arthur for not being more observant. When Arthur asked Silas if he was holding negotiating meetings with Wentworth, Silas told Lee that Wentworth had some pertinent questions about America's demands for reconciliation and he told Mr. Wentworth it had to be unqualified independence.

On December 17 Silas sent a note to Wentworth stating he was too ill that day to continue their talks. Gérard had been in a panic trying to reach Silas before the next meeting with Wentworth and the two finally met at Gérard's apartment. Gérard wanted Silas to know that Vergennes had granted there definitely would be a treaty and Vergennes was considering Gérard to start conducting negotiations for an alliance. Gérard wanted Silas to have a heads up, and to arrange a meeting with him the very next day, the 18th, using the excuse that more details were needed from the Americans concerning their funding of American military needs.

After their meeting at Gérard's apartment, Silas carried out his earlier arranged dinner meeting with Wentworth. This time the British agent ace went all out and spelled out his entire reconciliation plan in much greater detail, but still it fell short of complete independence from the British Empire. At the end of the meeting Wentworth pleaded with Silas to push for an interview with Franklin. Silas promised he would but said he doubted that Franklin would agree to a talk — at least not right away.

Gérard told Vergennes he had informed Deane of the possible start of negotiations and asked that Deane make arrangements to meet with the commissioners the next day. Vergennes's comment revealed the trust the French had in Silas. He said that Gérard should stay in close contact with Deane: "I do not suspect that any retinease exists on the side of our friend."[5] It would be a statement that the Foreign Minister was to repeat several times about Silas in the coming weeks. Deane would keep his colleagues "chilled out" while Vergennes waited for a reply from Madrid, knowing that there would be a treaty regardless of any circumstances and whether or not Spain joined in. Silas kept his word and Gérard was able to meet with all the commissioners the next day, December 18. The King's Council (ministry and diplomats) had made the decision for a treaty on December 17. But the ministry wanted to wait to hear from the other Bourbon monarch.

After the meeting with Gérard, Silas carried out his earlier arranged dinner meeting with Wentworth. This time the ace British agent went all out and laid out his plans for reconciliation. There was one item that aroused Silas's interest, Wentworth had his own version of a 21st century stimulus plan for updating American agriculture and commerce, but the plan had no real details worked out and the presentation continued but still left out complete and absolute independence from the British Empire.[6] It was their final meeting and, having come to no real common ground, Wentworth again pleaded with Deane to arrange a meeting with Franklin. Ignoring his own earlier attempts, Wentworth tried again on his own to get an interview with Franklin and got turned down a third time. This left the agent twiddling his thumbs for a while.

While Silas was meeting Wentworth, Beaumarchais entered the Passy stage with a personal problem. The famous *Amphitrite*, having delivered her much-needed supplies for Washington's army, returned with her first American trade cargo. There was really no question that the cargo belonged to Beaumarchais under Silas's first contracts in 1776, and Vergennes agreed. Franklin, however, immediately jumped in and claimed the cargo for the commissioners. With all the turmoil around him it was Franklin's chance to rattle Vergennes a little more and also make it pay-back time to Vergennes for treating his friend Dubourg badly and replacing him with that Beaumarchais. This was the first time Franklin actually bucked Silas, maintaining that Mr. Deane's instructions did not give him the authority to make any contracts with Beaumarchais in 1776. Of course Franklin knew this was stretching the rubber band a bit. As a member of the original Secret "Commerce" Committee, he knew chairman Robert Morris had arranged with Silas to make contracts with the French at a 5 percent commission.

Silas quietly pressured Vergennes through Gérard to get the cargo released to Beaumarchais, knowing the man was a secret French agent. Suddenly, Franklin released the cargo with the explanation that commissioner Deane controlled all aspects of trade and shipping for the American commission; thus ended a nuisance event that could have caused more delays in negotiating with the French ministry.

Vergennes remained silent for almost the next two weeks which made Franklin and Silas quite jumpy. Arthur Lee didn't care what was going on; he just kept pumping out lies to his brothers and friends in Congress via the London mail, which meant both sides got to read his mail through their excellent secret intelligence networks.

Christmas Day, Silas's 40th birthday, found Franklin and Deane at the beautiful home of their Passy neighbor, Admiral d'Estaing, as his dinner guests. The admiral clearly hated the British and Franklin took advantage of the moment to keep toasting the fact that the House of Bourbon and the Americans would soon reach an alliance.

Vergennes in the meantime was nervously waiting to hear from Spain. He was hoping against hope that Charles III, Louis XVI's uncle, would join France and the Americans in negotiating an alliance. On December 31 news finally arrived that Spain would not take part in negotiations. Franklin realized that it might mean a temporary delay while France reconsidered. The old sage decided to rattle Vergennes's cage hard and played his trump card. He announced he would now meet with Mr. Paul Wentworth.

On January 6, Franklin and Wentworth finally came face-to-face. A peculiar situation occurred shortly before the meeting which showed the trust both men had in Silas's judgment. They asked separately and secretly that Silas nonchalantly enter the room after some two hours of conversation had gone by.

During the meeting Wentworth was completely caught off guard by Franklin's strange ramblings; usually nobody said less and kept more to the point. But this time the old man was off the wall ranting about how the British were so barbarous. Wentworth wanted the Americans out from under the French ministry's thumb in the worst way. He asked if Franklin and Deane would agree to, and accept, a guaranteed safe conduct to visit London. Franklin implied that England could only deal with official commissioners from Congress. That did it. Wentworth gave up. The old man was immovable. On cue, Silas came into the room and proceeded to engage in a conversation concerning Silas's middle name—"trade." Wentworth did admit that the British and Americans could easily work out separate agreements concerning future commerce and trade.

At the end of the meeting, Silas stayed on with Bancroft, Wentworth and Franklin as Chaumont's dinner guests. The men made jokes and bets at dinner on whether or not the new United States would become truly independent. Wentworth returned to London knowing the American commissioners would plan no more political games. It was independence or nothing.

When Vergennes learned that Wentworth offered safe conduct to London for further negotiating talks he is reported as saying, "I don't know that I could survive the humiliation of signing the passports."[7]

Regardless of what effect Wentworth's meeting had on Franklin, it did a good job of faking out the French ministry. On January 7, the French Crown Council gave full approval to conduct an alliance with America. The commissioners were immediately informed that France would honor the assurance of a treaty given on December 18.

Again Gérard contacted Silas to let him know Gérard had full negotiating powers. For the second time he asked Silas to set up a meeting with all the commissioners the next day, but not to divulge the real purpose. The next afternoon, before the meeting got underway, Gérard surprised the Americans by requesting complete secrecy of the outcome of their discussions. There was an awkward silence and hesitation; then one by one each commissioner agreed by saying, "I promise."

Gérard explained that Vergennes needed to know the answer to two questions. In translation the first question asked was: "What would they, the Deputies, consider sufficient to reject all proposals of England, which did not include recognition of full and absolute independence both in policies and trade?"[8] The second question followed: "What would they consider equally necessary to produce the same effect on Congress and the American People?"[9] Ever alert, Franklin asked if France would be entering into war. Gérard dodged an answer, saying he was not empowered to discuss it at this time. He then left the room in order that the commissioners could confer privately, but said he would return in an hour.

This was the moment the Americans had been working so hard to achieve. Franklin grabbed a quill feather pen and began to write while Silas and Lee looked on, checking the leader of the commission's wording for absolute clarity. A couple of times the New Englander and Arthur Lee almost came to blows sniping at one another. The final epistle stated that an assurance of an immediate conclusion of a treaty of amity and commerce would stop the commissioners from considering any proposal that did not have complete independence, both political and commercial.

Before the hour was up an impatient Gérard walked back in. The commissioners showed him their answer. It was exactly what Vergennes wanted to know. The second question could wait. Gérard then said that he was at liberty to tell them the treaty would be concluded.

In reality, Silas and then Franklin knew that Vergennes was a little miffed at them for their continued audacity and arrogance in dealing with the French ministry. It was a time when the French and the English were really beginning to ask themselves if it was absolutely necessary to start another global war all over again after only some 15 years. But Vergennes still worked hard to keep negotiations going with the Americans and start new ones. Then, on January 18, negotiations finally got underway in earnest when Gérard brought the drafts to Passy.

Vergennes couldn't believe how slow the Americans were in going over the treaty articles. Of course, the Americans were deliberately slowing things down to get more leverage on certain points and legalities that Silas and Arthur, both being lawyers, wanted clarified. There were several issues where the commissioners had a hard time coming to any agreement. Silas and Lee went round and round on a treaty article where the Americans were to arrange for duty free molasses from the French West Indies. Franklin suggested that both countries forego export duties altogether. Lee went through the ceiling. He realized Franklin was playing him and if the compromise was not accepted by either side he would be to blame. There were other articles, especially those concerning trade regulations, that were finally left up to France and Congress to decide. By the end of January the Americans at last arrived at terms with Gérard. To speed up the negotiation process, six million livres had been granted to the commissioners.

Quietly, over the previous weeks, a second treaty was included in the negotiations. The first treaty of amity and commerce contained the most-favored nation clause and standard commercial legalities. The second was more than the Americans had originally dreamed about—a full military alliance to be triggered when France and England went to war. The big trade-off between France and the United States was the renouncing of any claim to Canada by the French and the Americans' guarantee of French possessions in the West Indies.

Once the treaties were finalized, Vergennes had every intention of keeping them under wraps until they were ratified by Congress. His target date was early May. But rumors of a treaty became routine. In spite of the rumors, confusion, and the refusal of Spain to participate, Vergennes pushed for actual signatures. He had the feeling he might have already lost time in getting negotiation information out to Congress. On the fifth of February, Gérard was wiped out with a brutal cold and had to postpone the signing of the treaties until the next evening—a historic date for the new United States, February 6, 1778.

The signing took place in the offices of the French Foreign Ministry in the Hôtel de Lautrec in Paris. The document was signed first by Gérard, then Franklin, then Deane. Lee hesitated, saying he should sign twice since he was a commissioner to both France and Spain. Franklin and Silas reacted in silent disgust, but quietly pointed out to Arthur that Spain was not a signatory. There was, however, a secret article reserving the right of the king of Spain to join the treaties at some future date.

The final treaty of amity and commerce followed, essentially with the same features that Franklin and John Adams had laid down in their Plan of 1776. In the second treaty of alliance, article two, was the real essential clause, and one of vital importance to the Americans, which stated the purpose of the alliance was for maintaining effectively the liberty, sovereignty, and independence — absolute and unlimited — of the United States in matters of operations and commerce. Both Silas and Franklin were particularly happy with the fifth article granting America the option of conquering northern America, meaning Canada and Bermuda.

Before the signing there was a satisfactory, private historic moment shared by all three commissioners. Silas and Arthur had dressed up in very formal attire for the occasion, but they couldn't help but notice that the head of the commissioners was wearing an old British coat of Manchester velvet. Silas, as well as Lee, was quite curious. When they asked Franklin why he was wearing the coat he replied, "Well, I would like this coat to have its moment of revenge. I wore it in the Cockpit the day Wedderburn abused us."[10]

A couple of weeks after the signing of the treaties, Vergennes learned the British were sending a commission headed by the Earl of Carlisle. They were going to submit to Congress conciliatory bills granting the equivalent of home rule within the British Empire. Vergennes kicked himself for already losing a month in dragged-out negotiations.

Late in the evening of February 26, Silas rushed to Versailles with more bad news. The ship that Vergennes had dispatched to America with the notice of pending alliance had been forced back to France after six weeks at sea. Vergennes had been so intent on secrecy he led the captain of the *Belle Poule* to believe he was just sailing from Bordeaux to Brest until he opened the secret orders at sea. The captain realized that with the provisions on board he couldn't cross the Atlantic. Deciding to return he ran into a violent windstorm off the coast that damaged the rigging, causing further delay in getting back to port.

At Passy the news of the *Belle Poule's* return caused Lee to jump all over Silas and Franklin for not informing him immediately. It was one of the few times the old sage lost his cool. Franklin, with obvious anger, slowly and deliberately explained to Lee that Mr. Deane hurried to Versailles minutes after the news of the *Belle Poule's* return reached Valentois. They saw no reason to stop and consult with anyone in such a crisis: "We think Mr. Deane deserves your thanks and neither of us deserves your censure."[11]

In the sense of letting the American Congress know early that the commissioners were about to make a breakthrough in negotiations for an alliance with France, the return of the *Belle Poule* Vergennes had sent out around the 10th of January was a diplomatic disaster. Because of the efficient British naval blockade of North America Congress knew very little, at least as a body, of what was taking place on the other side of the Atlantic. Officially this was true. Congress had no official direct correspondence from any of the commissioners. The blockade had done its job. But both Silas and the Lees had almost constant private and direct communications with various congressional delegates. Silas wrote most of his correspondence through Bingham. The Lees had their own private network of informants in London who forwarded the correspondence via the British Navy to the New York harbor.

Silas had now been working closely with Gérard for over a year-and-a-half, and, on occasion when he needed some personal advice, Vergennes himself. As a diplomat, Silas did not fully trust him or the minister of foreign affairs, but as a quasi-friend Silas held Vergennes in the highest esteem.

Once the copies of the treaties were signed, with Franklin's knowledge, Silas headed straight for Versailles the next morning. There he got Gérard to let him see Vergennes personally with Gérard present. That was nothing new; by this time Vergennes knew that Silas must have a plan of some kind. He was right. Silas wanted another ship, not for his navy but a frigate for delivering the treaties of amity, commerce and alliance. Always the planner with specific details, Silas asked Vergennes for a French frigate to sail for the North American coastline, knowing there was a lack of blockade ships in the Boston area. The warship should be able to make a landing somewhere on the Massachusetts coastline near Cape Cod, discharge the courier, and sail away. Vergennes gladly went for the plan and asked Sartine to make arrangements for the frigate.

Simeon Deane was returning to America after arranging private commercial contracts with French merchants, with the full support and influence of his brother. Consequently, Silas told Vergennes he was assigning Simeon to sail in the frigate with the responsibility of personally delivering the treaties to Congress for ratification.

The frigate had the same luck as the *Belle Poule,* running into a brutal windstorm that sent it back to Brest for two weeks for repairs before resuming the voyage. Arriving outside the port of Boston in late April, it quickly discharged Simeon and the treaties.

The next that history hears of Simeon and the treaties occurs when a soon-to-be ally of Silas appears in the Continental Congress by the name of Gouverneur Morris, a New Yorker. On April 29, Governor George Clinton reported to John Jay at Poughkeepsie, New York, that Simeon Deane, brother of Silas Deane in Paris, had suddenly appeared in Fishkill. He was traveling with a cavalry escort of Light Horse on his way to New York, where Congress had gone after being chased out of Philadelphia by General Howe. "Deane carried with him 'Dispatches from the Court to Congress' of great importance.... I may venture to tell you as a Truth.... [A] treaty is concluded between that Court and our Embassadors."[12]

Morris had anticipated the news of a treaty from his own private intelligence group. He wrote Jay from New York that "probably a treaty is signed with the House of Bourbon ere this."[13] On May 3, Morris sent a note to Robert L. Livingston that he didn't think they could have gotten more from the treaties if "the important word Louis had been put in his Thanks at the Bottom of a blank Paper."[14] The following day, May 4, Congress, by a unanimous vote, ratified both treaties.

The treaties signed, and his brother on his way with them to Congress, Silas planned to carry out Franklin's early wish of sending him to Holland with the hope of securing a Dutch loan for Congress. With the new treaties, the backing of Dumas and the Grand brothers, plus several Dutch merchants with whom Silas had contracts, he was fairly certain that success was just around the corner.

In any case, Silas knew before he could leave for Holland to meet his correspondence friend Dumas he needed to start gathering and getting accounts squared away and in open legal forms, knowing that the treaties would soon be official public knowledge. Since most purchases and forwarding of supplies had been done covertly, and in countless places all over Europe, the Connecticut merchant figured it would likely take two to three months.

During the stress of the treaty-making for months on end, Silas had been continually subjected to physical and mental strains. Sensing the danger to his general health, he had decided that after the treaties were signed, he would resign from public life and become a Caribbean merchant again with the possible goal of going international. After all, he already had contacts in many major houses throughout Europe. Pulling him in that direction was making a future for his son, Jesse, who would soon be arriving in France for his education. Silas wanted the very best for his only child and family members. Barnabus and Simeon were well established in business careers and his stepsons, Joseph and Samuel Webb, were doing well in privateering and involved in the West Indies trade.

It was a time when both Silas and Franklin had reached a point where anymore screwups might be more than either man could endure without going absolutely bonkers. In his usual straightforward style, Silas told Franklin he hoped he never had to see the inside workings of another European court. The old sage in turn showed the same kind of weariness with the French lifestyle when he stated, in a slightly more tactful touch, "I live here in great respect and dine every day with great folks, but I still long for home and for repose."[15] Consequently, having no immediate situation or problems to handle, they let their guard down momentarily and began thoroughly and honestly enjoying the Parisian night life without any purpose but pleasure. No secret agents were hovering any longer. Unfortunately, they had underestimated the hateful antics of Arthur Lee. The French secret service had intercepted Arthur's private message to Lord Shelbourne, his friend, telling him a treaty of alliance was about to be signed. Vergennes had immediately notified Silas and Franklin. Their correspondence showed how aware the men were of much of Lee's "out of country" correspondence, but not of the impact it had in Congress.

Stepping back a few weeks before Silas started meeting with Wentworth, Vergennes had been caught off guard when Stormont gave him an exact list of cargoes going to America just as they appeared in the commissioner's journals. At the same meeting, Stormont handed Vergennes a copy of a correspondence from the commissioners asking for an additional loan which Vergennes had yet to receive.

When the commissioners arrived at the Foreign Affairs office the next day, one can imagine the embarrassment. As a result, the foreign minister strongly suggested they get their house in order and get rid of the mole. Vergennes' agents had told their boss that the British had been working hard to turn Carmichael due to his open criticism of French policies, but Carmichael had refused.

To stay on the good side of Vergennes, the commissioners played it safe and decided Carmichael should return to America. To soften the hurt after all the good and efficient work Carmichael had done for the commissioners, they asked him to carry with him, to give to Congress, packets of all the official correspondence and records of the commission for the past year. Little did Silas know the "firing" of Carmichael would come back to haunt him within the year.

When Carmichael learned he was going to be the scapegoat for information leaks out of Passy, it jarred his memory. He remembered that when he was originally in London heading back to America, Arthur Lee, then an agent of the Committee of Secret Correspondence, gave him a letter book Arthur had kept of his relation with Beaumarchais. But Carmichael stopped in France and ended up working for Silas and forgot all about the letter book until Lee started sounding off about his suspicions concerning the Hôrtalez Affair. Carmichael then realized he had Lee over a barrel for all the lies he had given Congress and showed the letter book to Silas. Lee yelled hard and long to get it back, but Carmichael took it with him for the Congressional Committee of Foreign Affairs, where it conveniently disappeared from the eyes of the congressional body.

Unfortunately, Silas's political world and personal plans came to a sudden and permanent halt on March 4. The reason was a letter from Lovell with the order from Congress of December 8, 1777 (initiated by Richard Henry Lee), requesting commissioner Deane to immediately return to America to report to Congress the condition of affairs in Europe.

It didn't take a genius to figure out the recall was largely the results of Lee's disparaging efforts of character assassination to get Deane removed from his post. The rumors of Silas's impending recall had been circulating out of London for weeks. Silas checked with Franklin for advice. At first Deane thought he would stay put until Congress clarified the reasons for the recall. This would not happen, because Richard Henry Lee specified for the *Congressional Journal* that no reason be given and it passed. The old sage told Silas that, notwithstanding the state of the commercial accounts, it probably would be best if he went at once since he probably would not be in Philadelphia long and would be back by fall in time to finalize the commission's commercial accounts. The two could not know how wrong Franklin was or how powerful the Adams/Lee bloc had become.

News of Silas's recall set off a shock wave of worrisome reactions by Louis XVI and the entire French ministry. Gérard told Silas the French saw his recall as a victory for the powerful anti-alliance faction in Congress. If Congress rejected the treaties, France knew it would end up fighting England alone. The British Carlisle Peace Commission headed for America would gladly make far-reaching concessions to Congress.

To the French ministry, Commissioner Deane, not Franklin, became the symbol of a Franco-American alliance. Therefore the French ministry, on Beaumarchais' suggestion, intended to protect Silas from their common congressional enemies in any way possible. Silas was to receive the highest marks of regard, respect and affection the French could muster. About that time, probably around the 7th of March, Silas decided he wanted to talk with Vergennes to discuss the Foreign Affairs minister's personal reaction to his recall. Vergennes knew by this time Silas would have a plan to handle the recall. He was right again. Silas arrived at Vergennes's office in Versailles angry, bitter and disappointed with Congress, knowing it simply didn't have a clue or understanding of what Franklin and he had been doing over the past 18 months. (But they sure had an appreciation for all the work, including getting a treaty, that Mr. Arthur Lee had been doing.) Silas did have a very interesting plan that would benefit the United States far more than it would ever help him.

Vergennes knew Deane's extensive list of endeavors, but this time his plan(s) had to do with an open military action — a naval action to counter the British superiority — and Silas knew the French had been building and updating their navy. Basically Silas was suggesting and asking at the same time about the idea of sending the naval squadron at Toulin to the North American coast to face off with the British fleet. Vergennes liked the idea, but he needed to talk to the other members of the ministry and the king about it. Several meetings concerning timing, feasibility, and the strength of the squadron were held with members of the ministry and court. Silas was present at most since he was the initiator and had specific expectations for the squadron.

After the *Belle Poule* disaster, the commissioners for once all agreed that to level the race to America, France needed to make the treaties public. Vergennes gave in and on March 13 French Ambassador Noailles announced to the British government that the treaties with the United States had been signed.

With the secret plan underway, Vergennes, again with Beaumarchais' urging, began to make some special arrangements to put Silas in a good light to indicate to Congress that it would be an insult to France if he were to be treated badly. First, however, Vergennes saw to it that naval minister Sartine made Admiral D'Estaing head of the Toulin squadron.

Franklin and especially Silas, with his naval background, had become very friendly with their neighbors at Passy. Silas was delighted with the news that D'Estaing was heading the squadron with 14 ships that included a ship of the line, three frigates and 10 other assorted warships.

Having the naval part of the "secret plan" readied, Vergennes appointed his number two man, and by now Silas's good friend, Conrad-Alexandre Gérard de Rayvenal, as the new French royal minister plenipotentiary to the new United States. Further, Vergennes arranged that both Silas and Gérard would sail with D'Estaing on his flagship, the *Languedoc*. The sailing of the two men was a secret to be shared only with Franklin and Bancroft, which meant the British Secret Service also knew. Trying to cut as many leaks as possible, the foreign minister pleaded with Franklin, as head of the commission, not to tell Arthur Lee, or Whitehall would surely learn of the fleet's departure from Arthur's secretary spy within a week. Much to his later chagrin, Franklin did not tell Lee.

It was decided that the French fleet would sail directly to Delaware Bay. Comte D'Estaing told Silas he would need American pilots to guide the warships through the bay area. Always ready, Silas quietly engaged four captains from his quasi-navy. They were Captains Isaac All, Henry Johnson, his brother Elias Johnson and Samuel Nicholson's brother, John. The admiral couldn't help but admire Silas for his knowledge of the sea and ships, and, for lack of a better word, his "bluntness."

There is a letter from Silas to the admiral and comte during the voyage to America that clearly shows Silas's vast knowledge gathered over the years from sea captains and merchant friends. During the years 1776–1778, Deane had improved his knowledge even more through the information network he and Franklin had invented, but that Silas had designed and made a reality. The letter, dated May 11, 1778, onboard the *Languedoc*, almost in its entirety, reads:

> Sir, The situation of the British Forces in America, when the last Accounts came from thence was as follows. General Howe at Philadelphia, with

about Twelve Thousand Men and Five or six Frigates with Transports. General Clinton at New York with Four or Five Thousand Men, & Two Shipps of the Line, several Frigates, & Transports. General Pigott, at New Port with about Three Thousand Men, & Lord Howe in the harbor, with Three Shipps of the Line, & a Number of Frigates & Transports. The Force at Hallifax, & Canada, need not be considered at Present, as any thing to Our purpose. The Fleet under the command of Lord Howe consisted in the whole of Five Shipps of the Line, the Number of Frigates cannot so easily be ascertained, as it was constantly varying, and they were cruising at great distances from each other, some off Hallifax, and others off Carolina. This appears to have been the arrangement in the Month of February last; Lord Howe went to New Port on Account of the safety of that Harbor in Winter, & to be near at hand to give Orders for the embarking of General Burgoynes Army which were prisoners at Boston. It should be observed, that a Number of the Frigates were in Chesopeak Bay, to intercept the Trade of Virgina, & Maryland. The Bay of Chesopeak and The Bay or River of Delaware will admit Shipps of the largest size, & there is no Difficulty or Danger in going in to them, at this Season of the year, and Anchoring at the Mouth of them until intelligence can be had of the situation & Force of the Enemy. The Harbor of New York is also capable of receiving Shipps of the first rate the Channel is as may be seen by the Chart a good one, & I do not remember To have heard of any Accident in going in, or out of it, but at the same Time it is more difficult than either the Bay of Chesopeak or Delaware, & the difference is that it has only shoal or bank at the Entrance, whilst the others have their Shoals, & banks which are the most Dangerous after you have safely entered them, some way up from the Mouth. New London, Newport, Boston, Portsmouth and indeed almost all the Ports to the East of New York are exceedingly good Ones, and may be entered without danger, especially during this Season of the year. The question is which of these Ports is to be preferr'd taking all Circumstances into Consideration. It is a question of great importance, I have constantly considered it as such, & more attentively since I had the satisfaction to learn that a Fleet would be sent out, & since I have been honored, with having my Opinion asked on the Subject. The Result of my reflections is that it will be most for the benefit of Expedition, and all parties interested in the Event, that the Fleet go directly for the River Delaware....[16]

Count D'Estaing responded with a letter of commendation to Congress once the departure details were settled, Vergennes announced to Franklin and Deane personally that Silas was to receive from His Majesty a presentation box. At first the Connecticut Yankee was puzzled as to its meaning. Franklin, having more knowledge of European court etiquette, explained that for over the past hundred years, it was customary for the king to make these presentations to important personages and some ambassadors who had been of great service to the French monarchy.

The boxes had become the all-time symbol for the monarchial society of the 18th century. It was the ultimate upper echelon gift in French court circles to be presented, by the king, with a Parisian solid gold snuffbox inlaid with a miniature portrait of the king, surrounded with diamonds. The number of diamonds and jewels indicated how important the recipient had become to the monarchy. There is no known record of the number of diamonds and jewels on Silas's box, but we do know Franklin came home several years later with his "standard ambassador" gold snuffbox that had 72 diamonds. We can only imagine how Silas must have made out.

The real point of the box was its cash value. Monarchs did not want a present of cash to look like a bribe. But the king did expect the recipient would return the box to the royal exchequer for its cash value, which in today's money terms could be some 60,000 American dollars or more. Silas cherished his gold snuffbox for the prestige it represented. It remained in his possession until his death.[17] Ex-commissioner Deane was ecstatic. He was impressed and happy with all the accolades that came to him for his attaché case to present to Congress.

Only six weeks before, he had written Robert Morris that it was hard to do private business along with his public responsibilities, but after the treaties were signed he would resign from politics forever. Also, to his brother Simeon he had written, "I am most heartily tired of Public Business & only wish to retire without Loss or Disgrace."[18] BUT, now he was returning to America with positive correspondence from the highest and most influential individuals on the European side of the Revolution. The list of letters Silas would be carrying included ones from Ben Franklin, Bancroft, Vergennes Beaumarchais, Sartine, and even Maurepas, plus the king himself written directly to the president of Congress.

To Beaumarchais was left the final congressional needle. Vergennes and Silas asked separately for Beaumarchais to write a letter to Congress stating the relationship between him and Arthur Lee in full detail, and the fact that Hôrtalez et Cie were one and the same, and that the military aid definitely was not a gift.

Yet Silas was very worried that he was leaving Franklin in a wolf's den with the repercussions he was bound to experience from the "terrible duo" of Lee and Izard for keeping them "out of the loop." Silas was very concerned about not being able to close out the commissioners' accounts before leaving for Congress. He was so worried, in fact, that he wrote a long letter to Beaumarchais about it on March 29, just two days before he left Paris. In the letter, Deane said, "It is unhappy that a short time allowed me to prepare for my voyage will not admit of our making at least a general settlement of your accounts; but the absolute necessity of my setting out immediately, oblige me to leave my other transactions in the same unsettled state."[19]

VII. Franco-American Treaties at Last, 1778

Vergennes sent the news to Valentois that the commissioners were to be officially introduced to King Louis XVI and the treaties recognized. Although Silas had been recalled and replaced by John Adams, who had yet to arrive, it was only fitting and proper that the second American signer of the Franco-American treaties be included in the reception. The ceremonial presentation was held at Versailles on March 20, 1778. Although in many ways the treaty was one of the most important treaties of the 18th century and beyond, at that time it was a difficult diplomatic situation to carry out between a republic that had yet to be independent and the world's second most powerful monarchy. The presentation was a pleasant but down-sized affair managed by Vergennes, the king and the French diplomatic corps. There was a slight hitch due to the manner in which Franklin was dressed for the occasion, but all in all, as head of the mission, it definitely was Franklin's day all around, with Silas's backing.

Although the treaties had been signed and recognized, and just a couple of days before D'Estaing's fleet would leave Toulin, Franklin met with still another British emissary. This time it was his old and close friend William Pulteney, a member of Parliament. Pulteney wanted to discuss a new 18-point peace proposal with the condition that if the terms were not acceptable they would never be divulged. Franklin didn't take long to turn them down flat. Franklin did tell Vergennes but not Lee as the British Secret Service would also know.[20]

As usual Franklin did officially notify Silas of the terms and complained that Lee's constant ranting was driving him up a wall. Feeling guilty for breaking his word with his old friend, Franklin sent a note after Silas was already on his way, advising him to get rid of the Pulteney papers. Silas never did for whatever reason. As a result, the papers still exist.

Sending the sea captains on ahead, Silas left Paris on March 31 under an assumed name and headed directly for the coast. It had been arranged for him to meet Gérard on the way. Before leaving the city, from their banker Ferdinand Grand, Silas obtained an accounting of all monies received and paid on public accounts, which he took with him after leaving duplicate copies for Franklin and Lee. As Franklin was head of the commission Silas left him an explanation of his public paper accounts at that time. Most accounts were still unsettled and, therefore, no final general accounting could take place.

There has always been a question about how influential the British were in getting Silas recalled, and for what particular purpose. This remains uncertain. It was well known that the streets and traditional backrooms of Philadelphia were alive with loyalists and regular British agents constantly reporting back to Whitehall.

There is a very revealing, but speculative, correspondence written by

Chaumont to Vergennes on April 18, discussing the circumstances around Deane's recall. Chaumont observed in a conversation with Vergennes, translated and in part, "If we compare dates, we find the recall of Mr. Deane coincides with the period when Lord North was able to intrigue in Congress, guided by what he had read in the dispatches he had caused to be stolen. Mr. Deane's head was a good one to strike."[21] (He was referring to the Hynson heist.)

Only the Creator of the Universe knew what personal catastrophic circumstance lay ahead for Silas.

CHAPTER VIII

Congressional Recall Debacle, 1778–1780

On May 2, Congress returned to Philadelphia after over a year in exile, having been chased out of the city by General Howe. The general, having heard that Comte D'Estaing and the French squadron were coming up the coast, hurriedly marched his troops out of the city to avoid being trapped. They left the city in ruins. Congress wanted a scapegoat for its revenge and it didn't care who or why.

Then on July 9, the French fleet sailed into Delaware Bay and dropped anchor after a tedious 91-day voyage. Silas immediately sent word ahead to President Henry Laurens that the fleet had arrived with 4,000 soldiers and the new French minister plenipotentiary Conrad Alexandre Gérard. After another five days of planning and following Silas's suggestion of protocol for welcoming a foreign ambassador, Congress sent a congressional committee and military escort to accompany his excellency into Philadelphia with a 15-gun salute. Once welcomed to America, Gérard was given temporary lodging in the house of Deane's friend, the commandant of the city, General Benedict Arnold.

A mild illness, probably the usual intestinal situation, prevented Silas from going with Gérard in entering Philadelphia. When he did arrive he received a surprisingly cordial welcome. Arnold offered him the same accommodations as Gérard. Silas happily accepted, being in the company of two friends. Almost immediately though, several congressional delegates warned Silas to give Arnold a wide berth. He was under investigation by Congress and faced a possible court-martial for being too lenient with Philadelphia Tories, and conducting personal shady business deals with merchants within the city. Knowing how his friend usually operated, Silas ignored the charges. Unfortunately, that decision would later link Silas with previous knowledge of Arnold's defection, a perception that often remains in the present day, although it has been disproved many times over.

When the press formally announced the return of Silas, several old friends and merchant congressional delegates turned out to give him a cordial welcome back. Hearing of his return, Washington wrote him saying how much he appreciated all of his services to the revolutionary cause.

Three weeks after his return Silas wrote President Laurens reminding him that he awaited the pleasure of Congress. Now that Deane was out of France the Adams/Lee bloc had to decide what to do with Silas. They knew that Richard Henry Lee's recall was done almost strictly for personal prejudicial reasons and had little to do with any reality, but they still had to get rid of him. The conspiracy continued, with the goal of wearing Silas out with congressional delays and trumped-up charges by the Lee clan on the European side of the Atlantic. So it began in earnest. Finally, on August 14, over a month after Silas arrived back in the city, he was ordered to appear before congress. Mr. Silas Deane was introduced and seated just to the right of the president. Silas presented two letters from Franklin and Beaumarchais, which were read and tabled. When Silas began to present his report of European affairs, as recalled to do, he immediately encountered a motion to give a written report and withdraw. After a long debate among the entire body, the motion was defeated and Silas was ordered to appear the following Monday, August 17, and give from memory a general account of his activities in France. Reporting on Monday as ordered, he was suddenly told to withdraw. Four days later, the 21st, he was allowed to complete his report and was again told to withdraw. Little did Silas realize that in the months to come his character would be attacked and transformed in ways he could not yet imagine and that the months would continue to expand.

On September 8, Silas wrote President Laurens asking if he would be making further attendance. On September 11 he thanked the president in his final letter before Congress and explained he would be away from Philadelphia visiting friends before leaving for France. What Silas had feared all along became obvious to him: he had not been recalled to give a report on conditions in Europe — the former secret agent himself was the target of Congress. Actually it was an attempt by the Adams/Lee bloc to grab more power.

At the end of Silas's report Laurens warned Silas that as president he would reserve judgment until Congress heard from the "other side." The bloc knew that the delegates were not the delegates of 1774–1776; many of the old icons had moved on to state positions as governors or political leaders back home. Congress was easy to manipulate as long as they didn't know the background of specific issues.

The junto had to come up with some specific charge against Silas. Richard Henry Lee came to the rescue again. This time he heard that Carmichael was in town and while in France had publicly charged Silas with using public monies for private gain; of being "unprofessional" in his conduct; and of being responsible for the break-up among the commissioners at Passy because the French wanted Lee excluded from certain business transactions of the commission.

It was September 16 when Silas received an order to appear before Congress for questioning. It was the same old game. When he showed up on the day he was to be questioned, September 18, he was denied access again while Congress went over letters from Arthur Lee dated January 5, 6 and 31.

The charge concerning the honesty of Deane was too serious to avoid. Congress decided to examine Carmichael. The examination lasted seven days, through October 5. Expecting sensational disclosures, Silas's public enemies were bitterly disappointed. The result was a dismal failure. All Carmichael could say to critical questions was "I thought" or "I assumed."

While waiting on Congress in mid-September, Silas wrote to his old friend, and former president of Congress, John Hancock, saying that if the good people of the nation had any idea how their representatives conducted government business, they would not tolerate such treatment as he was now experiencing.

Not hearing from Congress, on October 7 Silas requested a chance to answer Izard's and Arthur Lee's charges. Congress ordered Deane's letter to lie on the table. Two days later he repeated his request, saying he planned to return to France the following month. On October 14, Congress ordered Silas's letters of October 12 read and copies sent back to Izard and Lee. His letters easily showed those two commissioners to be liars.

Still waiting on Congress, Silas wrote on November 1 to the president his serious ideas for the welfare of the new nation that would put it on a more stable and sound financial footing. He sent plans for a national bank secured by a foreign loan of five million dollars and suggested that a fleet of 40 ships be at sea within one year. He also highly recommended that the latest paper money issue of $40 million be redeemed. He feared complete bankruptcy otherwise. The letter and plans were read and then tabled.

For the first time, on November 19, Silas showed open hostility toward Congress for the treatment he was receiving. He wrote Congress: "Nothing would give me greater satisfaction than to learn by what part of my public conduct I have merited the neglect which my letters and most respectful solicitations, for months past, to be heard from Congress, have been treated."[1] Congress simply read the letter the next day without comment.

Silas's patience was exhausted. Now, after five months of abuse by Congress, he was thoroughly convinced that Titus Hosmer was right: his enemies were seeking to wear him out by delays. He wrote Barnabus of his plan to go public. At first Silas tried to rationalize it was the people's right to know the fractional work of Congress, but he finally admitted it gave him great pleasure to expose "the other side."

Silas did hold off and finally wrote one more letter on November 30. Congress resolved the following day it would extend its work hour by at least two hours more, starting at 6:00 P.M., to hear more on foreign affairs. Then, on December 5, the "Address of Silas Deane to the Free and Virtuous Citizens of America" appeared in the *Pennsylvania Packet*. It contained a blistering attack on the Lee clan and fully exposed the purpose and interest of the Adams/Lee junto. Deane's broadside made Congress the very center of conflict. The governmental side of the American Revolution was about to turn into a name-calling contest carried out in the newspapers.

The "Address" caught the Adams/Lee junto temporarily off guard. Months before, from Paris, William Lee had warned home base to go easy on how they dealt with Deane once he returned to Philadelphia. The advice had been ignored until the December 5 address, then Francis Lightfoot Lee, on the eighth of December, placed a request in the *Pennsylvania Packet* that the public suspend judgment until after a full investigation. The next day, Silas placed a notice in the *Packet* stating that since Congress had finally resolved to hear him he could not in good conscience continue his narrative.

When Congress convened again, President Henry Laurens laid before the body letters from respectable citizens saying that Deane's letter had excited anxieties that were highly derogatory and dishonorable to Congress. A motion to read the address in Congress lost by one vote because almost everyone had already read it. Laurens was livid and immediately resigned. John Jay was then elected the new president of Congress, which signaled a victory for the pro–Deane element in Congress. The newspaper war then began in earnest. The December 15 *Senex* (Robert Treat Paine of Massachusetts) went after the Lee brothers for holding too many offices at one time. He also stated that he was sure the public in general approved and agreed with Deane's address.

At this juncture, it is necessary to look back for a moment at what had taken place since the time Silas had been in Congress some 22 months earlier. There were certainly many circumstances, situations and conditions with which Congress had to deal. The Declaration of Independence had been proclaimed; the Americans had won a decisive victory at Saratoga; and the French Alliance Treaty was in effect. Now Congress faced a disastrous currency inflation and general war weariness. It was also a time of scandals within the departments of the Continental Army over excessive spending and speculation by officers. Congress, with its "holier than thou" republican principles (supposedly), went after any signs of military arrogance—no national army or generals were going to run the country.

For the first time in Congress two distinct parties had emerged with opposite views regarding foreign affairs. The Lee-Adams group formed their traditional "military diplomacy" (you should help me simply because I need help) and sought to keep a safe distance from European powers and their politics. The junto feared the influence of the French king, the Catholic Church and all European politics. They knew they had to accept the alliance, but still they suspected French motives.

Finally, on the morning of Wednesday, December 23, a somber but determined Silas arrived at Congress at 9:00 A.M. His friend John Jay now occupied the president's chair. He was also obviously surprised, and pleased, to see his early congressional friend General George Washington, who "just happened" to be visiting Congress. Mr. Deane read his narrative into record over three different days, from the 23rd to the 31st, with Congress still pulling the same deal of telling him suddenly to withdraw and giving no reason. Regardless of what went on in Congress, the dispute continued largely in the *Philadelphia Packet*.

The Lee hatchet man, Tom Paine, over-stepped the bounds of the "fight" and started quoting from the Committee of Secret Correspondence records as "Secretary of Foreign Affairs," insisting that the money for supplies sent by Silas and Beaumarchais was a gift from France. That insistence by Paine as he quoted Arthur Lee's correspondence to the Secret Committee made a new factor enter the imbroglio. Gérard immediately objected. The whole operation of secret aid was to conceal the fact. Gérard demanded that Congress deny its truth. Upon his strong demand Congress gave in and categorically denied having received aid from France before the alliance. Congress relieved Paine of his employment, but not before Paine resigned himself.

Paine kept one charge after another going in the newspaper and the responses kept coming back at him from Deane's supporters. Robert Morris and Governor Morris made hard and accurate charges. Silas himself took on Richard Henry Lee over the insult to the family name. Even a beating on the streets of the city by pro–Deane individuals didn't stop Paine from his nasty, vicious innuendos.

Congress simply refused to charge Silas with anything or release him. In March and again in April of 1779, Silas wrote President Jay that his financial situation was distressing, saying, "My own family and private affairs, as well as those of one entrusted to my care, long suffered by my absence; they must suffer to the last degree, if longer delayed."[2]

In the days and weeks that followed, Silas sent letter after letter to Congress requesting a hearing to explain his positions and refuting charges. The newspaper war increased to an even higher level of disquiet and hatred. Names like "Candour," "Lusitainia" and "Philathes" appeared. Henry Laurens came back on the scene in June when a resolution was introduced to prevent Deane from leaving the United States and to bring back Arthur Lee to testify about his charges against Silas. The motion had actually originated with Laurens, who did not want Silas to leave the country. In Laurens' mind, if he left without congressional permission he was "pleading guilty" to all charges.

While poor Silas was still waiting on Congress in February of 1779, Gérard told Congress that Spain was ready to enter the war against England unless the British agreed to a mediated settlement conducted by Spain. Congress formed a committee on peace terms and recommended that Franklin, Arthur Lee, William Lee and Ralph Izard all be recalled and a new plenipotentiary be appointed to negotiate with Great Britain. For the next six weeks Congress debated the recalls. It finally agreed to recall William Lee and Ralph Izard. Only eight delegates voted to recall Franklin. The debate over recalling Arthur Lee was the big issue and eventually Arthur was spared a recall by one vote. That vote indicated that the Adams/Lee bloc was no longer the majority in Congress. However, the moderate faction was still not strong enough to clear Silas of any charges. For the next eight months Silas hung in limbo, repeatedly asking Congress to let him return to France but to no avail.

When Spain formally entered the war in June of 1779, it became urgent that Congress appoint a peace commissioner. Gérard and pro-Deane delegates wanted the popular president of Congress, John Jay, appointed. But, the Adams/Lee radicals wanted Arthur Lee appointed plenipotentiary to Spain. Consequently, the same old polarization developed in Congress. But, in August, after much debate, a compromise was worked out as the radicals knew Arthur was a poor candidate. John Jay was to go to Spain and John Adams would be the peace commissioner.

On August 6, Congress also finally did what Silas had advocated for months. It was a resolution that passed with a lot of "noise" on both sides. The resolution stated that all commissioners, commercial agents and others in Europe should immediately transmit, without delay, all their accounts and vouchers in triplicate to the Board of Treasury for settlement. But, before transmission, a suitable person appointed by Congress should certify them. It was also resolved that the Board of Treasury be directed to report for Mr. Deane a reasonable allowance for his time and expense from March 1778 through August 1779. (Silas received a check for $10,500, five cents on the dollar, which he refused.)

Then on August 8, Samuel Harrington moved, and was seconded by John Fell, that "Honorable Silas Deane, Esquire, late one of the commissioners at the Court of Versailles, and political and commercial agent be excused from any further attendance on Congress, in order that he may settle his accounts without delay, agreeable to the forgoing resolutions."[3]

The motion was immediately amended to read "discharged" rather than "excused." Laurens' reasoning again was the fact that since the "foregoing resolution" had left no provision for Silas's return to France nor his expenses there, the motion left the settlement of his accounts an option with him. Of course, that left all responsibility for expenses and time squarely on Silas, leaving Congress open to any interpretation of his accounts they saw fit. Silas wrote to his brother Simeon on September 28, 1779:

> A Lee's Commission, is superceded, and Mr. Jay appointed Plenipotentiary to Spain, by which the Whole of the Family, are disposed of, though the Mischief, they have done, is in some instances irreparable yet their Dismission is a favorable Event, and gives almost universal Joy. I say almost for the Junto tho' broken are not destroyed. The removal of these men is some satisfaction to me, & in part repays me for what I have suffered, & the Indignities thrown upon me whilst pursuing my Opposition against them...."[4]

He had reasons for feeling bitter. His life had been shattered into a million pieces and his reputation spoiled. Two years had been wasted waiting on Congress while his own personal affairs and family were neglected. His personal finances were almost nonexistent after three years of uncompensated public service and he constantly faced the risk of arrest, or worse — assassination. The Connecticut Yankee had spent four long years away from his family and his wonderful Wethersfield home. Probably what really hurt the most was the fact that he received no words of thanks or recognition for all of his services to the revolutionary cause.

One wonders how Silas could just sit around for two years while Congress and individuals kept maligning his character. He didn't. He kept planning his future and finances and made deliberate steps to make things happen for him, but the old saying "if it weren't for bad luck, I'd have no luck at all" seemed to be Silas's fate. Fortunately, at least psychologically, Silas had many things besides politics to hold his attention.

"The states, of course, still needed supplies and Europe needed tobacco, and the trade could be transacted on one side of the Atlantic as well as the other."[5] With his brother Simeon, Robert Morris, John Holker, and De Chaumont, Deane now engaged in an elaborate commercial trading operation with contacts in France and Virginia.[6] Although Patrick Henry was politically and orally opposed to the Deane faction in Congress, as governor of Virginia at this time he helped Deane considerably with this new venture. It was during this interlude that the Philadelphia Committee discovered that a boatload of flour belonging to Silas Deane had been sold to the French fleet. When Congress received news of this transaction, not having had a chance to buy the flour, it immediately suspected that some of it would be used for private speculation purposes.

Silas wrote a final letter to Congress on November 23, 1779, in which he returned the warrant for $10,500 and explained that in spite of the conditions of his private funds he preferred to return to France as his own expense. Congress never answered. Before leaving, Silas went to Williamsburg to see his brother Simeon, who had also gotten into financial straits. While in Williamsburg, Silas tried to clean up his own personal and family affairs. To Barnabus he committed his only son, Jesse. Silas also asked Barnabus to take charge of his papers, inventories of the estate of Joseph Webb, and all accounts made out under his direction ready to be settled. He asked specifically that the inventory of notes payable to him be collected and preserved for the future. Silas showed the love and respect for his wives when he requested that a gravestone be erected to Elizabeth in the same fashion as that of Mehitabel, and that Elizabeth's family select the inscription as she "was equally dear to them as to me."[7]

The family matter that bothered and hurt Silas the most was the fact that his stepsons, Joseph and John, and his stepdaughter, Sarah, always felt Silas had robbed them of their inheritance by not having their fathers' estate settled before he went to France. Further confusion was caused by his leaving only an extended inventory of money received and paid out as of January 1776. Silas deeply resented being called a defaulter "when I have done not simply legal justice toward them, but have treated them with parental kindness."[8]

The winter of 1779–1780 was so severe that the convoy by which Silas planned to return to France was actually unable to sail until June 20, 1780. He spent the winter helping Simeon get a store started and formed the Simeon Deane and Company. (The company failed, with Simeon deep in debt and suffering from ill health and dying in June of 1787.) Still in Williamsburg waiting for the convoy to sail, Silas received a boost in his earlier plan to engage in some large-scale land speculation. Robert Morris suggested that he investigate selling undeveloped American lands in France. The organization formed for the venture would include Joseph Wharton and James Wilson. Silas would be the advance agent in Europe and have a quarter interest in any lands purchased. Wharton would run the business in Philadelphia by getting grants and descriptions. Silas could then sell off as much as he felt best.

While continuing to cope with the recall ordeal with Congress, a direct and indirect situation developed north of Philadelphia that clearly indicated Congress was not alone in its intrigues and conspiracies. These situations were a part of war, even coincidences if one believes in them. In July of 1779, the largest fleet assembled by the Americans during the Revolution, known as the Penobscot Expedition, was initiated by the state of Massachusetts. The ships in the armada were expected to swiftly defeat the British Fort George on

Penobscot Bay in Maine. But the fleet lost some 40 ships, suffering a defeat the size of which would not be seen again until Pearl Harbor.

After the defeat, Massachusetts wanted to know who was responsible for such a disaster. The state needed a scapegoat and means to pay for the cost of the fiasco. A committee of inquiry was formed and soon learned that the Continental Navy was holding a court-martial of Captain Dudley Saltonstall, the commodore of the doomed fleet. It was arranged by the Massachusetts General Court, with the Congressional Naval Board, to postpone the court-martial decision until the committee of inquiry had made its decision. The president of the court martial, Captain Samuel Nicholson of the frigate *Deane*, anchored in Boston Harbor, was ordered so to do.

Captain Saltonstall was a Continental Navy officer, a Connecticut Yankee outsider, whose brother-in-law Silas Deane had initially arranged for him to captain the *Alfred* in 1776. Because he was a captain in the Continental Navy, Massachusetts could ask Congress to pick up part of the tab for the cost of the expedition. Consequently, full blame fell squarely on the shoulders of Captain Dudley Saltonstall.

Evidently Saltonstall was never aware of the land commander of the expedition; General Lovell's duplicity in the matter; or the extent of Massachusetts' conspiracy to blame him for the expedition's defeat. If he and friends and family had known the injustice done him, the combined Massachusetts and Connecticut Saltonstall family branches would probably have had enough political power to challenge any Massachusetts charges.[9]

It was quite obvious, however, that family and friends were kept in the dark. On April 20, 1780, as Silas was finally preparing to leave for France, he wrote to Barnabus asking for information about the status of his brother-in-law. Silas ended the letter saying, "My compliments to all friends, in particular General Saltonstall's family. I wrote him and son Dudley by Capt. Rogers of Branford, but received no answer. Just tell me what became of D. Saltonstall's affair."[10] (Dudley became a successful privateer captain during the rest of the war, after which he went back to his family's maritime business. He died in 1796.[11])

Silas embarked on his return trip to France—full of trepidation, but with hope for the future.

CHAPTER IX

Return to France, Exile and Death, 1780–1789

After a monotonous 42-day sea trip, broken by the capture of two vessels and the loss of one merchantman, the convoy managed to make it past the British blockade — an unusual feat. They arrived in Bordeaux on the 25th of July.

Silas notified Franklin he was back in France and immediately headed to Paris for very personal and undisclosed reasons but showed up at Valentois just a few days later, where he received a very cordial welcome from all concerned. Franklin happily gave him his old room back. Silas found that, apparently, his character had not suffered at least on the European side of the Atlantic, and he greatly appreciated the hearty welcome from Chaumont and Beaumarchais. But his first priority was to get his financial situation in much better shape. His immediate concern was getting his accounts settled without delay.

He also kept his attention on planning for the future. As a merchant, he anticipated no real problem in establishing a mercantile business. He was already well known by many French merchant houses and he had a personal private account with Ferdinand Grand. Unfortunately, while he was in America he had given Chaumont power to draw on these funds. Typical of Chaumont, he had overextended the funds and declared technical bankruptcy; the money Silas and Simeon had poured into their venture in 1777 also vanished. Silas was now really broke. Vergennes, over the years before the treaty, had become very fond of Silas. Hearing of his plight from Beaumarchais he quietly sent ex-commissioner Deane 12,000 livres for immediate living expenses.

With inflation going wild and the deflation of the American currency 40:1, livre French interest in trade and investments with the United States faded fast, bringing Silas's prospects to zero. The biggest disappointment came when the contracts to supply American masts for the French and Spanish navies collapsed. The lack of naval convoys for delivery of the masts during the war years also helped bring about the failure of the contracts.

As if the loss of the masts contracts wasn't enough, Silas failed to have any real success with the sale of western lands. The planned large-scale land speculation with Joseph Wharton and James Wilson faltered as Silas continued to try to spark French speculators' interest. Unfortunately, the desire to sell in America was far greater than the desire to buy in France, due largely to the economic conditions of the war. Part of private citizen Deane's financial problems resulted from political and economic conditions, but the main reason was the absolute refusal of Congress to settle his accounts. Over time, the methods and tactics used by Congress to delay any settlement was detestable and would eventually break his spirit and support for the war.

As the domino effect of failure continued to plague Silas's plans for the future and his financial security, his bitterness towards Congress, France, and specific individuals grew. He began sounding off loudly in both private and public places, the major theme being that it was time to reunite with England. With France's failure to give any direct or substantial help militarily through 1778 and 1779, Silas kept verbalizing the adage "with friends like France who needs enemies." As the months slipped by, Silas became more abusive of France and Congress to the point that he realized he could be arrested and sent back to America for trial, but his "friends" just could not shut him up.

One particular situation involving a hitherto unknown "patriot" by the name of Mr. Searles constantly infuriated Silas when it came to telling the truth about conditions in America. Searles maintained that Washington had 20,000 men, that Americans could carry on the war alone, and that all merchants — American or French — were dishonest and speculators. He claimed he ought to know since he was a member of Congress and had been chairman of most of its committees.

Silas shouted the fact, hard and long, that there were many Americans in Paris from the individual states who also distorted the conditions in America. Deane's friends kept telling him to "shut up," but Silas was so disillusioned he couldn't help himself. He corrected other Americans in public as often as they lied. Silas felt it necessary and honorable since he had told Vergennes personally, shortly after he arrived back in Paris and Passy, that America was in a chaotic state. American forces finance and commerce needed supplies, money and a fleet SOP.

In a few short weeks, even though Franklin backed Silas constantly and spent considerable time with him at Valentois, the ex-commissioner soon lost most of his former supporters and gained dozens of new enemies. Beaumarchais felt sorry for him, but told Vergennes that Deane's ranting seemed to point to "something worse," especially in light of Deane's claiming France probably never intended to back America but only to use and dominate it.

All the correspondence that Silas wrote carried the same basic themes. In his depressed state of mind the letters showed his anger, frustrations and worries for his country. The language he used was coarse and dismal, with concern for the future of the war and the new republic. Could it survive? As a student of history, he could find no precedent. In Congress, there was an almost complete lack of reason, patriotism and justice. These qualities were replaced with factions, cabals and private interests. Silas was deathly afraid that if the war continued, America would have to surrender unconditionally.[1]

Once Silas became an ex-spy and commissioner, and his actions were more out in the open, considerably more correspondence appears between Silas and his friend and original counterpart in America, Major Benjamin Tallmadge. Silas told Tallmadge, now stationed at Washington's headquarters, that the young country was virtually trapped between two great monarchies historically, similar to "Scylla on the one hand and Charybdis on the other, and our pilots drunk with the intoxicating ideas of independent sovereignty, madly pushing us into that vortex in which our peace, liberty, and safety will be swallowed up and lost forever."[2] In Silas's mind America had no choice but to reunite with Great Britain. In openly saying so, he clearly showed he was not afraid of collateral cost to himself.

Regrettably, Silas, for whatever reason (and at present it remains unknown or unproven), wrote a series of letters to friends in America. The majority were written to old friends and relations in New England. Supposedly there were 11 letters in all, but some estimates go as high as 14 in number, with some letters ending up in Congress's hands theoretically unopened. All letters contained the same old issues with slight variations and emphasis. The dates on the letters span the period of May 10, 1781, to June 15, 1781, from Paris.

Silas had gone to Ghent on personal business and to meet with Joseph Barclay, the new congressional auditor, concerning his accounts. Deane was still in Ghent in late November when Bancroft wrote to him that the ship *L'Orient* bound for America had been seized by the British with important letters onboard. One month later, he learned that these letters were his and were now in the hands of the *Rivington Royal Gazette*, whose intent was to publish them. By the time Silas got this news the letters were already being published. It is odd, but true: sometimes individuals have premonitions of events. Such was the case with Silas in that some of his letters might find their way to publication. In a letter dated October 21, 1781, to Barnabus he wrote:

> It is high time that the curtain should be drawn up and that the actors behind the scene should be stripped of all disguise and false appearance, and the catastrophe of the piece should be placed in the full view of every

one. I have attempted to do this. I expect to be abused for it, and am sure I shall not be disappointed.... [S]hould that letter have been intercepted by the enemy, my sentiments will become more generally known that I wish for; but in one word be assured that we shall, unless we make peace immediately, become eventually dependent, and that unconditionally, either on France or England."[3]

Rivington received eleven letters in Silas's handwriting and on October 24, 1781, he began publishing them as a serial in the *Royal Gazette*. The series ran from October to December. They made juicy reading for Deane's enemies and dismayed his "used to be friends." The letters were so popular that Rivington republished them as a separate pocket volume entitled *Paris Papers*.

It would seem more than a coincidence that all of Deane's letters written in a period of just over four weeks would be intercepted at sea all at once. It is more likely they were turned over by someone who had access to Silas's correspondence. Theory has it that it was Bancroft, or possibly Wentworth, but it has not actually been proven. It does, however, somewhat coincide with two letters sent from Ghent during that time to an Edward Edwards by Silas. Obviously Silas knew Bancroft was a double spy. The question that will always remain is when he knew it. In this writer's mind it had to be clear to both Silas and Franklin when the same wording from the commissioner's file appeared in Stormont's possession. But Stormont was too valuable to Franklin and Deane to expose him.

To make the situation more complicated for Silas, and indirectly for Franklin, both men knew that the British now considered Silas a possible turncoat after the ex-commissioner put on the planned show to push France and England toward war and a treaty back in late 1777 and early 1778.

Months earlier, King George III and British officials started discussing how they could possibly use Mr. Deane. On March 3, 1781, the king in a letter wrote Lord North a statement that is very shopworn but is still used as proof that Silas was in British pay: "I think it is perfectly right that Mr. Deane should so far be trusted as to have three thousand pounds in goods for America."[4] It never happened. By 1781 Silas was in no position to influence any individual in America's Congress or state governments to reunite with England.

Still, in July 1781, King George wrote to Lord North that he had received "the intercepted letters from Mr. Deane for America."[5] But, the question still remains: why did the king use the words "from" and "intercepted letters," as they contradict themselves? At the present there are no provable theories.

As the furor continued, Silas wrote a long letter to Franklin explaining why he sent the letters. For weeks Franklin was at a loss as to how to respond.

When he finally did answer, he scolded Silas and said they could no longer be close friends. Silas was not really surprised and wrote that he was sorry they disagreed.

The two men, after going through four tortuous years together, never spoke or wrote to each other again. However, in the letter to Franklin, Silas made a veiled threat about releasing secrets of the commission. Franklin got it and panicked a bit. He wrote to Congress as a body and to the new superintendent of finance, Robert Morris, to please settle Deane's accounts to shut him up, but the Lee brothers and their allies kept the stall going. Shortly, Silas also lost another good friend in John Jay. This loss showed him that even the most famous icons can be duped into exposing the icon's shallow side. Jay believed everybody about Silas's supposed activities, except Silas himself.

Silas had arrived in Ghent early in October, but had intended on returning to France after he had completed his personal business. When the "intercepted letters" became published, the situation changed and Silas wrote Barnabus on October 20 that he was going to remain in Ghent. He was rather sick of Paris and he didn't want to embarrass Franklin in his situation and exacerbate his troubles any further. He wrote to Bancroft, just back from England on a "Franklin mission," asking him to take his little cash stash, sell his clothes and pay up his tailor and other minor retail debts.

When the war came to a close Silas was still in Ghent and Congress still had not decided to honor his accounts. He claimed he was owed 800,000, but Silas was happy the war had come to an end. He wrote to Barnabus that he had been a traitor to himself but never to the new republic. His brothers never lost faith in him, but he wished for the old days with Sam Parsons, Tallmadge and Wadsworth back home in Connecticut.

Silas was also bothered by the possibility that Rivington had messed around and altered the letters, making them far worse than they really were. Was it maybe a little payback for initiating with Arnold the raid on his print shop in 1775 that temporarily made him go to England? Of course it's doubtful that Silas ever knew Rivington actually worked with Tallmadge's famous Culper Ring from 1780 to the end of the war. Silas found he was right. Several letters had been changed in publication in New York, "not to serve Great Britain so much as to injure me; and for that purpose some of them were altered in many parts and the whole placed in the most unfavorable light."[6]

Early in March Silas made the decision to go to London. Jesse, who was still in France, needed surgery to remove a tumor. Bancroft told Silas there was no way he could return to France to see Jesse. Instead, Silas arranged passage for his son to return to America under Barnabus's care. The father hoped to see his son again in America someday.

Silas had tentative business plans in London he already had before hostilities broke out in the early 1770s. Now that the war was over he hoped to reestablish his old business contacts. Another very ambitious plan, which was half a century ahead of its time, was to build a canal to connect Lake Champlain and the St. Lawrence River. The governor of Canada, Lord Dorchester, was very interested and considered it a bold undertaking. At the time, Silas was considering land development in the Ohio River Valley and recruiting English settlers. But he went to London only after the peace commissioners at Paris had "no objections."

Silas Deane, a portrait "drawn from the life by Du Simitiere in 1779 in Philadelphia." Engraving circa 1781 by B.L. Provost (Library of Congress).

The day Silas arrived in London and had taken a room, he was shocked to see Benedict Arnold at his door. At first Silas was ready to slam the door in his face, but the 40-odd years of friendship halted the action. Arnold invited Deane to dine with him and several British officer friends. Silas refused. The next day Silas moved to a residence at 135 Fleet Street. Arnold kept sending invitations to his home. A second visit occurred at Deane's Fleet Street address. Like the first visit, Deane had two witnesses with very familiar names — Hodges and Sebor. Silas told Arnold that his visits were extremely embarrassing and that he should not return again. However, Deane did tell him that he might call with Mr. Sebor some evening to pay his respects to Mrs. Arnold, who had paid him many civilities while he was in Philadelphia, and he did so a few evenings later (with Mr. Joseph Sebor of New London, Connecticut, as a witness).[7]

For the next six years Silas would suffer continued harassment concerning his activities that became less and less countered by his supporters. Silas's appearance in London set off a firestorm of "tabloid mania" until his death. For most of his enemies, coming to London confirmed what they already believed: he was a traitor. Regardless of public reactions, Silas's main interest remained getting his accounts settled with Congress. In April 1783, "Mr.

Barclay," auditor (Joshua Johnson, a merchant, refused to serve) informed Deane that Congress had sent new instructions Silas should see. The instructions were another disappointment. Barclay was ordered to refer any questionable items directly to Congress, which reserved the right to approve or disapprove.

Thus Barclay's instructions made it impossible to settle with Silas. It was obvious to both Barclay and Silas that Congress had no intention of settling Deane's accounts. Regardless of this fact, in June of 1784 Barclay sent a copy of Deane's accounts, settled by Barclay, to Robert Morris, the superintendent of finance. A few months later, Morris sent Barclay's settled accounts to the president of Congress for its actions. After another audit by Congress, it sent the accounts to the Treasury Board for final approval. Congress, however, did not act on the Treasury Board's action and the accounts remained in limbo. Silas gave up hope of ever seeing his accounts settled.

In the meantime, Silas kept trying to refute the dozens of newspaper stories claiming he repeatedly visited Lord North, Duke of Portland, and Arnold, as well as claims that he even worked closely with Lord Sheffield on a pamphlet on American commerce, all of which were falsehoods.

A constant rumor that had some "inverted truth" to it was that Silas was working with the ministry as an advisor on American affairs. What had happened was that, while Silas was still in Ghent, Lord Shelbourne (Arthur Lee's friend) had been impressed with Silas's knowledge of American affairs in general, but specifically in commerce. Considering Deane's reputation, Sheffield decided not to involve Silas in any peace settlement questions of 1783. But almost immediately after Silas arrived in London, he supposedly favored an anti–American commercial policy with England. However, Silas and Sheffield had many conversations about America's commerce in the presence of many other people who could testify that Sheffield, in his pamphlet, wanted to keep the Navigation Acts, while Silas stressed the act needed overhauling completely.

Although Sheffield's pamphlet probably was the cause for most of the open resentment against Silas, Sheffield became one of Deane's few friends. During the rest of Silas's life, Sheffield and his family remained his close friends. During Silas's last illness, Sheffield helped financially and offered to pay for his return to America.

There was an incident that indicates just how much rejection Silas continued to face through the decade of the 1780s. In December of 1783, while Silas was visiting the factories in Birmingham, Henry Laurens, who had just returned from peace talks, saw Silas and the famous Dr. Priestly together. Laurens immediately contacted a Mr. Russel, a close friend of Priestly's, and told him that Silas was unworthy of any confidence in four different areas.

IX. Return to France, Exile and Death, 1780–1789

First, he had been poor and of no consequence until he entered "public life" (politics). Second, while in France he shipped two vessels with goods privately with public funds. Third, while he was in France he intercepted the commission's dispatches sent by Captain Folger, and substituted blank paper. And fourth, upon his return to America he used every means to avoid being called to account for his actions as an agent and commissioner in France. Silas now was sure that Laurens had always been a political enemy. It didn't take Mr. Deane long to refute all charges, which were not only false but also completely made up in the case of the intercepted dispatches.

After the Laurens episode of character abuse, Silas was beside himself trying to answer all falsehoods about his actions both political and private. Eventually, in 1784, he warned friends that he had had it and was going to publish another broadside pamphlet against Congress and the Adams/Lee junto. When his "Address to the Free and Independent Citizens of the United States" was published in England and America separately, Silas made it clear to his readers that the publications were written because his silence on so many subjects had been misconstrued to his disadvantage. This address was more than just a rehash of December 1778. This time Silas hammered the Adams/Lee junto harder and claimed he was a creditor of the public and not a defaulter. Silas also pointed out that his views were not all that different from those of George Washington at the end of the war when Washington said, "[I]t is yet to be decided if the Revolution must ultimately be considered a blessing or a curse." All Silas really wanted was the refuting by others of the falsehoods aimed at him.

During July of 1785, in spite of all the abuse, Silas wrote to his stepson Samuel Webb that he was studying English manufacturing techniques and inventions. He said he had even seen a machine that could spin 5,000 threads at once. And having become close with several inventors who were making big money, he was writing to contacts in America about setting up mills with different purposes. One thing that helped Silas to keep his sanity was the fact that he never once lost hope in reestablishing his fortune with an enterprise in America.

The most fascinating enterprise, as previously stated, was the proposal that Silas made to the English ministry of a plan for a navigation canal from Lake Champlain to the St. Lawrence River. As early as 1775, he had presented the project to Holdimand, and then his successor, Lord Dorchester, showing the lake could be opened to ships from England.

In 1785 Silas was doing a much more extensive study of a canal between the lake and the river. There was a 90-foot fall, but a canal would give England a 5,000 mile waterway. Giving the results of his study to Lord Sydney, Silas explained it would open an avenue from frontier country all the way to the

West Indies for cargoes of cattle, hogs and flour. Mr. Deane figured the canal could be built and open for traffic for 10,000. Should the project be approved, Silas asked for the office of building superintendent.

By the year 1785, Silas was beginning to have real trouble with his physical and mental health resulting largely from years of daily high stress and digestive problems. As the months and years slipped by, Silas was still full of bitterness bordering on physical rage and his body began to react and punish him to the point that he sometimes had trouble even walking across a room due to the general overall weakness to his body. In time the conditions grew worse.

In June of 1788 he wrote Sheffield that he was having night sweats and periods of anguish and shivering. Deane's physician thought he should make the voyage to America, but Silas felt he was too sick and weak to make such a trip then. Actually, he thought the doctor was baffled with his illness and figured Silas would probably die at sea. Deane knew he would need a good deal of fruit, milk, vegetables and personal care. With the heat, calms and strong gales of such a voyage, it was not for a sick person.

During all of this time, Sheffield continued to be Silas's sole means of support. When Deane first thought he could return to America, he refused Sheffield's offer to pay for his passage. In the meantime, Bancroft was "handling" the canal project and Silas's personal needs. On July 4, 1788, when Silas suddenly had a severe relapse of his unidentified illness, Thomas Jefferson, now minister in Paris, had a visitor from London. One Frenchman, named Foulloy, complained to Jefferson that Deane owed him 120 guineas. Because Silas had not paid up, Foulloy had taken an account book and a letter book from Silas's trunk and was offering them for sale to the Americans or the British for the amount owed him.

This was one of those weird situations that somehow always seemed to involve Silas indirectly, but in this case, by Jefferson's reasoning, Silas's personal papers were the property of the public (the United States). Actually the purchasing of stolen papers was a coverup to protect Bancroft (unknowingly) from being discovered by the British of being a double spy and Silas "over spending" public monies. Jefferson did not know Congress had never paid Silas a cent. From the letter book came the true story of the John the Painter affair and the fact the French ministry secretly, with Silas's help and planning, allowed Lafayette to get to America against official regulations.

After further bargaining, Jefferson bought the two books and asked Bancroft to "get" the other books. But Bancroft was protected now from being discovered by the British and said there were no other books. Silas never knew anything about the episode save for the fact that he had been robbed while he was sick.[8]

IX. Return to France, Exile and Death, 1780–1789

In the late fall of 1788, both Lord Sydney and Lord Dorchester approved of the canal plan. This was Silas's first piece of good news in several years. With the plan in a go-ahead mode, after secretly being stalled by Bancroft, Silas began to show signs of recovery and hoped in the spring he could sail for America. The winter of 1788-89 was the worst in 50 years and Silas's health was rocky, but things slowly fell into place.

In late June of 1789, Silas wrote three letters. The letters were sent to Jeremiah Wadsworth, George Washington and John Jay. They were a final plea for justice from Congress. At the same time, he also wrote a special letter to William S. Johnson asking to help clear his name and character.

During the month of March, Silas had received a letter from Barnabus (written in December 1788) that probably tipped the scales in Silas's decision to return to America. Barnabus wrote:

> Yours in August 10th is just Come to hand and the Contents of which give me pain Altho from Reports it was not unexpected, I must beg you to Leave London, what Can you Expect by Staying there but Beggery & Distress, I have not the Least Expectation of Your Ever doing any kind of Business. Again I judge from what is Past, I willingly find a Home for you if you will Come to this place where I have a good Home Partly Built, Your Creditors will not find it to be worth their Attention to put you in Gaol...[9]

In August Silas suddenly announced publicly that he was going to return to "North America." An unnamed friend in Boston paid for the voyage. On Tuesday, September 22, 1789, Silas left London with his friend Captain Theodore Hopkins and Captain Davis of the *Boston Packet*. According to several witnesses that day Silas "never looked better." He was talkative and happily looking forward to starting a new life back in America. At Gravesend, near the mouth of the Thames River, the men took lodging in the home of Captain Davis's father-in-law. After breakfast, on the morning of September 23, they boarded the *Boston Packet*.

As the ship departed the Thames, Silas became unsteady and grabbed the Captain's arm. Suddenly he turned and collapsed into Captain Davis's arms.

According to the captain's log, since probably lost in a fire, it is known that Silas fell into a deep coma and died shortly thereafter. All other details of how he died are still conjecture. The ship immediately returned to Deal for burial. Although there was no gravestone, interment is believed to be in St. George's churchyard. Captain Hopkins stayed behind, paid the burial charges, informed family members and close friends and forwarded the now famous trunk of Silas's papers (presumably to Barnabus) and other baggage.

A record of interment dated September 26, 1789, reads as follows: "Silas Deane Esquire. He was deputy of the State of Connecticut to the first and second American Congress; a Minister of Plenipotentiary from the United States of America to the Court of France in 1777, and 1778, died in the Downs of his passage from London to America. Register of Burials for the Parish of Deal."[10]

The appropriate epicedium of Silas Deane may well be the following: "He was second to very few in knowledge, plans, designs, and execution: deficient only in placing confidence in his compatriots, and doing them service, before he had got his compensation, of which no well-bred politician was ever guilty."[11]

Thus ended the life of Silas Deane, a life that should have been famous rather than erased from American history.

CHAPTER X

A Long Finale, 1789–1842

To say the reason and the circumstances surrounding Silas Deane's death were peculiar is an understatement. As a result, several versions as to why and how he died began to appear almost immediately.

The suddenness of his death after several witnesses had stated "he never looked better" made some individuals wonder if he had faked his death in order to return to America with a clean slate and identity. What quickly came to other minds was the possibility of some kind of cerebral accident which has carried through to the present.

Another version emerged when Bancroft told Dr. Priestly that Silas had been deeply depressed of late and had decided on suicide. This version of his death was quickly accepted and enlarged by Deane's old enemies. Edward Bancroft's version just didn't add up. He had stated to Dr. Priestly that Silas had overdosed on laudanum, but that would have meant a long, gradual death. Why would Bancroft stick with his suicide story? It was the same reason he tried to keep Silas in England earlier. The ex–secret American agent had many secrets about Dr. Bancroft's activities and Silas was well known for talking and writing too much when he should have remained quiet. Bancroft had to make sure that when Deane arrived in America he didn't expose him as a double agent. There was only one way to accomplish that. Bancroft was more than capable of it, and he knew how to murder without being present. The doctor was an expert on South American poisons and was known to have a quantity of curare. Before he left London, Silas could have asked Bancroft for some laudanum, which he had done several times previously, to calm his weak digestive system for the voyage. Seeing his opportunity, the doctor could have mixed in curare, which would have caused sudden asphyxiation.

Probably, once underway on the *Boston Packet*, Silas took the "doctored" laudanum to prevent seasickness. If so, it would account for the details expressed in several reports of Deane's collapse, supposedly taken from Captain

Davis's log, which was likely lost in a fire. It would definitely account for the phrase "suddenly collapsed" that appears in three versions.

The above is a very short version of a conjectural story of Deane's death by Professor Julian Boyd published in 1958 in the *William and Mary Quarterly*. The version was simplified in 2009 in Professor Joel Richard Paul's book, *Unlikely Allies*. Knowing Edward Bancroft had no allegiance to anything or anybody, except money and position, this writer would definitely vote for Professor Boyd's explanation of Deane's death. It is also pleasing to know that Lord Sheffield and his family were genuinely upset upon learning of the death of Silas — their friend.

Jesse Deane, son of Silas Deane, artist unknown. A glossy print of this portrait was given to the author by Mrs. Anna May Capen in 1965. The existence of the original portrait was unknown at that time but a search by the National Society of the Colonial Dames of America in the state of Connecticut was underway. The photograph had been placed in *Antique* magazine earlier by Colonial Dame Anna May Capen to help expedite the search.

Up until the late 1820s little was known about the Silas Deane case by the general public. Some highly prejudicial writings of the Lee family, accusations by Tom Paine, sketchy congressional records, and Deane's own 1779 and 1784 "Addresses" were the only sources available to the public. When Jared Sparks edited and published the *Diplomatic Correspondence of the American Revolution* in 1829, a more comprehensive picture of the controversies over the career actions of Silas Deane began to appear.

After Silas's granddaughter, Philaura Deane Alden, repetitioned Congress in 1840, a lengthy examination of all available documents (several papers no longer existed and the locations of others were unknown) took place. Finally, on February 17, 1841, the Senate Committee on Revolutionary Claims reported favorably, followed on July 27, 1841, by the Claims Committee of the House of Representatives. Just one year later, on August 10, 1842, "An Act for Settlement of the Accounts of Silas

X. A Long Finale, 1789–1842

The Webb-Deane-Stevens Museum is a complex of three authentic 18th century houses located in the center of Old Wethersfield, Connecticut. The museum is owned and operated by the National Society of the Colonial Dames of America in the State of Connecticut. They purchased the Webb House from the famous Wallace Nutting in 1919, the Stevens House in 1957, and the Silas Deane House in 1959 to form the present museum. All three houses are restored and furnished to reflect the lifestyles of merchant Webb, diplomat Deane and tradesman Stevens. All three houses are Registered National Historic Landmarks.

Deane" was signed into law by President John Taylor. Congress paid the Aldens $37,000, which today, presumably, would be nearly one million dollars. Congress found that "Mr. Deane performed highly important and valuable services for this country" and that a former audit was "exparte erroneous and a gross injustice to Silas Deane."[1]

Later in the 19th century further publications appeared more frequently with such individual names as Louis Loménie, Henri Doniol, John Durant, Francis Wharton, Charles Isham, Charles Stille and Benjamin Franklin Stevens. Their writing and research supplied more and more details to the case. By the mid–20th century there was a myriad of articles about Silas Deane — all trying to prove that certain charges or accounts against Deane were either true or false. Then, near the beginning of the 21st century, historians began to look hard and long at the entire picture of the various aspects of the European theater of the American Revolution, which includes the speed and greed of any war.

Historian Stacy Schiff in 2005 and Joel Richard Paul in 2009 have made extended and detailed studies of the American Revolution on the other side of the Atlantic and its cloudy period of 1774–1778. They have shown many true human sides of the reality of Silas Deane's political and commercial career, but there are still several unanswered questions of that "secret" time.

Silas Deane's sun has yet to set — and the band plays on.

Appendices

A: Key Personalities

John Adams (1735–1826): Replaced Deane in 1778. On-and-off friend. Both men were very high risk takers, especially with their pens and mouths. They meant what they said. Too honest to be politicians.

Samuel Adams (1722–1803): A throwback Puritan who valued virtue above all else. He desperately wanted a war for American independence, but never had a clue how to fight one. Sam was the main radical leader in the Congress of 1774; after 1775, he considered Deane a political enemy.

Benedict Arnold* (1741–1801): Famous as America's first defector and traitor. Deane's friend from boyhood through 1783.

Edward Bancroft* (1745–1821): The most amazing double agent (British mole) of the American revolutionary era, a fact not discovered until almost a century later. First a student, and then a lifelong friend of Deane, but only if Bancroft benefited more from the relationship.

Pierre Augustin Caron de Beaumarchais (1732–1799): A colorful character, famous playwright and French secret agent who, with Deane, arranged a network to secretly supply arms to the Continental Army. Deane and de Beaumarchais became mutually admiring friends.

William Bingham (1752–1804): A key partner of the Robert Morris group from Philadelphia. He was appointed American agent at Martinique in 1776. Bingham coordinated with Deane and the deposit points for secret French aid.

William Carmichael (?–1795): Wealthy Marylander on extended vacation to London and France. Recommended by Arthur Lee to Deane to help with his mission details. Became Silas's official secretary. Unintentionally betrayed by the American commissioners; took out his revenge on Deane.

Jacque Donatien le Ray de Chaumont (1725–1803): A real pro–American entrepreneur. With Vergennes's personal urging, worked with Deane in obtaining military supplies in 1776 and through 1778 with the three commissioners. He was Franklin and Deane's landlord at Passy.

Gustavus Conyngham (1747–1797): A reckless, unpredictable, brave and modest American sea captain in Deane's "Passy Navy." He terrified the British coastline and

---

* Indicates a Freemason

embarrassed the "neutral" French by sheer force of personality. Known as the Dunkirk Pirate, he took more than 60 prizes.

Barnabus Deane (birth and death dates unknown): He was the second of the five Deane sons. Became a very successful merchant like his older brother. Barnabus joined Silas in Wethersfield in 1768. He never wavered in his loyalty to Silas. Barnabus had the same kind of troubles with Congress as his brother did.

Elizabeth Saltonstall (Evards) Deane (1742–1777): Second wife of Silas Deane, married him in 1770 and launched him into much wider social circles and colonial politics. She was the granddaughter of a former Connecticut governor. Elizabeth died while Silas was still in France.

Jesse Deane (1764–1828): Silas Deane's only son, whom he adored and hoped one day to have follow in his footsteps as a wealthy, successful merchant. Unfortunately, Jesse was in poor health most of his life and unable to carry out his father's hopes.

Mehitabel Nott (Webb) Deane (1732–1767): First wife of Silas Deane. Daughter of the wealthy merchant/trader Nott family. Widow of Joseph Webb, a successful Wethersfield merchant. Married Silas in 1763 and introduced him to the commercial world. They had one son, Jesse, born in 1764.

Simeon Deane (1750–1787): Simeon was the number three Deane son, who Silas continuously helped to make his merchant career a success. He appeared in Silas's company at crucial stages in both their careers.

Baron Johann de Kalb* (1721–1780): It was De Kalb who introduced Lafayette to Silas Deane at Lafayette's request in 1776. De Kalb was representing French field marshal Count DeBroglie, who wished unsuccessfully to replace Washington. De Kalb was appointed mayor general by Deane and died at the Battle of Camden.

Charles-Henri, Comte D'Estaing* (1729–1794): American commissioners' neighbor at Passy and admiral of the French squadron sent to America in 1778. Deane sailed back to America in D'Estaing's flagship after his recall and gave D'Estaing detailed sailing directions for entering the Chesapeake Bay.

John Dickinson* (1732–1808): Conservative Philadelphia politician and a leading delegate to the Second Continental Congress. Very cautious about move toward independence, but as a member of the Committee of Secret Correspondence agreed to Silas's secret mission to obtain aid for the colonies and signed his commission.

Philippe-Charles Jean Baptiste Tronson du Coudray (1738–1777): French officer of artillery. To Silas Deane's regret he commissioned Du Coudray as a major general with a lot of promise and influence with the French court. Du Coudray's arrogance and attitude caused him to be hated by the famous American generals Greene, Knox and Sullivan. Drowned in Schuylkill River in September 1777.

Charles Guillaume-Fréderic Dumas (1721–1796): Franklin and Deane's intelligence source of European news from Leidon and The Hague. Strongly pro–American. Secret correspondence among them was almost continuous from 1775 to 1778.

Eliphalet Dyer (1721–1807): One of the founders of the Susquehanna Company in 1753. In 1774, Dyer was the first-named of the delegates appointed to represent Connecticut to the Continental Congress with Deane and Roger Sherman. He was an on-and-off friend of Deane.

Benjamin Franklin* (1706–1790): America's leading citizen and statesman during the Revolutionary Era. Silas Deane was one of perhaps a dozen individuals Franklin considered close enough to call a true and trusted friend. Silas, from their first meeting, became a close friend, admirer and political ally until the end of his life.

William Temple Franklin (1760–1823): Franklin's nephew and personal/private secretary in France. Deane, John Adams, Carmichael and Bancroft all found him to be an able assistant. He was known to be very socially oriented.

Joseph Galloway (1731–1803): An early ally of Franklin until he returned to America and the Continental Congress. Galloway turned loyalist. He had been the leading conservative delegate in the 1774 Congress, but was defeated in the Second Congress by the Adams/Lee bloc. Tired hard to persuade Deane to join his philosophy.

Conrad-Alexandre Gérard* (1729–1790): A very able diplomat and trusted undersecretary to Vergennes. Deane and Gérard became friends. He was the go-between for the French ministry and the American commissioners in negotiating the 1778 alliance. First foreign minister to the United States, 1778–1779.

Rodolphe-Ferdinand Grand (1726–1794): With his brother Georges based in Amsterdam, Grand was America's banker and financial agent collaborating closely with Vergennes. American commissioners' neighbor at Passy. He was responsible for some 38 million French livres in gifts passing through his hands to the Americans.

Charles Graviér Comte de Vergennes (1717–1787): French Foreign Minister from 1774 to 1787. Friend of the Americans, but France's interests always came first. Close to and friend of Beaumarchais. Saw to it that Deane and Beaumarchais secretly worked together. Through Gerard, worked closely with Deane (rather than Franklin): for 1778 Alliance.

John Hancock* (1737–1793): A prominent fellow merchant and friend from Boston who backed Deane from 1768 to 1779. President of the Continental Congress in 1776. Noted for his large signature on the Declaration of Independence.

Benjamin Harrison* (1726–1791): Virginia delegate to Continental Congress. Secret partner with Robert Morris. Williamsburg merchant member of the Committee of Secret Correspondence. Signed Deane's commission as secret agent.

William Hodges (1744–1797): A young man from Philadelphia sent by Congress with orders to buy two cutters to deliver dispatches back and forth between Passy and Congress. Deane commandeered him for the "Passy Navy" and to harass the English coast. First American to be impressed within the Bastille to pacify the British.

Titus Hosmer (1736–1780): A Connecticut lawyer, fellow Yale graduate and a close lifelong friend of Deane. Member of the Continental Congress, 1775–1776 and 1777–1779.

Ralph Izard (1741–1804): South Carolina planter. Appointed envoy to Tuscany in 1777, but remained in France until recall in 1779. Strong follower of Arthur Lee. Hated Franklin and Deane and would do and say anything to discredit them.

John Jay* (1745–1829): Member of the Continental Congress from 1774 to 1779. Lawyer/merchant from New York. Very close friend of Deane until after the "Intercepted Letters" in 1781. President of Congress in 1779 during Deane's recall period. Went on to become the first chief justice of the United States, 1789–1795.

William Samuel Johnson* (1727–1819): Lawyer and Connecticut supreme court judge, 1772–1774. As a member of the Connecticut Committee of Correspondence he was appointed to the First Continental Congress of 1774, but refused to serve. Sat out the war until 1784, when he was elected to Congress. Remained a colleague and friend of Deane until Deane's death.

John Paul Jones* (1747–1792): Deane obtained the first naval ship, the *Alfred*. Jones was the first naval officer to raise the Continental flag over the *Alfred*. Jones had mixed feelings about Deane, whom he accused of stealing his scheme of naval harassment along the English coastline. The opposite was true back in 1774–1775. They had a final falling out in March of 1778.

Marie-Joseph Paul Yves Roche-Gilbert du Motier de Lafayette* (1757–1834): After much secrecy and intrigue, was commissioned by Deane as a major general in the Continental Army. He is famous for his devotion to the American cause. Became extremely fond of Washington and adopted the general as his father. A real Franco-American hero.

Henry Laurens* (1724–1792): A mayor of South Carolina and merchant. President of the Continental Congress in 1777 and 1778. Resigned as president of the Congress because he hated Deane. Congress refused to censure him. Laurens was part of the Adams/Lee bloc.

Arthur Lee (1740–1792): A highly educated and strong patriot, but with a miserable personality that diffused any good that he intended. Commissioner to France with Franklin and Deane in 1776. Lee hated both men and made it his mission to politically destroy them.

Richard Henry Lee* (173?–1794): Member of the First and Second Continental congresses, 1774–1780. On May 17, 1776, made resolution declaring "that these United Colonies are, and of right ought to be free and independent States." Brother of Arthur Lee and hated Deane for attacking the Lee family name. Made the motion in Congress for Deane's recall.

William Lee (1739–1795): London alderman, 1775–1777. Appointed commercial agent at Nantes in 1777; commissioner to courts of Berlin and Vienna. Older brother of Arthur Lee. Sided with Arthur on most issues, but being a merchant worked rather well with Deane through 1778.

King Louis XVI* (1754–1793): Masonic French monarch at age 20 after the death of his grandfather, Louis XV. Married the famous Marie Antoinette. Louis personally liked Deane and gave him the diamond-studded snuffbox in appreciation of his relations with the court.

James Lovell (1737–1814): Member of the Continental Congress from Massachusetts and self-appointed secretary of the Committee of Foreign Affairs (formerly the Committee of Secret Correspondence):. Professed friendship for Deane, but secretly hated him. He was part of the Adams/Lee bloc.

Jeane Frédéric Phélypeaux de Pontchartrain Comte de Maurepas (1701–1781): Oldest of French king's advisors and influential minister of state. Very quick-tongued and demonstrative. Only lukewarm toward Vergennes' foreign policy. Told the French court and ministry to watch out for the "American in Paris; they will lead you down the garden path."

Robert Morris* (1734–1806): The leading merchant and financier of the American Revolutionary period. Close friend, admirer and commercial partner of Deane through 1778. A leading delegate to the Second Continental Congress.

Thomas Mumford* (1733–1828): Boyhood neighbor and friend of Deane. A constant and staunch supporter of Silas whenever his political enemies caused him problems, especially after Deane failed to be reelected in 1775 and again after his recall in 1778.

Thomas Paine (1737–1809): Famous author of *Common Sense*. Sided with the Adams/Lee bloc on the recall of Deane. Paine wrote seething articles in the local papers charging Deane with embezzlement, misconduct and worse. Deane's political allies and the French ambassador got Paine removed from his congressional secretary position for disclosing pre-alliance French and American secrets.

Samuel Holden Parsons* (1737–1789): Close political friend of Deane from the early 1760s through the Revolution. With Deane, one of the three men who initially helped Deane plan and finance the attack and capture of Fort Ticonderoga.

Charles William Peale* (1741–1827): The main portrait painter during the actual Revolution. Other famous painters, including West, Copley, Gilbert Stuart and John Trumbull, spent the war years in Europe. Captain Peale was with his friend Washington at Trenton, Princeton and Valley Forge. Painted Deane very early in 1776 in Philadelphia.

Israel Putnam* (1718–1790): Member of the Sons of Liberty and Connecticut chairman of the Committee of Correspondence in 1774. A longtime member of the Connecticut General Assembly. With Deane's strong influence he was appointed by Congress as the fourth Continental Army major general.

Peyton Randolph* (1721–1775): First president of the Continental Congress in 1774 and again in 1775, but because of his health, resigned. He died shortly afterward. Deane was impressed with his "character and demeanor."

John Ross (unknown birth and death dates): Legman in Europe for Robert Morris. He came down from Hamburg to straighten out Willing & Morris's finances in Nantes. Worked with Deane and Jonathan Williams to clear up which trade shipments belonged to whom: Congress, Morris or Passy.

Dudley Saltonstall (unknown birth and death dates): Commander of the Continental frigate *Warren*. Naval commission owed to the influence of his brother-in-law, Silas Deane. Scapegoat for the "Penobscot Fiasco" at Castine, Maine, in 1779. Became a successful privateer.

Antoine-Raymond-Gualbert-Gilbert de Sartine (1729–1801): The brilliant minister of the French navy, 1774–1780. Particularly close friend of Chaumont. Admired and enjoyed Deane's schemes and actions. Cooperated with Deane, and later Franklin, whenever he dared to openly support the Americans. Fired by Louis XVI in 1780 for spending too much money on the French fleet.

William Petty, Earl of Shelbourne (1737–1895): Colonial secretary and British prime minister, 1782–1783, and an early ally of Arthur Lee and Franklin (after the Revolution). Shelbourne sought out Deane for advice in resuming American commerce. The two men became good friends, but the Earl did not take Deane's advice. The Americans, however, were sure the Earl's negative ideas were Deane's.

Roger Sherman* (1721–1793): The only founding father to sign all four documents: the Articles of Association, the Articles of Confederation, the Declaration of Independence and the U.S. Constitution. Substitute as the third member of the 1774 Connecticut delegation to the First Continental Congress. He disliked Deane intensely and the feeling was mutual.

Baron Friedrich Wilhelm von Steuben* (1730–1794): Commissioned by Deane, but "raised" to a major general by Franklin. Arrived at Valley Forge in February 1778. Became Washington's drillmaster. He built the Continental Army into a fighting force equal to any European army.

Esyra Stiles (1727–1795): Early friend of Deane family during Silas's boyhood years. Graduated from Yale College in 1748 and ordained in 1749. Became Yale's president in 1778. From a very early date he heavily influenced Deane's interest in the Susquehanna Company's western lands speculation.

Earl of Mansfield, Viscount David Murray Stormont (1727–1796): British ambassador to Versailles, 1776–1778. Very knowledgeable diplomat who at first thought Deane to be quite inept at dealing with the French ministry. By mid-1777, however, Stormont stated Deane was even more dangerous than Franklin.

Benjamin Tallmadge (1754–1835): Silas Deane's counterpart secret agent in America under Washington. A personal friend of Deane from Wethersfield where he was superintendent of the high school until 1776. Tallmadge organized the famous Culper Spy Ring in New York for General Washington.

Charles Thomson (1729–1824): Known as the Sam Adams of Philadelphia. Early informer for Franklin while still in England. Deane and Thomson were both nominated as the first secretary of the Continental Congress in 1774. Deane dodged the honor, wanting more time to study and research issues that were before Congress. Thomson was voted secretary.

John Trumbull (1754–1843): Governor's youngest son and close friend of Deane's in Connecticut politics. A colonel in the Continental Army, but resigned in pique. Decided to study art. Painted the famous rendition of the Declaration of Independence with its authentic record of Revolutionary personage taken from life. Saw Deane again after the war in England while painting more Revolutionary events.

Jonathan Trumbull, Sr. (1710–1785): Famous governor of Connecticut during the American Revolutionary era. Admired and worked well with Deane from 1769 until the Second Continental Congress in 1775 when Deane backed military officers that the governor's group did not support. A Susquehanna Company member.

Joseph Trumbull (unknown birth and death dates): Governor Trumbull's son. Deane and his two fellow Connecticut delegates helped him become commissary general for the Continental Army.

Jeremiah Wadsworth (1743–1804): A Hartford, Connecticut, leading citizen and one of the greatest merchants of the 13 colonies along with Robert Morris and Hancock. Became commissary general of purchases during the Revolution. A close friend of Deane from the early 1760s. Business partner with Barnabus Deane and General Nathaniel Green, head of a Rhode Island mercantile family.

Thomas Walpole (1727–1803): British merchant, banker and MP who led a group of investors including Franklin, Bancroft and Deane seeking land grants in the Ohio region before and during the war. Speculated with Bancroft and Deane in British stocks using insider information about Franco-American relations.

George Washington* (1732–1799): Commander-in-chief of the Continental Army from May 1775 through the end of the Revolution. Deane's friend from 1774 to 1781. Washington stayed at Deane's home in Wethersfield on his way to take command of the new Continental Army at Cambridge, Massachusetts.

Samuel Balchley Webb* (1753–1817): Favorite stepson of Silas Deane. Webb had a brilliant military career starting as a lieutenant in the Lexington Alarm. In 1776, was appointed aide-de-camp to George Washington with his stepfather's influence. Captured in 1777 and exchanged in 1780. Made a brevet brigadier general in 1783.

Alexander Wedderburn (1733–1805): England's Solicitor General from 1771 to 1778. Openly condemned Franklin's actions as a colonial agent in the "cockpit" on January 29, 1774. Rushed to Paris in 1776 to personally spy on Deane's activities and Deane knew it.

Paul Wentworth* (?–1793): A British master spy originally from New Hampshire with over a dozen aliases, assorted disguises and invisible inks. Dogged Deane's activities through 1778. Desperately tried to bring Deane over to the British side.

Samuel Wharton (1732–1800): American-born London merchant involved with Thomas Walpole along with Bancroft and Deane in American western land deal schemes and stock market speculation in the Franco-American alliance.

Jonathan Williams, Jr. (1750–1815): Franklin's grandnephew and financial clerk in London. Deane asked Franklin to help him with the Commission's coordination of work in Nantes. Resulted in Williams' appointment as commercial agent in Nantes. He is noted for doing a great job and strongly admired Deane.

B: Deane's Original 1776 Instructions

FROM THE COMMITTEE OF SECRET
CORRESONDENCE TO SILAS DEANE

Philadelphia, March 3d, 1776

On your arrival in France, you will for some time be engaged in the business of providing goods for the Indian trade. This will give good countenance to your appearing in the character of a merchant, which we wish you continually to retain among the French, in general, it being probable that the court of France may not like it should be known publickly, that any agent from the Colonies is in that country. When you come to Paris, by delivering Dr. Franklin's letters to Monsieur Le Roy at the Louvre, and M. Dubourg, you will be introduced to a set of acquaintance, all friends to the Americans. By conversing with them, you will have a good opportunity of acquiring Parisian French, and you will find in M. Dubourg, a man prudent, faithful, secret, intelligent in affairs, and capable of giving you very sage advice.

It is scarce necessary to pretend any other business at Paris, than the gratifying of that curiosity, which draws numbers thither yearly, merely to see so famous a city. With the assistance of Monsieur Dubourg, who understand, English, you will be able to make immediate application to Monsieur de Vergennes, *Minister des Affairs Etrangères,* either personally or by letter, if M. Dubourg adopts that method, acquainting him that you are in France upon business of the American Congress, in the character of a merchant, having something to communicate to him, that may be mutually beneficial to France and the North American Colonies; that you request an audience of him, and that he would be pleased to appoint the time and place. At this audience if agreed to, it may be well to shew him your first letter of credence, and then acquaint him that the Congress, finding that in the common course of commerce, it was not practicable to furnish the continent of America with the quantity of arms and ammunition necessary for its defence, (the Ministry of Great Britain having been extremely industrious to prevent it,) you had been dispatched by their authority to apply to some European power for a supply. That France had been pitched upon for the first application, from an opinion, that if we should, as there is a great appearance we shall, come to a total separation from Great Britain, France would be looked upon as the power, whose friendship it would be fittest for us to obtain and cultivate, That the commercial advantages Britain had enjoyed with the Colonies had contributed greatly to her late wealth and importance. That it is likely great part of our commerce will naturally fall to the share of France; especially if she favours us with this application, as that will be a means of gaining and securing the friendship of the Colonies; and that as our trade was rapidly increasing with our increase of people, and in a greater proportion, her part of it will be extremely valuable. That the supply we at present want, is clothing and arms for twenty-five thousand men with a suitable quantity of ammunition and one hundred field pieces. That we mean to pay for the same by remittances to France or through Spain, Portugal, or the French

Islands as soon as our navigation can be protected by ourselves or friends; and that we besides want great quantities of linins and woollens, with other articles for the Indian trade, which we are now actually purchasing, and for which you ask no credit, and that the whole, if France should grant the other supplies, would make a cargo which it might be well to secure by a convoy of two or three ships of war.

If you should find M. de Vergennes reserved, and not inclined to enter into free conversation with you, it may be well to shorten your visit, request him to consider what you have proposed, acquaint him with your place of lodging, that you may yet stay sometime at Paris, and that knowing how precious his time is, you do not presume to ask another audience, but that if he should have any commands for you, you will upon the least notice immediately wait upon him. If at a future conference he should be more free, and you find a disposition to favor the Colonies, it may be proper to acquaint him, that they must necessarily be anxious to know the disposition of France, on certain points, which, with his permission, you would mention, such as whether if the Colonies should be forced to form themselves into an independent state, France would probably acknowledge them as such, receive their ambassadors, enter into any treaty or alliance with them, for commerce or defence, or both? If so, on what principal conditions? Intimating that you shall speedily have an opportunity of sending to America, if you do not immediately return, and that he may be assured of your fidelity and secrecy in transmitting carefully any thing he would wish conveyed to the Congress on that subject. In subsequent conversations, you may, as you find it convenient, enlarge on these topics, that have been the subject of our conferences with you, to which you may occasionally add the well known substantial answers, we usually give to the several calumnies thrown out against us. If these supplies on the credit of the Congress should be refused, you are then to endeavor the obtaining a permission of purchasing those articles, or as much of them as you can find credit for. You will keep a daily Journal of all your material transactions, and particularly of what passes in your conversation with great personages; and you will by every safe opportunity, furnish us with such information as may be important. When your business in France admits of it, it may be well to go into Holland, and visit our agent there, M. Dumas, conferring with him on subjects that may promote our interest, and on the means of communication.

You will endeavor to procure a meeting with Mr. Bancroft by writing a letter to him, under cover to Mr. Griffiths at Turnham Green, near London, and desiring him to come over to you, in France or Holland, on the score of old acquaintance. From him you may obtain a good deal of information of what is now going forward in England, and settle a mode of continuing a correspondence. It may be well to remit him a small bill to defray his expenses in coming to you, and avoid all political matters in your letter to him. You will also endeavor to correspond with Mr. Arthur Lee, agent of the colonies in London. You will endeavor to obtain acquaintance with M. Garnier, late *Chargé des Affairs de France en Angleterre*, if now in France, or if returned to England, a correspondence with him, as a person extremely intelligent and friendly to our cause. From him, you may learn many particulars occasionally, that will be useful to us.[1]

B. Franklin,
Benj. Harrison,
John Dickinson,
Robert Morris,
John Jay.

C: Deane's Unofficial Navy 1775–1778

Silas was involved with the need for an American navy through the auspices of the Continental Congress from the very beginning of the "idea" of a navy. In late 1775, in the eyes of some, Silas Deane became the "Father of the American Navy" by acquiring the first ship, Alfred, for the Continental Navy. After two-plus centuries, it still is not clear whether he purchased it or Robert Morris donated it at Silas's request.

Actually, the title "Father of the American Navy" cannot be given to any one man of the Revolutionary era. Washington used gunboats in the Boston Harbor area in 1775. Benedict Arnold built his own ships, used in the battle at Lake Champlain. John Paul Jones, of course, is recognized as the best-known naval officer of the Revolutionary era and eventually commanded the first ship, *Alfred*, before he became famous with the *Bonhomme Richard* in European waters. The United States made a big differentiation in navy names in 1789 with the establishment of the United States Navy.

Silas Deane had the most to do with establishing a viable American force of fighting sail from 1775 through 1778. He and John Langdon of Portsmouth obtained the first eight ships and, before leaving for France, laid the plans for six more Continental Navy ships. While in France, he was responsible for having three more ships built, directly purchased four ships and commandeered at least six American privateers, plus incorporated two captured British ships in the "European Theater American Navy." All these ships were overseen by Deane for orders and actions in European waters through March of 1978, "Admiral" Franklin gave his blessing to any harassment to the British Isles.

Below is a compilation of American ships in which Silas Deane had some direct concern or connection. The number beside the name indicates how many guns, and the asterisk indicates whether it was acquired or purchased by Deane:

Frigates: Description — A high-speed medium-sized sailing vessel usually with three masts.
  *1. *Indien* (later named *South Carolina*)— 40; built in Amsterdam.
  *2. *Deane* (later renamed *Hague*)— 32; arrived in America from France in May 1778.
  3. *Trumbull*— 28.
Sloop of War: Description — A single-masted vessel carrying guns on only one deck.
  *4. *Surprize*—10, acquired from England and fitted out at Dunkirk.
  5. *Ranger*—18.
Former Merchantmen:
  6. *Bonhomme Richard*— 42.
  *7. *Alfred*— 24 (first ship).
Brigs and Brigantines: Description — A two-masted vessel square-rigged on both masts with two or more head sails and differences in details.
  *8. *Lexington*—16.
  *9. *Reprisal*—16.
  *10. *Andrea Doria*—14 (first salute ship).
  *11. *Cabot*.
Schooner: Description — A ship with two or more masts fore and aft, the main mast taller than others.
  *12. *Wasp*—12.

* 13. *Fly.*

Sloop: Description — Single-masted vessel rigged fore and aft with a single head sail.
   * 14. *Providence*—12.
   * 15. *Hornet*—10.

Cutters: Description — Single-masted vessel rigged fore and aft with a running bowsprit, a mainsail, and two or more headsails.
   * 16. *Revenge*—14 (purchased in France).
   * 17. *Dolphin*—14 (purchased in Dover, England, and sent to Nantes for outfitting).

D: The Close Friendship Between Franklin and Deane

When it comes down to the real reason why Silas Deane was picked up by Franklin to go to France as America's first envoy, his contemporaries and many historians have been so far off the mark that the target isn't even in view.

It was one of those instant admirations for each other's abilities that quickly turned into one of those most unlikely close and lasting friendships. In fact, Silas became one of perhaps only a dozen true friends that Franklin ever had. As for Silas, he knew in spite of the age difference Franklin understood where he was coming from.

Recognizing that Franklin was always the number one man and chief-of-station and Deane was number two man in France and the main intelligence agent, listed below are the real reasons why the team of Franklin and Deane from 1776 to 1778 was so successful in ultimately obtaining an alliance with France. Unfortunately, one received high recognition and the other received condemnation.

1. Both men came from a common, ordinary background.
2. Both men were successful businessmen and not particularly agrarian-oriented.
3. Both men were very pragmatic in their outlook and only slightly altruistic.
4. Both men were always concerned with profit. For Silas it was purely economic; for Franklin it was the benefits derived.
5. Both men had more faith in the American people than they did in Congress.
6. Both men liked and deeply admired George Washington and his abilities.
7. Both men had high intellect in very specific areas and knew enough to stay out of others.
8. Both men deeply admired another popular patriot until that admiration went sour; with Franklin it was Jefferson, with Silas it was Robert Morris.
9. Both men continually speculated in American western lands unsuccessfully.
10. Both men could be incredibly naïve.
11. Both men had a dream for the future of the new United States of America. For Silas it was a world economic empire; for Franklin it was a future large and strong republic of free people.
12. Both men were intriguers and schemers in the most positive sense—"They loved it when a plan all came together."
13. Both men could be poor judges of character.
14. Both men were very socially oriented creatures, but only on the surface.

Chapter Notes

The notes for each chapter have two parts. The first is a list of key sources. The second is the exact source of the particular facts or quotes, and follows a regular note-numbering scheme.

As base information applicable to the particular chapter time period, all chapters use the seven volumes of the Deane papers for the story line source. That includes the five volumes from the collections of the New York Historical
Society and two volumes from the collections of the Connecticut Historical Society, in addition to the Deane manuscript boxes.

Quotes from Clark's biography are utilized extensively in the first four chapters as the primary source, as he had access to the original family copies that came home in Deane's trunk and were lost in the Deane House library fire of November 15, 1932.

Preface

1. Alan Axelrod, *The Real History of the American Revolution* (Sterling: New York, 2007) p. xi: "Author's Note."

Introduction

1. Christopher Hodapp. *Solomon's Builders* (Berkeley, CA: Ulysses Press, 2007), 109.

Chapter I

Adams, Sherman W. *The History of Ancient Wethersfield, Connecticut.* Ed. Henry R. Stiles. Vol. 1. New York: Grafton Press, 1835, rev. 1904.
Clark, (Rev.) George L. *Silas Deane: A Connecticut Leader in the American Revolution.* New York: G., Putnam's Sons, 1913 (first full biography.)
Gordon, Robert B. *A Landscape Transformed: The Ironmaking District of Salisbury, Connecticut.* New York: Oxford University Press, 2001. (This was an area of Connecticut in which the Deane family was deeply involved and was of major historical importance.)
James, Coy Hilton. *Silas Deane: Patriot or Traitor?* East Lansing: Michigan State University Press, 1975 (only the second biography ever published).
Van Dusen, Albert E. *Connecticut.* New York: Random House, 1961.

1. Ledyard and the Town Historical Society records, folders.
2. Allen Johnson and Dumas Malone, eds., *Dictionary of American Biography,* 34 vols. (New York: 1930). 5:173–175.
The New England Historical and Genealogical Register, 104 vols. (Boston: 1847–).
F.B. Dexter, *Biographical Sketches of the Yale Graduates with Annals of College History,* vol. 2 (New York: Henry Holt, 1896).
3. Ibid.

4. Gordon, *Landscape Transformed*, 11–44.
   5. *Public Records of the Colony of Connecticut, 1636–1776*, ed. James H. Trumbull and Charles J. Hoadly, 15 vols. (Hartford: 1850–1890), 14:94.
   6. Ibid., 14:412.
   7. Ibid., 14:161.
   8. Ibid., 14:94.
   9. Ibid.
   10. Van Dusen, *Connecticut*, 129–130 (Susquehanna Question).
   11. Ibid., 116–120 (Great Awakening).
   12. Jasper Ridley, *The Freemasons: A History of the World's Most Powerful Secret Society* (New York: Arcade Publishing, 2001), 74–75.
   13. Ibid., p. 104.
   14. Ibid., p. 103.

Chapter II

Barrow, Thomas C. *Connecticut Joins the Revolution*. Chester, CT: Pequot Press, 1973.
Bullock, Steven C. *Revolutionary Brotherhood*. Chapel Hill: University of North Carolina Press, 1996.
Clark, George L. *Silas Deane: A Connecticut Leader in the American Revolution*. New York: Knickerbocker, 1913.
Collier, Christopher. *Connecticut in the Continental Congress*. Chester, CT: Pequot Press, 1973.
Dunkelberger, George S. *An Early History of St. John's Lodge, No. 4. A.F. & A.M.* Hartford, CT: Case, Lockwood & Brainard, 1973.
Gordon, Robert B. *A Landscape Transformed: The Iron District of Salisbury, Connecticut*. New York: Oxford University Press, 2001.
James, Coy Hilton *Silas Deane: Patriot or Traitor?* East Lansing: Michigan State University Press, 1975.

   1. Gordon, *Landscape*, 25–32
   2. Clark, *Silas Deane*, 10.
   3. Ibid., 3.
   4. Barrow, *Connecticut Joins*, 16–18.
   5. Dunkelberger, *St. John's Lodge #4*, 27, 54.
   6. Collier, *CT in Congress*, 8, 9.
   7. Clark, *Silas Deane*.
   8. Bullock, *Brotherhood*, 59–63.

Chapter III

Barrow, Thomas C. *Connecticut Joins the Revolution*. Chester, CT: Pequot Press, 1973.
Bullock, Steven C. *Revolutionary Brotherhood*. Chapel Hill: University of North Carolina Press, 1996.
Clark, George L. *Silas Deane: A Connecticut Leader in the American Revolution*. New York: G. Putnam's Sons, 1973.
Collier, Christopher. *Connecticut in the Continental Congress*. Chester, CT: Pequot Press, 1973.
Daughan, George C. *If By Sea*. Philadelphia: Basic Books, 2008.
Gerlack, Larry R. "A Delegation of Steady Habits: The Connecticut Representatives to the Continental Congress, 1774–1789." *Connecticut Historical Society Bulletin* 32, no. 2 (Hartford, April 1967).
Heaton, Ronald E. *Masonic Membership of the Founding Fathers*. Silver Spring, MD: Masonic Service Association, 1997.
James, Coy Hilton. *Silas Deane: Patriot or Traitor?* East Lansing: Michigan State University Press, 1975.
Paul, Joel Richard. *Unlikely Allies*. New York: Riverhead Books, 2009.
Ridley, Jasper. *The Freemasons: A History of the World's Most Powerful Secret Society*. New York: Arcade, 2001.

Smith, Paul H., ed. *Letters of Delegates to the Continental Congress, 1774–1789.* 26 vols. Washington, DC: Library of Congress, 1976–2000.
Volo, James M. *Blue Water Patriots: The American Revolution Afloat.* Lanham, MD: Rowman & Littlefield, 2006.
Weider, Lois M. *The Wethersfield Story.* Stonington, CT: Pequot Press, 1966.

1. Gerlack, *Delegation of Steady Habits* 32, no. 2.
2. Clark, *Silas Deane,* 24.
3. Ibid.
4. Ibid.
5. Ibid.
6. Ibid.
7. Ibid.
8. Ibid.
9. Collier, *Connecticut in Congress,* 14.
10. H. Smith, *Letters of Delegates, August 31–September 5* (hereinafter *LDC*), vol 1, p. 15–19.
11. Clark, *Silas Deane,* 29.
12. Ibid., 31.
13. Smith, *LDC,* vol. 1, p. 18.
14. Heaton, *Masonic Founding Fathers,* viii.
15. Collier, *Connecticut in Congress,* 18.
16. Clark, *Silas Deane,* 28.
17. CHS Collections, vol 2.
18. Clark, *Silas Deane,* 29.
19. Willard Sterne Randall, *Benedict Arnold: Patriot and Traitor* (New York: William Morrow, 1990), 72–75.
20. Collier, *Connecticut in Congress* 30.
21. Ibid., 21.

Chapter IV

Augur, Helen. *The Secret War of Independence.* New York: Duell, Sloan and Pearce, 1955.
Barrow, Thomas. C. *Connecticut Joins the Revolution.* Chester, CT: Pequot Press, 1973.
Callahan, North. *Connecticut's Revolutionary War Leaders.* Chester, CT: Pequot Press, 1973.
Clark, (Rev.) George L. *Silas Deane: Connecticut Leader in the American Revolution.* New York: G., Putnam's Sons, 1913.
Collier, Christopher. *Connecticut in the Continental Congress.* Chester, CT: Pequot Press, 1973.
Daughan, George C. *If By Sea.* New York: Basic Books, 2008.
Gordon, Robert B. *A Landscape Transformed: The Ironmaking District of Salisbury, Connecticut.* New York: Oxford University Press, 2001.
Isaacson, Walter. *Benjamin Franklin: An American Life.* New York: Simon & Schuster, 2003.
O'Toole, G.J.A. *Honorable Treachery.* New York: Atlantic Monthly Press, 1991.
Paul, Joel Richard. *Unlikely Allies.* New York: Riverhead Books, 2009.
Schoenbraun, David. *Triumph in Paris: The Exploits of Benjamin Franklin.* New York: Harper & Row, 1976.
Scrodes, James. *Franklin: The Essential Founding Father.* Washington DC: Regnery, 2002.
Van Vlack, Milton C. "North Canaan's Place in Connecticut History." *Connecticut Western News.* May Series, 1958 (Re: Salisbury Iron District).
___. "A Survey of Writings Concerning the Controversial Envoy Silas Deane, 1776–1789." Master's thesis, Trinity College, 1958 (housed in Connecticut Historical Society Collections).
Volo, James M. *Blue Water Patriots: The American Revolution Afloat.* Lanham, MD: Rowman & Littlefield, 2006.

1. Because of the remarkable organization of the Committees of Correspondence secretaries and express riders like Bissel, widely scattered settlements were informed of the outbreak of hostilities with amazing accuracy and speed. It took just two-and-a-half weeks for nearly the entire population of the 13 colonies to hear their country was at war with England.
2. Callahan, *Connecticut Revolutionary War Leaders,* 40.

3. Coy Hilton James, *Silas Deane: Patriot or Traitor?* (East Lansing: Michigan State University Press, 1975), 5.
4. Connecticut Historical Society Collections (hereafter CHS), MSS, Deane's Diary.
5. Collier, *Connecticut in Congress*, 21.
6. Journal, *Connecticut in Congress*, 49–52.
7. The delegates to the 1774 Congress knew above all they had to show a united front.
8. Collier, *Connecticut in Congress*, 25.
9. Clark, *Silas Deane*, 32–33.
10. Collier, *Connecticut in Congress*, 26.
11. Ibid., 27.
12. Ibid., 28.
13. "Delegation," CHS *Bulletin* 32, no. 2 (April 1967), 37.
14. Smith, *LDC*, vol. 1, p. 567.
15. Journal C.C. (Franklin motion 7/15/75).
16. Collier, *Connecticut in Congress*, 29.
17. Ibid.
18. Edmund S. Morgan, *Benjamin Franklin* (New Haven, CT: Yale University Press, 2002), 227.
19. Clark, *Silas Deane*, 31.
20. Ibid.
21. Collier, *Connecticut in Congress*, 11.
22. Ibid.
23. *Hartford Courant,* April 17, 1960, Jay's Letter.
24. Attributed to John Adams' expression.
25. CHS Collections, vol. 2, 1870, 321.
26. CHS, MSS box, 3rd folder, no. 35.
27. Volo, *Water Patriots*, 105–106.
28. Gordon, *Landscape*, 25.
29. Morgan, *Franklin,* 228–230.
30. Ibid., 229.
31. Augur, *Secret War*, 102–108.
32. O'Toole, *Honorable,* "End Games."
33. CHS, vol. 2, 1870, p. 360.

Chapter V

Adams, William Howard. *Gouverneur Morris: An Independent Life*. New Haven, CT: Yale University Press, 2003.
Augur, Helen. *The Secret War of Independence*. New York: Duell, Sloan and Pearce, 1955.
Clark, George L. *Silas Deane: A Connecticut Leader in the American Revolution*. New York: G. Putnam's Sons, 1913.
Collections of the Connecticut Historical Society. *The Deane Papers, Correspondence between Silas Deane, His Brothers and Their Business and Political Associates, 1771–1795*. Vol 23. Hartford, CT: Published by the Society, 1930.
Collections of the Connecticut Historical Society. *Correspondence of Silas Deane, Delegate to the First and Second Congress at Philadelphia, 1774–1776*. Vol 2. Edited by J. Hammond Trumbull. Hartford, CT: Published by the Society, 1930.
Daughan, George C. *If By Sea*. New York: Basic Books, 2008.
Fuye, M. de la, and E.A. Barbeau. *The Apostle of Liberty: A Life of Lafayette*. Translated by Edward Hyams. New York: Thomas Yoseloff, 1956.
Isaacson, Walter. *Benjamin Franklin: An American Life*. New York: Simon & Schuster, 2003.
James, Coy Hilton. *Silas Deane: Patriot or Traitor?* East Lansing: Michigan State University Press, 1975.
Morgan, Edmund S. *Benjamin Franklin*. New Haven, CT: Yale University Press, 2002.
New York Historical Society Collections (hereafter NYHS). *The Deane Papers*. Edited by Charles Isham. 5 vols. New York: Published by the Society, 1887–1891.

Patton, Robert H. *Patriot Pirates*. New York: Pantheon Books, 2008.
Paul, Joel Richard. *Unlikely Allies*. New York: Riverhead Books, 2009.
Schiff, Stacy. *A Great Improvisation*. New York: Henry Holt, 2005.
Smyth, Albert H. *Writings of Benjamin Franklin*. New York: Macmillian, 1907.
Srodes, James. *Franklin: The Essential Founding Father*. Washington DC: Regnery, 2002.
Van Vlack, Milton C. "A Survey of Writings Concerning the Controversial Envoy Silas Deane, 1776–1789." Housed in Collections of the Connecticut Historical Society. Master's thesis, Trinity College, 1958.
Volo, James M. *Bluewater Patriots: The American Revolution Afloat*. Lanham, MD: Rowman & Littlefield, 2006.
Warner, Jessica. *John the Painter: Terrorist of the American Revolution*. New York: Thunder's Mouth Press, 2004.
Wharton, Francis. *The Revolutionary Diplomatic Correspondence of the United States*. Vols. 1–5. Washington: Government Printing Office, 1889.

1. This was a reaction by Lee from the snubbing by Franklin when a colonial agent.
2. John J. Meng, "A Footnote to Secret Aid in the American Revolution," *American Historical Review* 33 (1938), 791–796.
3. Paul F. Cadman and Allan Forbes, "Hortales and Company," in *France and New England*, vol.2 (Boston: State Street Trust Company, 1927), 128.
4. John Durand, *New Materials for the History of the American Revolution* (New York: Henry Holt, 1889), 89.
5. Ibid., 90.
6. Dubourg did move good "contracts," but his association with Penet virtually nullified his help to the Americans after 1776.
7. NYHS Collections, *Deane Papers*, vol. 1, p. 109, and vol. 2, pp. 167–176.
8. Smyth, *Franklin's Writings*, vol. 5, p. 313.
9. Wharton, *Diplomatic Correspondence*, vol. 2, p. 116.
10. Augur, *Of Independence*, 131–132.
11. Ibid.
12. Wharton, *Diplomatic Correspondence*, vol. 2, p. 207.
13. NYHS Collections, vol. 1, p. 220.
14. Ibid. Dumas and Deane were friends who never met face-to-face.
15. Ibid.
16. Clark. *Silas Deane*, 75.
17. Ibid, 74.
18. Ibid.
19. Ibid, 76
20. Ibid, 77
21. CHS Collections, vol. 23, pp. 25–31.
22. Thirty-five days was fast for a "normal" crossing, but the crossing could easily run up to three months-plus, due to the British blockade.
23. "Affairs de l'Amerique, December 7, 1780"; "*Duesions du Roi*, 1766–1792."
24. CHS Collections, Vol. 23.

Chapter VI

Augur, Helen. *The Secret War of Independence*. New York: Duell, Sloan and Pearce, 1955.
Connecticut Historical Society Collections. *Deane Papers*. Vol. 2. Hartford, CT, 1870.
Daughan, George C. *If By Sea*. New York: Basic Books, 2008.
Hodapp, Christopher. *Solomon's Builders*. Berkeley, CA: Ulysses Press, 2007.
Isaacson, Walter. *Benjamin Franklin: An American Life*. New York: Simon & Schuster, 2003.
Morgan, Eedmund S. *Benjamin Franklin*. New Haven, CT: Yale University Press, 2002.
O'Toole, G.J.A. *Honorable Treachery*. New York: Atlantic Monthly Press, 1991.
Patton, Robert H. *Patriot Pirates*. New York: Pantheon Books, 2008.
Schiff, Stacy. *A Great Improvisation*. New York: Henry Holt, 2005.

Schoenbraun, David. *Triumph in Paris: The Exploits of Benjamin Franklin.* New York: Harper & Row, 1976.
Scrodes, James. *Franklin: The Essential Founding Father.* Washington, DC: Regnery, 2002.
Stevens, Benjamin Franklin. *Facsimiles of Manuscripts in European Archives Relating to America, 1773–1783.* Vols. 1–4. London: C. Whittingham, 1889–1898.
Van Doran, Carl. *Secret History of the American Revolution.* New York: Viking, 1941.
Volo, James M. *Blue Water Pirates: The American Revolution Afloat.* Lanham, MD: Rowman & Littlefield, 2006.
Wharton, Francis. *The Revolutionary Diplomatic Correspondence of the United States.* Vols. 1–4. Washington: Government Printing Office, 1889.

1. Schoenbraun, *Triumph,* 71.
2. Ibid., 81.
3. Ibid., 82.
4. Ibid., 83.
5. Schiff, *Improvisation,* 50.
6. *NDAR,* 8, p. 725, March 31, 1777.
7. Van Doran, *For Independence,* 598.
8. Augur, *Of Independence,* 181.
9. *Hartford Courant,* April 16, 1960.
10. Stevens, *Facsimiles,* vol. 1, p, 241, #1562.
11. Augur, *Secret War,* 187.
12. Ibid.
13. Ibid., 190.
14. Ibid., 192.
15. Ibid.
16. CHS, *Deane Papers,* vol. 2., p. 160, August 9, 1777.
17. Wharton, *Revolutionary Corr.,* vol. 1, p. 106, October 4, 1777.
18. Ibid.
19. Ibid.
20. Ibid.
21. CHS, *Deane Papers,* vol. 2, p. 164, October 1, 1777.
22. Ibid., 199, October 24, 1777.
23. Ibid., 213, October 26, 1777.
24. Schoenbraun, *Triumph,* 165.

Chapter VII

Adams, William Howard. *Gouverneur Morris: An Independent Life.* New Haven, CT: Yale University Press, 2003.
Connecticut Historical Society Collections. *Deane Papers.* Vols. 2 and 23. Published by the Society, Hartford, CT: 1870 & 1930.
Augur, Helen. *The Secret War of Independence.* New York: Duell, Sloan and Pearce, 1955.
Isaacson, Walter. *Benjamin Franklin: An American Life.* New York: Simon & Schuster, 2003.
James, Coy Hilton. *Silas Deane: Patriot or Traitor?* East Lansing: Michigan State University Press, 1975.
Jay, John. *John Jay: The Making of a Revolutionary; Unpublished Papers, 1745–1780.* Edited by Richard B. Morris. 2 vols. New York: Harper & Row, 1980.
Srodes, James. *Franklin: The Essential Founding Father.* Washington DC: Regnery, 2002.
Stevens, Benjamin Franklin. *Facsimiles of Manuscripts in European Archives Relating to America, 1773–1783.* Vols. 1–4. London: C. Whittingham, 1889–1898.

1. This is the most accurate in sequence of several accounts of how Wentworth made contact with Silas.
2. Stevens, *Facsimiles,* #s 698–1868.
3. CHS Collections, *Deane Papers,* vol. 2, 94.
4. Ibid., vol. 2, pp. 272–273.

5. James, *Or Traitor?*, 52.
6. It is possible that the British used this knowledge of Silas's interests to pressure him later.
7. Also, Vergnennes was remembering the "John the Painter affair."
8. James, *Silas Deane*, 53.
9. Ibid.
10. Isaacson, *Franklin*, 347. The phrase "a little revenge" is so famous because it indicates even our icons have a dark side.
11. C. Espagne, vol. 588, f 338AAE, pp. 126–133.
12. Jay, *Unpublished*, vol. 1, p. 494.
13. Ibid., 475.
14. Ibid.
15. Franklin's letter to Catherine Green clearly indicates the stress both he and Silas had been under for 18 months.
16. CHS, vol. 2, p. 128.
17. Ibid., vol. 33, pp. 246–247.
18. Augur, *Of Independence*, 278.
19. CHS, *Deane Papers*, vol. 2, p. 439.
20. Frederick B. Talles, "Franklin and the Pulteney Mission: An Episode in the Secret History of the American Revolution," *Huntington Library Quarterly* 17 (1953), 37–59.
21. James, *Or Traitor?* 27, 246–247.

Chapter VIII

Abernathy, Thomas Perkins. *Western Lands and the American Revolution*. New York: D. Appleton-Century, 1937.
Buker, George E. *The Penobscot Expedition*. Annapolis, MD: Naval Institute Press, 2002.
Connecticut Historical Society Collections. *Deane Papers*. Vols. 2 and 23 (1870 and 1930).
Clark, George L. *Silas Deane: A Connecticut Leader in the American Revolution*. New York: G. Putnam's Sons, 1913.
Ingraham, Edward S., ed. *Papers in Relation to the Case of Silas Deane*. Philadelphia: Seventy-six Society, T.R. and G. Collins, 1855.
James, Coy Hilton. *Silas Deane: Patriot or Traitor?* East Lansing: Michigan State University, 1975.
Journals of Congress. Inclusive 1774–1787.
New York Historical Society Collections. *Deane Papers*. Edited by Charles Isham. 5 vols. New York: Published by the Society, 1887–1891.
Wharton, Francis. *The Revolutionary Diplomatic Correspondence of the United States*. Vols. 1–4. Washington: Government Printing Office, 1889.

1. Ingraham, *Case of Silas Deane*, 228
2. Wharton, *Diplomatic Corr.*, vol. 3, pp. 139, 144.
3. *Journals*, vol. 14, pp. 929, 930.
4. CHS Collections, *Deane Papers*, vol. 23, p. 149.
5. Abernathy, *Western Lands*, 213.
6. Ingraham, *Case of Silas Deane*, 124–126.
7. NYHS Collections, *Deane Papers*, vol. 4, p. 130, April 20, 1780.
8. Ibid., 162–165, June 2, 1780.
9. Buker, *Penobscot*, 19–32.
10. NYHS Collections, *Deane Papers*, vol. 4, p. 132.
11. James, *Or Traitor?*, 68–97. (James has probably given us one of the best, if not the best, running accounts of the recall proceedings in Congress, 1778–1780.)

Chapter IX

Augur, Helen. *The Secret War of Independence*. New York: Duell, Sloan and Pearce, 1955.
Boyd, Julian. "Silas Deane: Death by a Kindly Teacher of Treason?" *William and Mary Quarterly* 16, series 3 (April, July, October 1959).
Bullock, Steven C. *Revolutionary Brotherhood*. Chapel Hill: University of North Carolina Press, 1996.

Clark, George L. *Silas Deane: A Connecticut Leader in the American Revolution.* New York: G., Putnam's Sons, 1913.
Isaacson, Walter. *Benjamin Franklin: An American Life.* New York: Simon & Schuster, 2003.
James, Coy Hilton. *Silas Deane: Patriot or Traitor?* East Lansing: Michigan State University Press, 1975.
Paul, Joel Richard. *Unlikely Allies.* New York: Riverhead Books, 2009.
Schiff, Stacy. *A Great Improvisation.* New York: Henry Holt, 2005.
Schoenbraun, David. *Triumph in Paris: The Exploits of Benjamin Franklin.* New York: Harper & Row, 1976.
Scrodes, James. *Franklin: The Essential Founding Father.* Washington DC: Regnery, 2002.

1. NYHS. *Deane Papers,* vol. 4, pp. 340–344, May 20, 1781.
2. Ibid., 388–389, May 20, 1781, to Tallmadge.
3. Ibid., 507, October 21, 1781, to Barnabus.
4. Ibid., 502.
5. Ibid., 503
6. NYHS, *Deane Papers,* vol. 5, p. 134, to Chaumont.
7. Ibid., 213. October 19, 1783, to Franklin.
8. The complete and detailed version of Silas's stolen papers can be found in Boyd's *Jefferson Papers,* vol. 13.
9. CHS Collections, vol. 23, p. 235, Barnabus to Silas, December 6, 1788.
10. Clark, *Silas Deane,* 253.
11. Taken from the last paragraph of an obituary that appeared in *Gentlemen's Magazine* 59 (September 1789), vol. 2, p. 866 (sometimes credited to Bancroft).

Chapter X

American Mercury, Hartford, Conn: Barlow and Babcock, December 28, 1789.
Burch, Samuel. *Papers Relating to the Case of Silas Deane and His Heirs, 1775–1842.* Manuscript Division, Library of Congress (a very detailed history).
Clark, George L. *Silas Deane: A Connecticut Leader in the American Revolution.* New York: G., Putnam's Sons, 1913.
James, Coy Hilton. *Silas Deane: Patriot or Traitor?* East Lansing: Michigan State University Press, 1975.
Paul, Joel Richard. *Unlikely Allies.* New York: Riverhead Books, 2009.
Stokes, Anson Phelps. *Memorials of Eminent Yale Men.* New Haven, CT: Yale University Press, 1914.
Urban, Sylvanus, ed. "Essays." *Gentlemen's Magazine and Historical Chronicle* 60 (1790), London: Printed by John Nichols, pp. 383–386 (Bancroft's suicide story).
___. "Obituary." *Gentlemen's Magazine and Historical Chronicle* 59 (1789), London: Printed by John Nichols, p. 866 (Bancroft's first version of Deane's death).
U.S. Congress. House of Representatives. Committee of Revolutionary Claims. *Committee Report on Settlement of Acounts of Silas Deane.* House Report 952 to accompany S.155, 27th Congress, 2nd Session. Washington: Government Printing Office, 1842.
U.S. Congress, Senate. Committee of Revolutionary Claims. Report made by Mr. Smith of Connecticut, Senate report 201 to accompany S.155, 26th Congress, 2nd Session. Washington: Blair & Rives, 1841.

1. See NYHS, *Deane Papers,* vol. 1, p. 13, for original copy.

Appendix B

1. Quoted from Jared Sparks, *The Diplomatic Correspondence of the American Revolution* (Boston: Nathan Hale, Gray and Bowen, 1829), I, 5–9.

Bibliography

Abernethy, Thomas Perkins. "Commercial Activities of Silas Deane in France." *American Historical Review* 39 (April 1934).
_____. "The Origin of the Franklin-Lee Imbroglio." *North Carolina Historical Review* 15 (1938).
_____. *Western Lands and the American Revolution.* New York: D. Appleton-Century, 1937.
"Accounts of Franklin, Deane and Adams, December 1776 to June 1778." Collections of the Connecticut Historical Society. Given to the Society in 1874 by special act of Congress. Independent Unpublished Manuscript Ledger.
Achenbach, Joel. *The Grand Idea: George Washington's Potomac and the Race to the West.* New York: Simon & Schuster, 2004.
Adams, Charles Francis, ed. *Familiar Letters of John Adams and His Wife Abigail Adams During the Revolution.* New York: Hurd & Houghton, 1876.
_____. *The Works of John Adams.* Vol. 3. Boston: Little, Brown, 1853.
Adams, James Truslow. *New England in the Republic, 1776–1850.* Boston: Little, Brown, 1926.
Adams, John. *Diary and Autobiography.* Edited by L.H. Butterfield. 5 vols. Cambridge: Cambridge University Press, 1961–66.
Adams, Randolph G., ed. *Political Ideas of American Revolution.* New York: 1958.
Adams, Sherman W. *The History of Ancient Wethersfield, Connecticut.* Edited by Henry R. Stiles. 2 vols. New York: Grafton Press, 1904.
Adams, William Howard. *Gouverneur Morris: An Independent Life.* New Haven, CT: Yale University Press, 2003.
Adams, Willie Paul, ed. "The Spirit of Commerce, Requires His Property Be Sacred: Gouverneur Morris and the American Revolution." *Amerikastudien/American Studies* 21 (1976).
Affairs Étrangeres Correspondence Politique, Etats-Unis. Manuscript Division, Library of Congress, No. 98 (Chaumont and Vergennes).
Ahlstrom, Sydney E. *A Religious History of the American People.* New Haven: Yale University Press, 1973.
Alberts, Robert C. *The Golden Voyage: The Life and Times of William Bingham.* Boston: Houghton, Mifflin, 1969.
Alden, Horatio. *Memorial of the Heirs of Silas Deane.* No place, no publisher, 1835.
Aldridge, Alfred Owen. "Jacques Barbeu Dubourg, A French Disciple of Benjamin Franklin." *Proceedings of the American Philosophical Society* 95 (1951).
Alexander, John K. *Samuel Adams: America's Revolutionary Politician.* Lenham, MD: Rowman & Littlefield, 2002.
Allen, Gardner Weld. *A Naval History of the American Revolution, 1913–1940.* Vol. 2. Reprint. New York: Russell and Russell, 1962.
Allis, Margerite. *Historic Connecticut.* New York: Grosset & Dunlap, 1934.
Alsop, Susan. *Yankees at the Court: The First American in Paris.* Garden City, NY: Doubleday, 1982.
Ambler, Charles. *George Washington and the West.* Chapel Hill: University of North Carolina Press, 1936.
American Maritime Documents, 1776–1860. Mystic, CT: Mystic Seaport Museum, 1992.

American Mercury 7, no. 286 (Monday, December 28, 1789). Hartford, CT. Printed by Elisha Babcock. "London, October 20, Silas Deane Obituary."
Ammon, Harry, ed. "Letters of William Carmichael to John Cudwalder." *Modern History Magazine* 8 (June, 1913).
Andersen, Bethanne. *Patience Wright: America's First Sculptor and Revolutionary Spy*. New York: Henry Holt, 2007.
Anderson, Dennis Kent, and Godfrey T. Anderson. "The Death of Silas Deane: Another Opinion." *New England Quarterly* 57 (1984).
Anderson, Fred. *Crucible of War*. New York: Alfred A. Knopf, 2000.
_____. *The War That Made America*. New York: Penguin, 2006.
Anderson, James H. *Colonel William Crawford*. Ohio Archaeological and Historic Publications, 1896.
Andrews, C.M. "A Note on the Franklin-Deane Mission to France." *The Yale University Library Gazette* 2 (April 1928).
Andrews, Jeanmarie. "A New View of George Washington." *Early American Life* (October 2006).
Anthony, Preston, et al. *Navies of the American Revolution*. Englewood Cliffs, NJ: 1975.
Apple, Joe A. "Silas Deane: America's First Diplomat." *Social Education* 14 (April 1950).
Appleby, Joyce. "Liberalism and the American Revolution." *New England Quarterly* 49 (March, 1976).
_____. "The Social Origins of American Revolutionary Ideology." *Journal of American History* 64 (March 1978).
Arch, Nigel, and Joanna Marschner. *Splendor at Court: Dressing for Royal Occasions Since 1700*. London & Sydney: Unwin Hyman, 1987.
Augur, Helen. "Benjamin Franklin and the French Alliance." *American Heritage* 8 (April 1956).
_____. *The Secret War of Independence*. New York: Duell, Sloan & Pearce, 1955.
Axelrod, Alan. *The Real History of the American Revolution: A New Look at the Past*. New York: Sterling, 2007.
Baack, Ben. "Forging a Nation State: The Continental Congress and the Financing of War of American Independence." *Economic Review* 54, no. 4 (2001).
Baigent, Michael, and Richard Leigh. *The Temple and the Lodge*. Arcade, 1989.
Bailey, Thomas A. *A Diplomatic History of the American People*. New York: F.S. Crofts, 1942.
Bailyn, Bernard. *Faces of Revolution: Personalities and Themes in the Struggle for American Independence*. New York: Knopf, 1990.
Bakeless, John. *Turncoats, Traitors and Heroes: Espionage in the American Revolution*. New York: 1959.
Baker, William A. *Colonial Vessels*. Barre, MA: 1962.
Ballagh, James Curtin, ed. *The Letters of Richard Henry Lee*. Vols. 1 and 2. New York: DaCapo Press, 1970.
Barrow, Thomas C. *Connecticut Joins the Revolution*. Chester, CT: Pequot Press, 1973.
Batham, C.N. "The Compagnonnage and the Emergence of Craft Masonry in France." *AQC* 86 (London, 1874).
Batterbary, Ariane Ruskins. *Spy for Liberty: The Adventurous Life of Beaumarchais, Playwright and Secret Agent for the American Revolution*. New York: Pantheon Books, 1965.
Baxter, William T. *The House of Hancock: Business in Boston, 1724–1775*. Cambridge, MA: Cambridge University Press, 1945.
Beach, Stewart. *Samuel Adams*. New York: Dodd, Mead, 1965.
Beaumarchais, Pierre-Augustin Caron de. *The Figaro Trilogy*. Oxford: Oxford University Press, 2003.
Bell, Herbert C. "West Indies Trade Before the American Revolution." *American Historical Review* 22 (January 1917).
Bell, William Clark. "John the Painter." *Pennsylvania Magazine of History and Biography* 68 (1939).
Bemis, Samuel Flagg. "British Secret Service and the French-American Alliance." *American Historical Review* 29 (?) (1924).
_____. *The Diplomacy of the American Revolution*. New York: D. Appleton-Century, 1935.
_____. *A Diplomatic History of the United States*. New York: A. Holt, 1942.

_____, ed. "Edward Bancroft Memorial to the Marquis Carmarthen." *American Historical Review* 29 (?) (1924).
Bendickson, L. "The Restoration of Obliterated Passages and Secret Writing in Diplomatic Missives." *Franco-American Review* 1 (1937).
Bendiner, Elmer. *The Virginia Diplomats*. New York: Alfred A. Knopf, 1976.
Benemeli, J.A.I. *La Masoneria Espanöla en el Siglo* 18 (Madrid, 1979).
Berger, Carl. *Broadsides and Bayonets: The Propaganda War of the American Revolution*. Philadelphia: University of Pennsylvania Press, 1961.
_____. "The Campaign to Win Indians' Allegiance." In *Broadsides and Bayonets: The Propoganda War of the American Revolution*. Philadelphia: University of Pennsylvania, 1961
Berkley, Andrew S., and James P. Shenton. *The History of the United States* Vol. 1. New York: G.P. Putnam & Sons, 1966.
Bernheim, A. "Note on Early Freemasonry in Bordeau (1732–1769)." *AQC* 101 (London, 1989).
Bernier, Oliver. *Lafayette: Hero of Two Worlds*. New York: Dutton, 1973.
Bidwell, Bruce W. *History of the Military Intelligence Division, Department of the Army General Staff, 1775–1941*. Frederick, MD: University of Publications of America, 1986.
Bigelow, John. *Beaumarchais the Merchant; Letters of Théreneau de Francey, 1777–1780*. New York, 1870.
_____. "Franklin's Home and Hast in France." *Century Illustrated Monthly* 35 (1888).
Bill, Shirley A., and Louis Gottschalk. "Silas Deane's Worthless Agreement with Lafayette." *Prologue* 4 (Winter 1972).
Bizardel, Yvon. *Les Américains à Paris sous Louis XVI et pendant la revolution*. Self-published, 1978.
Bloom, Richard. "Silas Deane: Patriot or Renegade." *American History Illustrated* (November 1978).
Bobrick, Benson. *Angels in the Whirlwind*. New York: Simon & Schuster, 1997.
Bodley, Temple. *Our First Great West in the Revolutionary War, Diplomacy and Politics*. Louisville: Morton, 1938.
Bolles, Albert S. *The Financial History of the U.S. from 1774 to 1789*. New York: D. Appleton, 1896.
Boorstin, Daniel J. *Hidden History Explores Our Secret Past*. New York: Vintage Books, Random House, 1989.
Boudinot, Elias. *The Journal or Historical Recollections of American Events During the Revolutionary War*. Private Press, 1894 (350 copies issued).
Bourne, Russel. "The Penobscot Fiasco." *American Heritage* 25, (October 1974).
Bouteiller, Earl Kenneth. "The Mission of Silas Deane." Master's thesis, Trinity College, 1931.
Boutwell, Georgiana A. "Silas Deane and the Coming of Lafayette." *New England Magazine* 8. New Series (1893).
Bowen, Catherine Drinker. *John Adams and the American Revolution*. Boston: 1950.
Bowen, Hassell E., Gordon Dennis, Michael Conrad and Mark L. Hayes. *Sea Raiders of the American Revolution: The Continental Navy in European Waters*. Washington DC: Naval History Center, 2003.
Bowman, Larry G. *Captive Americans: Prisoners During the American Revolution*. Athens: Ohio University Press, 1976.
Boxer, Charles. *The Dutch Seaborne Empire, 1600–1800*. New York: 1965.
Boyd, Julian P. "Death by a Kindly Teacher of Treason?" *William and Mary Quarterly* 21, nos. 2, 3, and 4; 3rd Series (April, July and October 1959).
Boyd, Julian P., ed. *The Susquehannah Papers, 1750–1772*. 4 vols. Wilkes-Barre: 1930–1933.
Boyd, Julian P., et al., eds. *The Papers of Thomas Jefferson*. 30 vols. as of 2006. Princeton: Princeton University Press, 1950–(vols. 1–4, 15).
Brandt, Clare. *The Men in the Mirror: A Life of Benedict Arnold*. New York: Random House, 1994.
Brecker, Frank W. *Securing American Independence: John Jay and French Alliance*. Westport, CT: Praeger, 2003.
Breen, T.H. *Tobacco Culture: The Mentality of the Great Tidewater Planters on the Eve of the Revolution*. Princeton, NJ: Princeton University Press, 1985.
Bridenbaugh, Carl. *Cities in Revolt: Urban Life in America, 1743–1776*. 1955. New York: Oxford University Press, 1971.
_____. *The Spirit of '76: The Growth of American Patriotism Before Independence*. New York: 1975.

"Brief Biographies of Connecticut Revolution Naval and Privateer Officers: Dudley Saltonstall" Pt. 4, vol. 1, *Records and Papers of the New London County Historical Society*. New London, CT: New London County Historical Society, 1893.

Broglie, Prince de. "Narrative of the Prince de Broglie, 1782." Translated by E.W. Balch. *Magazine of America History* 1 (March 1871).

Brookhiser, Richard. *Gentleman Revolutionary: Gouverneur Morris, the Rake Who Wrote the Constitution*. New York: Simon & Schuster, 2003.

Brown, Alan. "The British Peace Officer of 1778: A Study in Ministerial Confusion." *Paper of the Michigan Academy of Science, Arts and Letters* 40 (1955–56).

Brown, Margaret L. "William Bingham, Agent of the Continental Congress in Mertinique." *Pennsylvania Magazine of History and Biography* 61 (1937).

Brown, Richard D. *Knowledge Is Power: Diffusion of Information in Early America, 1700–1865*. New York: Oxford University Press, 1989.

Brown, William Moseley. *George Washington, Freemason*. Richmond: 1952.

Bruin, Fred D. "St. Eustatius: A Golden Link with the Independence of the United States." *De Halve Maen, Quarterly Journal of Holland Society of New York* 58, no. 2 (1984).

Brumgardt, John R., ed. *The Revolutionary Era: A Variety of Perspectives*. Riverside, CA: 1976.

Brymer, Douglas, ed. "Observations Respecting a Navigable Canal from Lake Champlain to the St. Lawrence." *Deane to Dochester, October 25, 1785*. Ottawa: Canadian Archives, Series Q, 1889.

Buck, Phillip W. *The Politics of Mercantilism*. New York: Henry Holt, 1942.

Buel, Richard. *Dear Liberty: Connecticut's Mobilization for the Revolutionary War*. Middletown, CT: Wesleyan University Press, 1980.

Buell, Richard Jr. "Democracy and the American Revolution: A Frame of Reference." *William and Mary Quarterly* 21, 3rd Series (1964).

_____. *In Irons: Britain's Naval Supremacy and the American Economy*. New Haven, CT: Yale University Press, 1998.

Buker, George E. *The Penobscot Expedition: Commodore Saltonstall and the Massachusetts Conspiracy of 1779*. Annapolis, MD: Naval Institute Press, 2002.

Bullock, Steven C. "The Ancient and Honorable Society: Freemasonry in America, 1730–1860." PhD. diss., Brown University, 1986.

_____. *Revolutionary Brotherhood: Freemasonry and Transformation of the American Order, 1730–1840*. Omhumdro Institute of Early American History and Culture. Chapel Hill: University of North Carolina Press, 1996.

_____. "The Revolutionary Transformation of American Freemasonry, 1752–1792." *William and Mary Quarterly* 47, 3rd Series (July 1990).

Buranelli, Vincent, and Nan Buranelli. *Spy Counter Spy: An Encyclopedia of Espionage*. New York: McGraw-Hill, 1982.

Burch, Samuel. Papers Relating to the Claims of Silas Deane and His Heirs, 1775–1842. No. 9126, Manuscript Division, Library of Congress.

Burham, J.H. "A Curious Proposition in 1776." *Illinois Historical Society Journal* 2 (October 1909).

Burnett, Edmund C. "Ciphers of the Revolutionary Period." *American Historical Review* 22 (January 1917).

_____. *Letters of the Members of the Continental Congress*. Washington DC: Carnegie Institution, 1921–36.

_____. "Note on the American Negotiations for Commercial Treaties, 1776–1786." *American Historical Review* 16 (1910–11).

Burnett, Edmund Cody. *The Continental Congress*. New York: Macmillan, 1941.

_____. *The Continental Congress*. New York: Macmillan, 1942.

_____, ed. *Letters of the Members of the Continental Congress*. 8 vols. Washington DC: Carnegie Institution of Washington, 1921–1936.

Burns, Eric. *Virtue, Valor and Vanity: The Founding Fathers and the Pursuit of Fame*. New York: Arcade, 2007.

Butler, John A. *Sailing on Friday: The Perilous Voyages of America's Merchant Marine*. Washington: Brassey's, 2000.

Butterfield, C.W., ed. *Washington-Crawford Letters: Correspondence Between George Washington and William Crawford, 1767–1781, Concerning Western Lands.* Cincinnati: Robert Clark, 1877 (chronologically arranged and carefully annotated and copyrighted, 1997 by Arthur W. McGraw; preface by CWB crucial).
Calhoun, Robert McCuer. *The Loyalists in Revolutionary America, 1760–1781.* New York: Harcourt & Brace Jovanich, 1973.
Callahan, North. *Connecticut Revolutionary War Leaders.* Chester, CT: Pequot Press, 1973.
Callaway, M. Jr. "Benedict Arnold and Freemasonry: Correction of a Long-standing Error." *AQC* 80 (London, 1968).
Calloway, Colin G. *The American Revolution in Indian Country.* Cambridge: Cambridge University Press, 1995.
Calusen, Henry C. *Masons Who Helped Shape Our Nation.* Washington: 1976.
Carleton, Marcia W. *Silas Deane, 1737–1789.* S.I. National Society of the Colonial Dames of America in the State of Connecticut, 1971 (Pamphlet).
Carson, Cary, Ronald Hoffman, and Peter J. Albert. eds. Of Consuming Interest: The Style of Life in the Eighteenth Century. Charlottesville: University Press of Virginia 1994.
Carson, Hampton L. "The Case of the Sloop Active." *Pennsylvania Magazine of History and Biography* 16 (893)
Central Intelligence Agency. *Intelligence in the War for Independence.* Washington DC: Public Affairs Office of the CI, 1997.
Cerza, A. "The American War of Independence and Freemasonry." *AQC* 89 (London, 1977).
_____. "The Boston Tea Party and Freemasonry." *AQC* 92 (London, 1986).
Chambers, William Nisbet. *Political Parties in a New Nation, 1776–1789.* Oxford: Oxford University Press, 1969.
Charles, Joseph. *The Origins of the American Party System.* New York: 1961.
Chessnutt, David R., and C. James Taylor, eds. *The Papers of Henry Laurens.* 16 vols. Columbia: University of South Carolina Press, 1968–2003.
Chinard, G., ed. *The Treaties of 1778.* Institut de Francais de Washington. Baltimore: Johns Hopkins Press, 1928.
Chinard, Gilbert. *Honest John Adams.* Boston: 1933.
Chitwood, Oliver Perry. *Richard Henry Lee: Statesman of the Revolution.* Morgantown: West Virginia University Library, 1967.
Clark, (Reverend) G.L. Paper read before the D.A.R. and published in full by the *Hartford Daily Courant*, June 10 1904, entitled "Silas Deane, Patriot."
Clark, George L. *Silas Deane: A Connecticut Leader in the American Revolution.* New York: G.P. Putnam's Sons, 1913.
Clark, William Bell. "American Naval Policy, 1775–76." *American Neptune* 1 (1941).
_____. *Lambert Wickers: Sea Raider and Diplomat.* New Haven, CT: 1932.
Clark, William Bell, and James Morgan, eds. *Naval Documents of the American Revolution.* 2 Vols., Washington DC: U.S. Government Printing Office, 1964.
Cogan, Charles. *French Negotiating Behavior.* Washington: U.S. Institute of Peace Press, 2003.
Coggins, Jack. *Ships and Seamen of the American Revolution.* Harrisburg, PA: 1969.
Cohen, Sheldon S. "Samuel Peters Comments on the Death of Silas Deane." *New England Quarterly* 40, no. 3 (1967).
Collier, Christopher. *Connecticut in the Continental Congress.* Chester, CT: Pequot Press, 1973.
_____. "Inside the American Revolution: A Silas Deane Diary Fragment, April 20 to October 25, 1775." *Connecticut Historical Society Bulletin* 4 (1964).
_____. *Roger Sherman's Connecticut.* Middletown, CT: Wesleyan University Press, 1971.
_____. "Silas Deane Reports on the Continental Congress." *Connecticut Historical Society Bulletin* 29, no. 1 (January 1964).
Conyngham, Gustavus. "Narrative." *Pennsylvania Magazine of History and Biography* 20 (1898).
Conynghan, D.H. "Reminiscences." *Proceedings and Collections of the Wyoming Historical and Geological Society.* Vol. 8, Wilkes-Barre: 1904.
Cook, Don. *The Long Fuse: How England Lost the American Revolution, 1760–1785.* New York: Atlantic Monthly Press, 1995.

Cooper, Helen A. *John Trumbull: The Hand and Spirit of a Painter*. New Haven, CT: Yale University Art Gallery, 1982.
Correspondence of Henry Laurens of South Carolina. New York: Printed for the Zenger Club, 1861.
Corwin, E.S. "The French Objective in the American Revolution." *American Historical Review* 16 (1915).
Cousins, Norman, ed. *In God We Trust: The Religious Beliefs and Ideas of the American Founding Fathers*. New York: Harper, 1958.
Cox, Cynthia. *The Real Figaro: The Extraordinary Career of Caron de Beaumarchais*. New York: Coward, McCann, 1963.
Crane, Verner W. *Benjamin Franklin and a Rising People*. Boston: Little, Brown, 1954.
Crankshaw, Mildred Rowley. *Silas Deane, Patriot*. A Play. Wethersfield, CT.: Wethersfield Historical Society, 1961.
Crary, Catherine Snell. "The Tory and the Spy: The Double Life of James Rivington." *William and Mary Quarterly* 16, 3rd Series (January 1959).
Crowley, J.E. *This Sheba, Self: The Conceptualization of Economic Life in Eighteenth Century America*. New York: 1974.
Currey, Cecil B. *Code Number 72: Ben Franklin, Patriot or Spy?* Englewood Cliffs, NJ: Prentice Hall, 1972.
Cushing, Henry Alonzo, ed. *The Writings of Samuel Adams*. 4 vols. New York: Putnam, 1904.
Dangerfield, George. Chancelor Robert Livingston of New York, 1746–1813. New York: Harcourt Brace, 1960.
Daniel, John. *Scarlet and the Beast*. Vol. 1. JKI, 1995.
Darnton, Robert. *George Washington's False Teeth: An Unconventional Guide to the Eighteenth Century*. New York: W.W. Norton, 2003.
Daughan, George C. *If By Sea: The Forging of the Revolution to the War of 1812*. New York: Basic Books, 2008.
Davidson, James West, and Mark H. Lytle. "The Strange Death of Silas Deane." In *After the Fact: The Art of Historical Detection*. New York: Knopf, 1982.
Davidson, Philip. *Propaganda and the American Revolution*. Chapel Hill: University of North Carolina, 1941.
Deane, Silas *An Address to the Free and Independent Citizens of the United States of North America to Which Is Added a Letter to the Hon. Robert Morris, Esq., With Notes and Observations*. London: J. Debrett, 1784.
_____. *An Address to the Free and Independent Citizens of the United States of North America*. Hartford: Hudson and Goodman, 1784.
_____. "Deane to Patrick Henry, MSS, January 2, 1775." Miscellaneous Collections, Clements Library, University of Michigan.
_____. "Deane to Samuel H. Parsons, April 13, 1774." MSS Box from the Collections of the Connecticut Historical Society, Hartford, CT.
_____. Silas Deane Diary, 1775–1776. Collections of the Connecticut Historical Society, Hartford, CT.
The Deane Papers: Correspondence Between Silas Deane His Brothers and Their Business and Political Associates, 1771–1795. Vol. 23. Collections of the Connecticut Historical Society. Hartford: Published by the Society, 1930.
Deas, Anne Izard, ed. *Correspondence of Ralph Izard of South Carolina from the Years 1774 to 1804: With a Short Memoir*. New York: 1884.
Decker, Malcolm. *Benedict Arnold: Son of the Havens*. New York: 1961.
DePuy, Henry W. *Ethan Allen and the Green-Mountain Heroes of '76*. New York: 1970.
Destler, Chester, M. *The Provision State*. Chester, CT: Pequot Press, 1973.
Destler, Chester McArthur. "Barnabus Deane and the Barnabus Deane Company." *Connecticut Historical Society Bulletin* 35, no. 1 (January 1970).
Dexter, F.B., ed. *Literary Diary of Ezra Stiles*. New York: 1966.
Dexter, Franklin B. *Biographical Sketches of the Graduates of Yale College with Annals of the College History*. Vol. 2. New York: Henry Holt, 1896.
Dickersen, Olivia M. *The Navigation Acts and the American Revolution*. Philadelphia: University of Pennsylvania Press, 1951.

Dill, Alonzo T. *William Lee, Militia Diplomacy.* Williamsburg: 1976.
Doerflinger, Thomas M. *A Vigorous Spirit of Enterprise: Merchants and Economic Development in Revolutionary Philadelphia.* Chapel Hill: University of North Carolina Press, 1986.
Doll, Peter N. *Revolution, Religion and National Identity: Imperial Anglicanism in British North America, 1745–95.* Madison, NJ: Fairleigh Dickinson University Press, 2000.
Doniol, Henri, ed. *Historie de la Particiaption de la France á l'Establessment des Etats-Unis d'Amerique Correspondence Diplomatic et Documents.* 6 vols. Paris: Imprimerie Nationale, 1884–1892.
Donne, W. Bodham, ed. *The Correspondence of King George III with Lord North from 1768 to 1783.* 2 vols. London: 1867.
Dos Passos, John. "Robert Morris and the 'Art Magic.'" *American Heritage* 7, no. 6 (October 1956).
Dow, George Francis, and John Rokmen. *Sailing Ships of New England, 1607–1907.* New York: Skyhorse, 2007.
Doyle, Joseph B. *Frederick William von Steuben and the American Revolution.* New York: Burt Franldin, 1970.
Dreer, Ferdinand J. "Letters of Silas Deane." *Pennsylvania Magazine of History and Biography* 1 (1877).
Dull, Jonathan R. *A Diplomatic History of the American Revolution.* New Haven: Yale University Press, 1985.
_____. "Franklin in France: A Reappraisal." *Proceedings of the Annual Meeting of the Western Society of French History* 4 (1976).
_____. *The French Navy and American Independence: A Study in Arms and Diplomacy, 1774–1787.* Princeton: Princeton University Press, 1975.
Dunin, Elonka. *The Mamouth Book of Secret Codes and Cryptograms.* New York: Carroll & Graf, 2006.
Dunkelberger, George S., comp. *An Early History of St. John's Lodge, No. 4, Hartford, Connecticut, 1762–1937.* Hartford, CT: Case Lockwood & Brainard, 1937.
Dupuy R. Ernest, Gay Hammerman, and Grace P. Hayes. *The American Revolution: A Global War.* New York: David McKay, 1996.
Durand, John. *New Materials for the History of the American Revolution taken from Documents in the French Archives.* New York: Henry Holt, 1889.
Du Simitière, Pierre Eugène, and Burnet Reading. *Thirteen Portraits of American Legislators, Patriots, and Soldiers, Who Distinguished Themselves in Rendering Their Country Independent.* London: W. Richardson, 1783.
Earle, Alice Morse. *Customs and Fashions in Old New England.* Detroit: Single Tree Press, 1968.
East, Robert A. "The Business Entrepreneur in a Changing Colonial Economy, 1763–1795." *Journal of Economic History* 6 (1946).
_____. *Business Enterprises in the American Revolutionary Era.* New York: 1938.
Edler, Friedrich. *The Dutch Republic and the American Revolution.* Baltimore: 1911.
Ellis, Joseph J. *American Creation.* New York: Alfred A. Knopf, 2007.
_____. *His Excellency.* New York: Alfred A. Knopf, 2004
Engal, Marc, and Joseph A. Ernst. "An Economic Interpretation of the American Revolution." *William and Mary Quarterly* 24, 3rd Series (January 1972).
Ettwein, John. "The Resignation of Henry Laurens, President of Congress, 1778." *Pennsylvania Magazine of History and Biography* 13 (1889).
Fales, Edward D. Jr. *Arsenal of the Revolution: The History of the Seventeen "Iron Country Towns" of Connecticut, New York and Massachusetts Highlands.* Lakeville, CT: Lakeville Journal Press, 1976.
_____. *Iron Country: 1720 to 1972.* Lakeville, CT: Lakeville Journal Press, 1972.
Fallows, Samuel. *Samuel Adams.* Milwaukee: H.G. Campbell, 1903.
Fay, B. *LaFranc-Maconnerie et la revolution intellectuelle du XVIII siecle.* Paris: 1961.
Fay, Bernard. *Franklin, the Apostle of Modern Times.* Boston: Little, Brown, 1929.
Feintuck, Burt, and Donald H. Walters, eds. *The Encyclopedia of New England.* New Haven: Yale University Press, 2005.
Fenton, S.J. "The Military Services and Freemasonry." *AQC* 60 (London, 1950).

Ferguson, E. James. "Business, Government and Congressional Investigation in the Revolution." *William and Mary Quarterly* 16, 3rd series (1959).
_____. *The Power of the Purse: A History of American Public Finance, 1776–1790*. Chapel Hill: University of North Carolina Press, 1961.
Ferguson, E. James, and Elizabeth Miles Nuyoll. "The Investigation of Government Corruption During the American Revolution." *Congressional Studies* 8, no. 2 (1981).
Ferguson, James, et al., eds. *The Papers of Robert Morris, 1781–1784*. 9 vols. Pittsburgh: University of Pittsburgh Press, 1973–1999.
Ferling, John. *John Adams: A Life*. New York: Henry Holt, 1996.
Fischer, Paul A. *Behind the Lodge Door*. Shield, 1988.
Fiske, John. "The French Alliance and the Conway Cabal." *Atlantic Monthly* 64, no. 18.
Fitzmaurice, Lord Edmund. *Life of William, Earl of Shelburne*. 3 vols. London: 1875–76.
Flegial, Fred Gerard. "Silas Deane: Revolutionary of Profiteer?" Master's thesis, Western Michigan State University, 1976.
Flexner, James Thomas. *George Washington*. Vol. 2, *In the American Revolution, 1775–1783*. Boston: Little, Brown, 1967.
Fliegelman, Jay. *Prodigals and Pilgrims: Against Patriarchal Authority, 1750–1800*. Cambridge: Cambridge University Press, 1982.
Flower, Milton E. *John Dickinson: Conservative Revolutionary*. Charlottesville: University Press of Virginia, 1983.
Foner, Eric. *Tom Paine and Revolutionary America*. New York: Oxford University Press, 1976.
Force, Peter, ed. *American Archives*. Fifth Series, July 4, 1776 – September 3, 1783. 3 vols. Washington: 1848 –1853.
_____, ed. *American Archives*. Fourth Series, March 7, 1774 – July 4, 1776.
Ford, Corey. *A Peculiar Service*. Boston: Little, Brown, 1965.
Ford, Paul Leicester, ed. *Edward Bancroft, A Narrative of the Objects and Proceedings of Silas Deane, Commissioner of the United Colonies to France, Made to the British Government in 1776*. Brooklyn: 1891.
_____, ed. *Writings of John Dickinson*. 2 vols. Philadelphia: 1895.
Ford, Worthington Chauncey, ed. *Correspondence and Journals of Samuel Blachley Webb*. 3 vols. Lancaster, PA: Wickersham Press, 1894. reprint, 1938.
Ford, Worthington Chauncey, and Gaillard Hunt, eds. *Journals of the Continental Congress, 1774–1789*. 34 vols. Washington DC: 1904–1937.
_____. *Family Letters of Samuel Blachley Webb, 1764–1807*. 1892. New York: 1912.
_____, ed. *Letters of William Lee, 1766–1783*. New York: 1891.
_____, ed. *Reply of William Lee to the charges of Silas Deane, 1779*. Brooklyn: Historical Printing Club, 1891.
Forrest, Morgan, ed. *Connecticut as a Colony and as a State or One of the Thirteen*. Vol 2. Hartford: Society of Connecticut, 1904.
Fortescue, Sir John. "Confession of James Atkyns." In *The Correspondence of King George the Third, 1760–1783*. Vol 3. London: Macmillan, 1902.
_____. *The Correspondence of King George the Third from 1760 to December 1783*. 6 vols. London: Macmillan, 1928.
Fowler, William M. "Dudley Saltonstall." in John A. Garrity and Mark C. Carness, eds. *American National Biography*. Vol 19. New York: Oxford University Press, 1999.
Fowler, William M., Jr. *Rebels Under Sail: The American Navy During the Revolution*. New York: Scribner, 1976.
_____. *Sam Adams: Radical Puritan*. New York: Longman, 1997.
Franklin, Benjamin. *The Writings of Benjamin Franklin*. Edited by Albert Henry Smith. 10 vols. New York: 1907.
French, Allen. *The First Year of the American Revolution*. Boston: 1934.
_____. *The Taking of Ticonderoga in 1775*. Cambridge: Cambridge University Press, 1928.
French, Thomas E. "Arthur Lee's Berlin Visit." *The Lure of the Litchfield Hills*. Vol. 20, no. 4 (Winter 1962).
_____. "Silas Deane Patriot or Traitor?" *The Lure of the Litchfield Hills* (Winter 1961).

———. "The Two Captains." *The Lure of the Litchfield Hills* 22, no. 6 (Winter 1963).
Friedenberg, Daniel M. *Life, Liberty and the Pursuit of Land*. Buffalo: Prometheus Books, 1992.
Fritz, Jesen. *Why Not Lafayette?* New York: Putnam, 1999.
Fruchtman, Jack, Jr. *Thomas Paine: Apostle of Freedom*. New York: Four Wells Eight Windows, 1994.
Fuye, Maurice de la, and Emile A. Babeau. *The Apostle of Liberty: A Life of La Fayette*. Translated ny Edward Hymans. New York: Thomas Yoseloff, 1956.
Garrett, Wendell, ed. "Antiques in Wethersfield." *Antiques* (March 1976).
Gaustad, Edwin S. *Benjamin Franklin: Inventing America*. Oxford: Oxford University Press, 2004.
Gawalt, Gerard W., ed. *John Paul Jones: Memoir of the American Revolution Presented to King Louis of France*. Washington, DC: Library of Congress, 1979.
Genet, George Clinton. "Beaumarchais's Plan to Aid the Colonies." *Magazine of American History* 2a (1878).
Gentlemen's Magazine 59, no. 2 (September 1789): page 866, Silas Deane's obituary.
"Gerard: Narrative of a Conference with the American Commissioners." *Stevens Facimiles No. 1831* (January 9, 1978).
Gerlach, Larry R. "A Delegation of Steady Habits: The Connecticut Representatives to the Continental Congress, 1774–1789." *Connecticut Historical Society Bulletin* 32, no. 2 (April 1967).
———. "Firmness and Prudence: Connecticut, the Continental Congress and the National Domain, 1776–1786." *Connecticut Historical Society Bulletin* 31, no. 3 (July 1966).
Gilbert, Felix. "The New Diplomacy of the Eighteenth Century." *World Politics* 4 (1951).
Gionfriddo, Paul, and William Lobb. "*Silas Deane: The Improbable Hero*." 90-minute radio docudrama narrated by actor Robert Vaughn, WNPR Connecticut Public Radio, January 9, 2007.
Gipson, Lawrence, Henry. *The Coming of the American Revolution, 1763–1775*. New York: Harper Torchbook, 1962.
Glatthaar, Joseph T., and James Kirby Martin. *Forgotten Allies: The Oneida Indians and the American Revolution*. New York: Hill and Wang, 2006.
Godfrey, William G. *Pursuit of Profit and Preferment in Colonial North America*. Waterloo, Ontario: John Bradstreets, Quest, 1982.
Goldstein, Kolman. "Silas Deane: Preparation for Rascality." *The Historian* (November 1980).
Gordon, John Steele. "Land of the Free Trade." *American Heritage* 44, no. 4 (July/August 1993).
Gordon, Robert B. *A Landscape Transformed: The Ironmaking District of Salisbury, Connecticut*. New York: Oxford University Press, 2001.
"Grand's Accounts to Deane, March 26, 1778." Deane Letterbooks from the Collections of the Connecticut Historical Society, Hartford, CT.
Grant, Ellsworth. "They Gave Us Liberty: Silas Deane." *Hartford Courant*, editorial page, Sunday, June 27 1976.
Grant, James. *John Adams: Party of One*. New York: Ferrar Straus and Giroux, 2005.
Grant, Steve. "Hero? Crook? Silas Deane, an Enigmatic Figure in State History, Gets His Own Voluminous Website" (www.silasdeane-online.org). *Hartford Courant*, Section D, February 5, 2005.
Greene, Jack P., ed. *The American Revolution: Its Character and Limits*. New York: 1987.
Greene, Jack P., and J.R. Pole. eds. *The Blackwell Encyclopedia of the American Revolution*. Cambridge, MA: Basil Blackwell 1994.
Greene, William. "Journal of a Visit to Paris." *Massachusetts Historical Society Proceedings* 54 (1972).
Grendel, Frederic. *Beaumarchais: The Men Who Was Figaro*. Translated from the French by Roger Graves. London: Macdonald & Jane's, 1977.
Hagger, Nicholas. *The Secret Founding of America: The Real Story of Freemasons, Puritans and the Battle of the New World*. London: Watkins, 2004.
Hale, Edward E., and Edward E. Hale, Jr. *Franklin in Paris*. 2 vols. Boston: 1887.
Hall, Charles Swain. *Benjamin Tallmadge: Revolutionary Soldier and American Businessman*. New York: Columbia University Press, 1943.

Hallahan, William H. *The Day the American Revolution Began.* New York: William Morrow, 2000.
Hallowell, Edward M., and John R. Ratey. *Driven to Distraction.* New York: Pantheon Books, 1994.
Halsted, Janet Gertrude. "Silas Deane: Intelligence Agent and Ambassador form the Continental Congress." Master's thesis, Southern Connecticut State University, 1999.
Hardman, J., and M. Price. eds. *Louis XVI and the Comte de Vergennes Correspondence, 1774–1787.* New York: Oxford University Press, 1998.
Hardman T. *French Politics, 1774–1789: From the Accession of Louis XVI to the Fall of the Bastille.* London: Oxford University Press, 1995.
Harmer, Harry. *Tom Paine: The Life of a Revolutionary.* London: Haus, 2006.
Hartog, J. *History of St. Eustatius.* Aruba: U.S. Bicentennial Committee of the Netherlands, Aruba, Netherlands Antilles, 1976.
Hartz, Louis. "American Political Thought and the American Revolution." *American Political Science Review* 66 (1952).
Harvey, Robert. *A Few Bloody Noses: The American Revolutionary War.* London: Robinson, 2004.
Hassler, Edgar W. *Old Westmoreland: A History of Western Pennsylvania During the Revolution.* Pittsburgh: 1900.
Hawke, David Freeman. *Everyday Life in Early America.* New York: Harper & Row, 1988.
_____. *Paine.* New York: Harper & Row, 1974.
Hawke, David. *The Colonial Experience.* Indianapolis: 1966.
Haywood, H.L. *Famous Masons and Masonic Presidents.* Richmond, VA; 1945.
Heaton, R.E. *Masonic Membership of the Founding Fathers.* Silver Spring, MD: 1974.
Heimertt, Alan, and Perry Miller, eds. *The Great Awakening.* Indianapolis: 1967.
Heitman, Francis B. *Historical Register of Officers of the Continental Army.* Washington, DC: 1914.
Hemenway, C.C., ed. *Story of Connecticut.* Hartford, CT: Hartford Times, 1936 (Pictures and text by Robert N. Holcomb).
Henderson, H. James. *Party Politics in the Continental Congress.* New York: McGraw-Hill, 1974.
Hendrick, Barton. "America's First Ambassador." *Atlantic Monthly* 66 (April 1935).
Hendrick, Burton J. "Worse Than Arnold." *Atlantic Monthly* 156 (September 1935).
Henkels, Samuel F. *The Confidential Correspondence of Robert Morris.* Philadelphia: 1917.
Henretta, James I. *The Evolution of American Society, 1700–1815.* Lexington, Mass: 1973.
Hibbert, Christopher. *Redcoats and Rebels.* New York: Avon, 1991.
Hielscher, Udo. *Financing the American Revolution.* New York: Museum of American Financial History, 2003.
Higginbottam, Don. *The War of American Independence: Military Attitudes, Policies and Practices, 1763–1789.* New York: MacMillan, 1977.
Higgs, Robert. *Crisis and Leviathan: Critical Episodes in the Growth of American Government.* New York: Oxford University Press, 1987.
Hill, David Jayne. "A Missing Chapter of Franco-American History." *American Historical Review* 21 (1916).
Hoadley, C.J., ed. *Public Records of the Colony of Connecticut.* 2 vols. Hartford: 1857.
Hoadly, Charles J. "Silas Deane." *Pennsylvania Magazine of History and Biography* 1 (1877).
Hodapp, Christopher. *Solomon's Builders.* Berkeley, CA: Ulysses Press, 2007.
Hoffman, Ronald, and Peter Albert. *Diplomacy and Revolutions: The Franco-American Alliance of 1778.* Charlottesville: University of Virginia Press, 1981.
Holbrook, Sabra. *Lafayette.* New York: Atheneum, 1977.
Holcomb, Robert N. *Story of Connecticut.* Vol. 2, *1765–1825.* Hartford, CT: Hartford Times, 1936.
Holmes, David L. *Faith of the Founding Fathers.* New York: Oxford University Press, 2006.
Horsman, Reginald. *Diplomacy of the New Republic, 1776–1815.* Arlington, Illinois: Harlen Davidson, 1985.
Hosley, William N. Jr. *The Great River: Art and Society of the Connecticut River Valley, 1635–1820.* Hartford, CT: Wadsworth Atheneum, 1985.

Howard, Hugh. *Houses of the Founding Fathers*. New York: Artisan, 2007.
_____. Photography by Roger Strong III. "Revolutionary Real Estate." *Smithsonian* 38, no. 9 (December 2007).
Howard, Nora. *Stories of Wethersfield: Four Centuries of American Life in Connecticut's "Most Ancient Town."* Wethersfield, CT: White, 1997.
Howell, Kenneth, and Elinar W. Carlson. *Men of Iron Forbes and Adam*. Lakeville, CT: Pocketknife Press, 1980.
Howell, T.B., ed. *A Complete Collection of State Trials*. Vol. 20. London:1814.
Hudson, Ruth Strong. *The Minister from France: Conrad Alexandre Gérard*. Eulid, OH: Lutz, 1994.
Huntington Library Quarterly. Vol. 24 (1966–67). "Secret Intelligence, 1777: Two Documents."
Hurt, Douglas R. *The Ohio Frontier*. Bloomington: Indiana University Press, 1996.
Hutson, James H. "Intellectual Foundation of Early American Diplomacy." *Diplomatic History* 1 (Winter 1977).
_____. *John Adams and the Diplomacy of the American Revolution*. Lexington: University Press of Kentucky, 1986.
Idzerda, J. Stanley, ed. *Lafayette in the Age of the American Revolution: Selected Letters and Papers*. 5 vols. Ithaca: Cornell University Press, 1977–1980.
Ingraham, Edward Duncan, ed. *Papers in Relation to the Case of Silas Deane Now Published from the Original Manuscripts*. Philadelphia: Seventy-Six Society, 1855.
Isham, Charles. "A Short Account of the Life and Times of Silas Deane." *American Historical Association Papers*. Vol. 3, 1889.
_____. *Silas Deane*: A Paper read before the American Historical Association of Boston and Cambridge, 1887.
_____, ed. *The Deane Papers*. 5 vols. Collections of the New York Historical Society. New York: Published by the Society, 1887–1891.
Issacson, Walter. *Benjamin Franklin: An American Life*. New York: Simon & Schuster, 2003.
Jacob, Margaret. *Living the Enlightenment*. New York: Oxford University Press, 1991.
_____. *The Origins of Freemasonry*. Philadelphia: University of Pennsylvania Press, 2006.
James, Coy Hilton. *Silas Deane: Patriot or Traitor?* Ann Arbor: Michigan State University Press, 1975.
Jameson, J. Franklin. *Privateering and Piracy in the Colonial Period*. 1923. New York: 1970.
Jameson, John Franklin. "St. Eustatius in the American Revolution." *American Historical Review* 8 (July 1903).
Jay, William. *The Life of John Jay*. New York: J&J Harper, 1830.
Jennings, Francis. *The Ambiguous Iroquois Empire*. New York: W.W. Norton, 1984.
_____. *Benjamin Franklin Politician*. New York: W.W. Norton, 1996.
Jenson, Carl. "The Silas Deane House, Wethersfield, Being Restored by the Connecticut Society of Colonial Dames, Drips 'History.'" *Hartford Courant*, Estate Section, Sunday, October 24 1965.
Jillison, Charles A. *Ethan Allen*. Syracuse, NY: 1969.
Jillson, Calvin, and Rick K. Wilson. *Congressional Dynamics: Structure, Coordination and Choice in the First American Congress, 1774–1779*. Stanford, CA: Stanford University Press, 1994.
Johnson, Allen, and Dumas Malone, eds. *Dictionary of American Biography*. 34 vols. New York: Charles Scribner's Sons, 1928–1974 (Volume 5).
Johnson, Herbert A. *John Jay: Colonial Lawyer*. New York: Garland, 1989.
Johnston, Henry P., ed. *The Correspondence and Public Papers of John Jay*. 4 vols. New York: G.P. Putnam's Sons, 1890–93.
Johnston, Henry Phelps. *Yale and Her Honor Roll in the American Revolution, 1775–1783*. New York: Privately Printed, 1888.
Johnstone, Ruth Y. "American Privateers in French Ports, 1776–1778." *Pennsylvania Magazine of History and Biography* 53 (October 1929).
Jones, Alice Hanson. *American Colonial Wealth: Documents and Methods*, 3 vols. New York: Arno Press, 1977.
_____. *Wealth of a Nation to Be: The American Colonies on the Eve of the American Revolution*. New York: Columbia University Press, 1980.

Jones, Colin. *The Great Nation: France from Louis XVI to Napoleon.* New York: Columbia University Press, 2002.
Journals of the American Congress from 1774–1788. Washington, DC: 1823.
Kahn, David. *The Codebreaker: The Comprehensive History of Secret Communication from Ancient Times to the Internet.* New York: Scribner 1996.
Kammen, Michael G. *A Rope of Sand: The Colonial Agents, British Politics and the American Revolution.* Ithaca, NY: Cornell University Press, 1968.
Kapp, Friedrich. *The Life of John Kalb, Major General in the Revolutionary Army.* New York: 1884.
Keane, John. *Tom Paine: A Political Life.* Boston: Little, Brown, 1995.
Kelly, J. Frederick. *Early Domestic Architecture of Connecticut.* New Haven: Yale University Press, 1924.
_____. *Early Domestic Architecture of Connecticut.* New York: Dover, 1924.
Kennedy, Lawrence F. ed. *Biographical Directory of the American Congress, 1774–1971.* Washington DC: Government Printing Office, 1971.
Kennedy, Roger G. *Mr. Jefferson's Lost Cause: Land, Farmers, Slavery and the Louisiana Purchase.* New York: Oxford University Press, 2003.
Kenyon, Cecilia M. "Republicanism and Radicals in the American Revolution: An Old Fashion Interpretation." *William and Mary Quarterly* 19, 3rd series (April 1962).
Kerr, Wilford Benton. *Bermuda and the American Revolution, 1760–1783.* Princeton: Princeton University Press, 1936.
Ketchum, Richard M. *Saratoga.* New York: Henry Holt, 1997.
Kierner, Cynthia A. *Traders and Gentlefolk: The Livingstons of New York, 1675–1790.* Ithaca: Cornell University Press, 1992.
Kite, Elizabeth S. *Beaumarchais and the War for American Independence.* Vol. 2. Boston: Richard G. Badger, Gorman Press, 1918.
_____. "Benjamin Franklin Diplomat." *Catholic World* 142 (1935).
_____. "French 'Secret Aid,' Precursor to the French-American Alliance, 1776–1777." *French American Review* (April 1948).
_____. "How the Declaration of Independence Reached Europe." *Daughters of the American Revolution* 62, no. 7 (July 1928).
_____. "Lafayette and His Companions on the *Victoire*." *Records of the American Catholic Historical Society* 45, no. 1 (March 1934).
Kite, Elizabeth Sarah. "America's First Envoy to France." *Common-weal* 4 (August, 26 1925).
_____. "Silas Deane: Diplomatist and Patriot Scapegoat of the Revolution." *Daughters of the American Revolution* 60 (1926).
Kloppenberg, James T. "Christianity, Republicanism, and Ethics in Early American Discourse." *Journal of American History* 74 (June 1987).
Knapp, Mary E. "John the Painter and Silas Deane." *Yale University Library Gazette* 39 (April 1955).
Konstam, Angus, and Angus McBride. *Privateers and Pirates, 1730–1830.* Oxford: Osprey, 2001.
Krebs, Albert. "Un Alsacien trop oublié: Conrad-Alexandre Gérard, Artisan de l'indépendance des Etats-Unis." *Revue d'Alzace* 95 (1956).
Labourdette, Jean-Francois. *Vergennes: Ministre principal de Louis XVI.* Paris: Editions Desjonquiefes, 1990.
Lacey, Barbara E. "Gender, Piety and Secularization in Connecticut Religion, 1720–1770." *Journal of Social History* 24 (Summer 1991).
LaFontaine, E.C., de. "Paul Jones." *AGC* 44 (1934).
Laland, Patricia O. "Virginia's Stratford: Home of the Lees." *Early American Life* (April 2004).
Lambert, Frank. "Subscribing for Profits and Piety: The Friendship of Benjamin Franklin and George Whitefield." *William and Mary Quarterly* 50, 3rd series (July 1993).
Langguth, A.J. *Patriots: The Men Who Started the American Revolution.* New York: Simon & Schuster, 1988.
Latako, Andreas. *Lafayette: A Life.* Translated from the German by E.W. Dickes. Garden City, New York: Doubleday, Doran, 1936.
Leamon, James S. *Revolution Downeast: The War for American Independence in Maine.* Amherst: University of Massachusetts Press, 1993.

Leckie, Robert. *"A Few Acres of Snow": The Saga of the French and Indian War.* Hoboken, NJ: John Willey & Sons, 1999. Reprn., Castle: 2006.

———. *George Washington's War: The Saga of the American Revolution.* New York: Harper Perenial, 1993.

LeCorbeiler, Clare. *European and American Snuff Boxes.* New York: Viking: 1978.

Lee, Arthur. *Extracts from a Letter Written to the President of Congress, by the Hon. Arthur Lee, Esquire, inAanswer to a Libel, Published in the Pennsylvania Gazette, on the Fifth of December, 1778 by Silas Deane, Esquire.* Philadelphia: Francis Bailey, 1780.

Lee, R.H. *Memoir of the Life of Richard Henry Lee, and His Correspondence with the Most Distinguised Men in America and Europe, Illustrative of Their Character and the Events of the American Revolution.* 2 vols. Philadelphia: 1825.

Lee, Richard Henry. *Life of Arthur Lee.* 2 vols. Boston: Wells & Lilley, 1829.

Leffman, Henry. *"The Real Thomas Paine, Patriot and Publicist: A Philosopher Misunderstood." Pennsylvania Magazine of History and Biography* 46 1922.

Lemay, J.A. Leo. *Deism, Masonry and Enlightenment.* Newark: University of Delaware Press, 1987.

Lemish, Jesse. "Jack Tar in the Streets: Merchant Seamen in the Politics of Revolutionary America." *William and Mary Quarterly* 25 (July 1968).

"Letter to Silas Deane to his Brother Simeon Deane." *Pennsylvania Magazine of History and Biography* 17 (1893).

Lever, Maurice. *Beaumarchais: A Biography.* Translated by Susan Emanuel. New York: Farrar, Straus and Giroux, 2009.

Livermore, Shaw. *Early American Land Companies: Their Influence on Corporated Development.* New York: Commonwealth Fund; London: Oxford University Press, 1939.

Livsey, R., ed. *The Prisoners of 1776: A Relic of the Revolution Compiled from the Journal of Charles Herbert.* Boston: 1854.

Lockridge, Kenneth A. *Literacy in Colonial New England.* New York: 1977.

Loménie, Louis de. *Beaumarchais and His Friends.* Translated by Henry S. Edwards. London: Addey, 1856.

———. *Beaumarchais et son Temps.* 4 vols. Paris: Michel Lévy frèves, 1856.

Lopez, Claude-Anne. "Saltpeter, Tin and Gunpowder: Addenda to the Correspondence of Lavorsier and Franklin." *Annals of Science* 16 (1960).

Louis XVI. *Louis XVI and the Comte de Vergennes: Correspondence, 1774–1787.* Edited by John Hardman and Munro Price. Oxford: Voltaire Foundation, 1998.

Love, William Deloss. *The Colonial History of Hartford.* U.S. Bicentennial ed. Chester, CT: Pequot Press, 1974.

Lutnick, Solomon. *The American Revolution and the British Press, 1775–1783.* Columbia: University of Missouri Press, 1967.

Maclay, Edgar S. *A History of American Privateers.* New York: D. Appleton, 1899.

Mahan, Alfred T. *The Major Operation of the Navies in the War of American Independence.* London: 1913.

Maier, Pauline. *From Resistance to Revolution: Colonial Radicals and the Development of American Opposition to Britain.* New York: Alfred A. Knopf, 1972. Reprn., Vintage Books, 1974.

———. *The Old Revolutionaries: Political Lives in the Age of Samuel Adams.* New York: Vintage Books, 1982.

Main, Jackson Turner. *Political Parties Before the Constitution.* Chapel Hill: University of North Carolina Press, 1973.

———. *The Social Structure of Revolutionary America.* Princeton, NJ: Princeton University Press, 1965.

Malloy, William M., comp. *Treaties, Conventions, International Acts, Protocols and Agreements Between the United States of America and Other Powers, 1776–1909.* Vol. 1. New York: Greenwood Press, 1970. Reprn.

Mann, Bruce H. *Neighbors and Strangers: Law and Community in Early Connecticut.* Chapel Hill: University of North Carolina Press, 1987.

Marshall, Peter. "Lord Hillsborough, Samuel Wharton and the Ohio Grant." *English Historical Review* 80 (1965).

Martin, Asa E. "American Privateers and the West Indies Trade, 1776–1777." *American Historical Review* 39 (July 1934).
Martin, Gaston. "Commercial Relations Between Nantes and American Colonies." *Journal of Economic and Business History* 4 (August 1932).
Martin, James Kirby. *Benedict Arnold: Revolutionary Hero.* New York: 1997.
Martin, Margaret E. *Merchants and Trade of the Connecticut River Valley, 1750–1820.* Northampton, MA: 1939.
Martindale, Meredith. "Benjamin Franklin's Residence in France." *Antiques,* August 1977.
_____. "L'Hôtel de Valentinois et ses environs au Benjamin Franklin." *Bulletin de la Société Historique d'Auteuil et de Passy* 15, no. 2 (1978).
Matson, Cathy D., and Peter S. Onuf. *A Union of Interests: Political and Economic Thought in Revolutionary America.* Lawrence: University of Kansas Press, 1990.
Maurer, David. "Connecticut's Ancient River Town." *Colonial Homes,* April 1996.
_____. "The Many Faces of Historic Wethersfield, Connecticut's Ancient River Town." *Colonial Homes,* April 1966.
McClellan, William S. *Smuggling in the American Colonies at the Outbreak of the Revolution.* New York: Williams College Press, 1912.
McCullough, David. *John Adams.* New York: Simon & Schuster, 2001.
_____. *1776.* New York: Simon & Schuster, 2005.
McDougill, Walter, A. *Freedom Just Around the Corner: American History 1585–1828.* New York: Simon & Schuster, 2004.
McEvers, Hugh. "Silas Deane's Scheme Too Revolutionary: Sold Jay on Attacking England." *Hartford Courant,* Sunday, June 2 1962.
McMahon, Darrin M. "From the Happiness of Virtue to the Virtue of Happiness, 400 BC–1780 AD." *Daedalus,* Winter 2003.
Meacham, Jon. *American Gospel: God, the Founding Fathers and the Making of a Nation.* New York: Random House, 2006.
Melville, Phillip S. "Eleven Guns for the Grand Union." *American Heritage* 9, no. 6 (October 1958).
Meng, John J. *The Comte de Vergennes: European Phases of His American Diplomacy, 1774–1780.* Washington DC: Catholic University Press, 1935.
_____. "A Footnote to Secret Aid in the American Revolution." *American Historical Review* 43 (1938).
_____. "French Diplomacy in Philadelphia, 1778–79." *Catholic Historical Review* 24 (1938).
Meng, John Joseph. *Despatches and Instructions of Conrad Alexandre Gérard, 1778–1780.* Baltimore: Johns Hopkins Press, 1939.
Merrill, James H. "Some Thoughts on Colonial History and American Indians." *William and Mary Quarterly* 46, 3rd series (1989).
Middlebrook, Louis F. *History of Maritime Connecticut During the American Revolution.* 2 Vols. Salem, MA: Essex Institute, 1925.
Middlekauff, Robert. *Benjamin Franklin and His Enemies.* Berkley: University of California Press, 1996.
_____. *The Glorious Cause: The American Revolution, 1763–1789.* New York: Oxford University Press, 1982.
Middleton, Arthur Pierce. *Tobacco Coast: A Maritime History of the Chesapeake Bay in the Colonial Era.* Baltimore, London: Johns Hopkins University Press and Maryland State Archives, 1984.
Middleton, Richard. *Colonial America: A History, 1585–1776.* 3rd ed. Oxford, England: Blackwell, 2002.
Millar, John F. *American Ships of the Colonial and Revolutionary Period.* New York: 1898.
Miller, Hal. "Silas Deane: Father of the American Navy." *Connecticut Circle,* February 1944.
Miller, Hunter, ed. *Treaties and Other International Acts of the United States of America.* Washington DC: Government Printing Office, 1931.
Miller, John C. *Origins of the American Revolution.* Boston, 1948.
_____. *Triumph of Freedom, 1775–1783.* Boston: Little, Brown, 1948.

Miller, John T., and Mark Molesky. *Our Oldest Enemy: A History of America's Disastrous Relationship with France*. New York: Doubleday, 2004.
Miller, Lilian, B., ed. *Selected Papers of Charles Willson Peale and His Family*. 5 vols. New Haven, CT: Yale University Press, 1939–2000.
Miller, Margaret. "The Spy Activities of Dr. Edward Bancroft." *Journal of Modern History* 22 (1928).
Miller, Nathan. *Broadsides: The Age of Fighting Sale, 1775–1815*. New York: John Wiley, 2001.
———. *Sea of Glory: The Continental Navy Fights for Independence, 1775–1783*. New York: 1974.
———. *Spying for America: The Hidden History of U.S. Intelligence*. New York: Marlowe, 1997.
Moise, Sidney. *Freemasonry of the American Revolution*. Washington DC: 1924.
Montross, Lynn. *The Reluctant Rebels: The Story of the Continental Congress, 1774–1789*. New York: Barnes & Noble, 1950.
Morgan, Edmund S. "The Puritan Ethic and the American Revolution." *William and Mary Quarterly* 14, 3rd series (October 1967).
———. *Benjamin Franklin*. New Haven, CT: Yale University Press, 2002.
———. *The Gentle Puritan: A Life of Ezra Stiles, 1727–1795*. 1962. New York: W.W. Norton, 1984.
Morgan, Edmund, S., and Helen M. Morgan. *The Stamp Act Crisis: Prologue to Revolution*. New York: 1965.
Morris, James M. *History of the U.S. Navy*. North Dighton, MA: Publications Group, Rev, ed., 2002.
Morris, Richard B. *Seven Who Shaped Our Destiny: The Founding Fathers as Revolutionaries*. New York: Harper & Row, 1973.
———, ed. *John Jay: The Making of a Revolutionary; Unpublished Papers, 1745–1780*. 2 vols. New York: Harper & Row, 1980.
Morris, S. Brent (PhD, 33°). *The Complete Idiot's Guide to Freemasonry*. New York: Alpha, 2006.
Morrison, Samuel Elliot. *John Paul Jones: A Sailor's Biography*. Boston: Little, Brown, 1959.
Morse, Sidney G. "Yankee Privateersmen of 1776." *New England Quarterly* 17 (1944).
Morton, Brian N. "Roderique Hortalez to Secret Committee: An Unpublished French Policy Statement of 1777." *French Review* 50 (May 1777).
Morton, Brian N., and Donald C. Spinelli. *Beaumarchais and the American Revolution*. Lanham, MD: Lexington Books, 2003.
———. *Beaumarchais: A Biography*. Ann Arbor, MI: Olivia and Hill, 1988.
———, eds. *Correspondence of Pierre Augustin Caron de Beaumarchais*. 4 vols. Paris: Nizet, 1969.
Mulkearn, Lois, ed. *George Mercer Papers Relating to the Ohio Company*. Pittsburgh: 1954.
Nash, Gary B. *The Unknown American Revolution*. New York: Viking, 2005.
———. *The Urban Crucible: Social Change, Political Consciousness and the Origins of the American Revolution*. Cambridge: Harvard University, 1979.
Neeser, R.W., ed. *Letters and Papers Relating to the Cruises of Gustavous Conyngham*. Vol. 6. New York: Naval History Society, 1915.
Neeser, Robert W., ed. *Letters and Papers Related to the Cruises of Gustavus Conyngham*. New York: Associated Faculty Press, 1970.
Nelson, Craig. *Thomas Paine: Enlightenment, Revolution and the Birth of Modern Nations*. New York: Viking, Penguin, 2006.
Nelson, James L. *George Washington's Secret Navy: How the American Revolution Went to Sea*. New York: McGraw Hill, 2008.
Nettels, Cortes P. *The Economic History of the United States: The Emergence of a National Economy, 1775–1815*. New York: Holt, Rinehart and Winston, 1962.
Neustadt, Katherine D. *Carpenter's Hall: Meeting Place of History*. Philadelphia: 1981.
New England Historical and Genealogical Register. 104 vols. Boston, 1847–.
Newman, A. "Politics and Freemasonry in the Eighteenth Century." *AQC* 104 (London, 1992).
Nordholt, J.W. Schultz. *The Dutch Republic and American Independence*. Chapel Hill: University of North Carolina Press, 1982.
Oakley, Imogen. *Historic Homesteads*. Philadelphia: University of Pennsylvania Press, 1962.
Oberholtz, Ellis Paxon. *Robert Morris: Patriot and Financier*. New York: Macmillan, 1968.

Olson, Alison Gilbert, and Richard Maxwell Brown, eds. *Anglo-American Political Relations, 1765–1775*. New Brunswick: 1970.
Onuf, Peter, S., ed. *Patriots, Radicals and Loyalists*. New York: Garland, 1991.
O'Shaughnessy, Andrew Jackson. *An Empire Divided: The American Revolution and the British Caribbean*. Philadelphia: University of Pennsylvania Press, 2000.
O'Tolle, G.J.A. "Benjamin Franklin: Spymaster or British Mole?" *International Journal of Intelligence and Counter Intelligence* 3, no. 1 (Spring 1989).
_____. *Encyclopedia of American Intelligence and Espionage*. New York: Facts on File, 1989.
_____. *Honorable Treachery*. New York: Atlantic Monthly Press, 1991.
_____. "Intrigue in Paris." In *Secret New England: Spies of the American Revolution*. Edited by Edmund R. Thompson. Portland, ME: Provincial Press, 2001.
_____. "Kahn's Law: A Universal Principal of Intelligence?" *International Journal of Intelligence and Counter Intelligence* 4, no. 1 (Spring 1990).
Ousterhout, Anne M. "Frontier Vengeance: Connecticut Yankees vs. Pennamites in the Wyoming Valley." *Pennsylvania History* 62 (Summer 1995).
Palmer, Dave R. *George Washington and Benedict Arnold*. Washington DC: Regnery, 2006.
Paltist, Victor Hugo. "The Use of Invisible Ink for Secret Writing During the American Revolution." *Bulletin of the New York Public Library* 39, no. 5 (May 1935).
Paris Papers, or Mr. Silas Deane's Late Intercepted Letters to His Brothers and Other Intimate Friends in America. New York: 1782. ("This being a reprint by James Rivington from his *Royal Gazette* for October 24–December 12, 1781.")
Parrington, Vernon L. *Main Currents in American Thought The Colonial Mind 1 1620–1800*. New York: Harcourt, Brace and World, 1954.
Patton, Robert H. *Patriot Pirates: The Privateer War for Freedom and Fortune in the American Revolution*. New York: Pantheon Books, 2008.
Paullin, Charles O., ed. *Outletters of the Marine Committee and Board of Admiralty*. Vol. 2. New York: 1941.
Paullin, Charles Oscar. *The Navy of the American Revolution*. Cleveland: 1906.
Pavlovsky, Arnold M. "Between Hawk and Buzzard: Congress as Perceived by Its Members, 1775–1783." *William and Mary Quarterly*, 3rd series: 349–364.
Peale, Charles Willson. *The Short Talk Bulletin* 80, no. 1 (January 2002). (Silver Spring, MD: Masonic Service Assoication of North America.)
Peckman, Howard H. "Documents of Freedom." *American Heritage* 16, no. 4 (June 1965).
Pennsylvania Gazette. 1728–1789. "A Reprint Edition, in Cooperation with the Historical Society of Pennsylvania." 25 vols. Philadelphia: Microurance, 1968.
Pennsylvania Packet, or General Advertiser. July 4–December 31, 1778–79 (7/4/78–12/31/79).
Papers Appertaining to the Silas Deane Claim. Facsimiles of Letters and papers covering 1775 to 1777 relating to Deane's diplomatic mission to France. No publisher, 1890.
Perkins, Elizabeth. *Border Life*. Chapel Hill: University of North Carolina, 1997.
Perkins, James Breck. *France in the American Revolution*. Boston: Houghton Mifflin, 1911.
_____. *France in the American Revolution*. 1911. Repr., Whitefish, Montana: Kessinger, 2006.
Perrault, Gilles. *La Revanche américaine: Le Secret du Roi*. Paris: Fayard, 1996.
Perry, Charles, ed. *Founders and Leaders of Connecticut, 1633–1783*. Boston: D.C. Heath, 1934.
Petrie, Donald A. *The Prize Game: Lawful Looting on the High Seas in the Days of Fighting Sail*. New York: Berkeley, 1999.
Phillips, Kevin P. *The Cousin's War: Religions Politics and the Triumph of Anglo-America*. NY: Oxford University Press, 2001.
Pierre, Manuel. *La police de Paris dévoilée*. 2 vols. Paris: Gerney: 1791.
Plumb, J.H. "The French Connection." *American Heritage* 26, no. 1 (December 1974).
Plus, Mark. *Samuel Adams: Father of the American Revolution*. New York: Palgrave MacMillan, 2006.
Pocock, J.G.A *Virtue, Commerce and History: Essays on Political Thought and History, Chiefly in the Eighteenth Century*. Cambridge: Cambridge University Press, 1985.
_____. "Virtue and Commerce in the Eighteenth Century." *Journal of Interdisciplinary History* 3 (Summer 1972).

Potts, Louis W. *Arthur Lee: A Virtuous Revolutionary*. Baton Rouge: Louisiana State University Press, 1981.
Prelinger, Catherine M. "Benjamin Franklin and the American Prisoners of War in England During the American Revolution." *William and Mary Quarterly* 32, 3rd series (April 1915).
Price, Jacob M. "*Economic Functions of the Growth of American Port Towns in the Eighteenth Century.*" *Perspectives in American History* 8 (1974).
Price, M. *Preserving the Monarchy: The Comte de Vergennes 1774–1787*. Cambridge: Cambridge University Press, 1995.
Public Document of the 27th Congress, 2nd Session, in the Senate of the United States, February 3, 1842. Ordered to be printed: *Revolutionary Claims Committee Report* to accompany Senate Bill 155 submitted by Mr. Phelps.
Public Records of the Colony of Connecticut and the Public Records of the State of Connecticut, 1773–1787. Hartford: 1887–1945.
Purcell, L. Edward. *Who Was Who in the American Revolution*. New York: Facts on File, 1993.
Radford, Phyllis. "The Troubles of Silas Deane." *New England Galaxy* 13, no. 3 (1972) (Sturbridge, MA).
Rakove, Jack. *The Beginnings of National Politics: An Interpretive History of the Continental Congress*. New York: Knopf, 1979.
———. "French Diplomacy and American Politics: The First Crisis, 1779." *Mid-America* 60 (1978).
"Ralph Izard–Henry Laurens Correspondence." *South Carolina Historical and Genealogical Magazine* 21–22 (1920–21).
Ralston, Hayden. "The Apostasy of Silas Deane." *Magazine of History* 16 (March 1913).
Randall, E.O. "Washington's Ohio Lands." *Ohio Archaeological and Historical Quarterly* 19 (July 1990).
Randall, William Sterne. *Benedict Arnold, Patriot and Traitor*. New York: William Morrow, 1990.
Raphael, Ray. *The First American Revolution: Before Lexington and Concord*. New York: New Press, 2002.
Records of the Bureau of Accounting, Fiscal Section. "Mr. Deane's Accounts with Mr. Bareley's Observations," Record Group 39, National Archives.
Relin, David Oliver. "Not Necessarily the News." *Scholastic Search (American History)* 21, no. 1 (September 1992).
Renault, Francis Paul. *L'espionage naval au XVIIIe siècle*. Paris: 1936.
"Revolutionary Debts." 15th Congress, 1st Session, House Document 1823, Series 9, No. 3. Repeated in the 20th Congress, 1st Session, House Document and Debt to Silas Deane.
Reynolds, Donna L. "Wethersfield People and Their Portraits." *Antiques*, March 1976.
Rhoden, Nancy L., and Ian K. Steele. eds. *The Human Tradition in the American Revolution*. Wilmington, DE: Scholarly Resources, 2000.
Richardson, Nancy. "A Pride of Boxes." *House and Gardens*, May 1983.
Ridley, Jasper. *The Freemasons*. New York: 2001.
Riggs, A.R. *The Nine Lives of Arthur Lee, Virginia Patriot*. Williamsburg: 1976.
Riley, James C. *International Government Finance and the Amsterdam Capital Market, 1740–1815*. Cambridge: Cambridge University Press, 1980.
Risch, Erna. *Supplying Washington's Army*. Washington DC: 1981.
Ritcheon, Charles R. *Aftermath of Revolution: British Policy Toward the United States, 1783–1795*. Dallas: Southern Methodist University Press, 1986.
Roberts, Allen E. *G. Washington: Master Mason*. Richmond, VA: Macoy & Masonic Supply Co., 1976.
Ross, Winfield. "Life in Early America: The Real Benjamin Franklin." *Early American Life* 37, no. 1 (February, 2006).
Rossiter, Clinton. "The Political Theory of Benjamin Franklin." *Pennsylvania Magazine of History and Biography*, July 1952.
Roth, Philip A. *Masonry in the Formation of Our Government*. Milwaukee: 1927.
Rouzeau, L. "Aperçus du role de Nantes dans la guerre d'indépendance d'Amerique, 1775–1783." *Annales de Bretagne* 14 (1967).

Rownan, John S., eds. *The Founding Fathers: The Men Behind the Nation*. North Dighton, MA: World, 2005.
Royster, Charles. *The Fabulous History of the Dismal Swamp Company*. New York: Vintage Books, 2000.
Sabine, Lorenzo. *Biographical Sketches of Loyalists of the American Revolution*. Vol. 1, 2nd ed. Boston: Little, Brown, 1864.
Saltonstall, Leverett. *Ancestry and Descendents of Sir Richard Saltonstall: First Associate of the Massachusetts Bay Colony and Patentee of Connecticut*. Cambridge: Riverside Press, 1897.
Sanderson, John P. *The Views and Opinions of American Statesmen on Foreign Immigration*. Philadelphia: 1856.
Savelle, Max. "Colonial Origins of American Diplomatic Principles." *Pacific Historical Review* 3 (1934.)
Schaper, Thomas J. *France and America in the Revolutionary Era: The Life of Jacques-Donatien Lezy de Chaumont*. Providence: Berghohn Books, 1995.
Schiff, Stacey. *A Great Improvisation: Franklin, France and the Birth of America*. New York: Henry Holt, 2005.
Schlesinger, Arthur M. *The Colonial Merchants and the American Revolution, 1773–1776*. New York: 1917.
Scott, Kenneth. comp. *Rivington's New York Newspaper: Excerpts from a Loyalist Press, 1773–1783*. New York: 1973.
Secret Journals of Congress, May 10, 1775 to October 26, 1787; Papers of the Continental Congress. National Archives, Washington, DC.
Secret Journals of the Acts and Proceedings of Congress [of the Confederation]. 4 vols. Boston: 1821.
Seeman, Erik R. *Pious Persuasion: Laity and Clergy in the Eighteenth Century New England*. Baltimore: Johns Hopkins University Press, 1999.
Seleskey, Harold E. *War and Society in Colonial Connecticut*. New Haven: Yale University Press, 1990.
Sellers, Charles C. The Artist of the Revolution: The Early Life of Charles Willson Peale. Hebron, CT: 1939.
Selser, Vernon G. "*Did Americans Originate the Conditional Most Favored Nation Clause?*" Journal of American History, V 1933.
Shalhope, Robert E. "Republicanism and Early America Historiography." *William and Mary Quarterly* 39, 3rd series (April 1982).
Shelburne Papers. Vol. 38. Clement Library, Ann Arbor, Michigan.
Shewmake, Antoinette, ed. and trans. *For the Good of Mankind: Pierre-Augustin Caron de Beaumarchais: Political Correspondence Relative to the American Revolution*. Lanham, MD: University Press of America, 1987.
Shipperson, Archibald B. *John Paradise and Lucy Ludwell of London and Williamsburg*. Richmond: 1942.
Silas Deane Manuscript Papers. Boxes 384–389. Collections of the Connecticut Historical Society, Hartford, CT.
"Silas Deane's Account and Documents." Account Ledger Book No. 6037 given to the Connecticut Historical Society, Hartford, CT, by special act of Congress in 1874.
Silas Deane's address "To the Free and Virtuous Citizens of America." *Pennsylvania Packet*, December 5, 1778.
Silverstone, Paul H. *The Sailing Navy: 1775–1854*. Annapolis, MD: Naval Institute Press, 2001.
Sizer, Theodore, ed. *The Autobiography of Colonel John Trumbull*. New Haven, CT: Yale University Press, 1953.
Skousen, Mark, comp., ed. *The Completed Autobiography by Benjamin Franklin*. Washington DC: Regnery, 2006.
Sloane, Eric. *American Yesterdays*. New York: Funk & Wagnalls, 1956.
Smith, Paul, ed. *Letters of the Delegates to Congress, 1774—1789*. Washington DC: Library of Congress, 1976—2000.
Smith, Paul H. "Benjamin Franklin: Gun Runner." *Pennsylvania Magazine of History and Biography* 95 (1971).

_____, ed. *Letters of the Delegates to Congress, 1774–1789.* 26 vols. Washington DC: U.S. Printing Office, 1976–2000.

_____, ed. *Letters of Delegates to Congress, 1774–1789.* 24 vols. to date, Washington DC: Library of Congress, 1996-.

Snowman, A. Kenneth. *Eighteenth Century Gold Boxes of Europe.* New York: Faber & Faber, 1971.

"Some Accounts of James Hutton's Visit to Franklin in France in December 1777." *Pennsylvania Magazine of History and Biography* 32 (1908).

Somma, Ann Marie. "A Patriot Long Forgotten." *Hartford Courant*, Section B, "Connecticut," January 8, 2007.

Sosin, Jack M. *Agents and Merchants: British Colonial Policy and the Origins of the American Revolution.* Lincoln: University of Nebraska Press, 1965.

Sparks, Jared. *The Diplomatic Correspondence of the American Revolution.* 6 vols. Boston: Nathan Hale, Gary and Bowen, 1829.

_____. *Library of American Biography.* Boston, MA: Little, Brown, 1845.

_____. *The Life of Gouverneur Morris, with Selections from His Correspondence and Miscellaneous Papers.* Vol 1. Boston: 1832.

Stahr, Walter. *John Jay: Founding Father.* New York: Palgrave Macmillan, 2005.

Stemper, W.M. "Conflicts and Developments in Eighteenth Century Freemasonry: American Context." *AQC* 104 (London, 1992).

Stephenson, O.W. "The Supply of Gunpowder in 1776." *American Historical Review* 30, no. 2 (January 1925).

Stevens, Benjamin Franklin, ed. *Facsimiles of Manuscripts in European Archives Relating to America, 1773–1783.* 25 vols. London: C. Whittingham, 1889–1898.

Stille, Charles. "Silas Deane, Diplomatist of the Revolution." *The Pennsylvania Magazine of History and Biography* 18 (1894).

Stimson, Henry L., and George Bundy. *On Active Service in Peace and War.* New York: Harper & Brothers, 1947.

Stinchcomte, William. *The American Revolution and the French Alliance.* Syracuse: Syracuse University Press, 1969.

Stinchcombe, William C. "John Adams and the Model Treaty." *Diplomatic History* 1 (Winter 1977).

_____. "A Note on Silas Deane's Death." *William and Mary Quarterly* 32, no. 4 (1973).

Stoblecki, Edith J. *Paul Revere and Freemasonry.* Boston: Paul Revere Memorial Association, 1985.

Stoeckel, Herbert J. "James Bond Minus 175 Years: Escapades of America's First Spy in Europe, Silas Deane of Wethersfield, reads like an Ian Fleming Mystery." *Hartford Courant Magazine,* September 20, 1964.

Stokes, Anson Phelps. *Memorial of Eminent Yale Men.* New Haven: Yale University Press, 1914.

Stoll, Ira. *Samuel Adams: A Life.* New York: Free Press, 2008.

Storch, Neil T. "The Recall of Silas Deane." *Connecticut Historical Society Bulletin* 38, no. 1 (January 1973).

Stourzh, Gerald. *Benjamin Franklin and American Foreign Policy.* Rev. ed. Chicago: University of Chicago Press, 1969.

_____. *Benjamin Franklin and American Foreign Policy*, 2nd edition. Chicago: University of Chicago Press, 1964.

Stout, Harry S. "Religion, Communications and the Ideological Origins of the American Revolution." *William and Mary Quarterly* 34 (1977).

Streeter, Floyd B. "The Diplomatic Career of William Carmichael." *Maryland History Magazine* 8 (June 1913).

Summerson, John. *The Architecture of the Eighteenth Century.* New York: Thames & Hudson, 1994.

Sumner, William Graham. *The Financier and the Finances of the American Revolution.* 2 vols. New York: Dodd, Mead, 1976.

Syrett, David. *The Royal Navy in European Waters: During the American Revolution.* Columbia: University of South Carolina, 1998.

Tabbert, Mark. *Freemasons: Three Centuries of Building Communities.* 2005.
Talbott, Page. *Benjamin Franklin: In Search of a Better World.* New Haven, CT: Yale University Press, 2005. (This extensive Ben Franklin biographic source list reluctantly provides a rich source of pertinent information concerning Deane's responsibilities and actions not found in his own writings.)
Tallmadge, Benjamin. *Memoir of Colonel Benjamin Tallmadge.* 1808. New York: Arno Press, 1968.
Tatsch, J. Hugo. *Freemasonry in the Thirteen Colonies.* New York, 1929.
Taylor, Alan. *American Colonies: The Settling of North America.* New York: Penguin, 2001.
Thomas, Evan. *John Paul Jones.* New York: Simon & Schuster, 2003.
Tolles, Frederick B. "Franklin and the Pulteney Mission: An Episode in the Secret History of the American Revolution." *Huntington Library Quarterly* (1953).
Tolson, Jay. "Inside the Masons." *U.S. News & World Report.* September 5, 2005.
Towler, William, Jr. *The Baron of Beacon Hill: A Biography of John Hancock.* Boston: Houghton Mifflin, 1980.
Triber, E. Jayne. *A True Republican: The Life of Paul Revere.* Amherst: University of Massachusetts, 1998.
Trumbull, J. Hammond, ed. *Correspondence of Silas Deane, Delegate to the First and Second Congress at Philadelphia, 1774–1776.* Vol. 2. Collections of the Connecticut Historical Society. Hartford: Published by the Society, 1870.
Trumbull, James H., and Charles J. Hoadley. eds. *Public Records of the Colony of Connecticut 1636–1776.* 15 vols. Hartford: 1850–1890.
Tuchman, Barbara W. *The First Salute: A View of the American Revolution.* New York: Ballantine, 1988.
Tyler, John W. *Smugglers and Patriots: Boston Merchants and the Advent of the American Revolution.* Boston: Northeastern University Press, 1986.
Unger, Harlow Giles. *John Hancock: Merchant King and American Patriot.* NJ: Castle, 2005.
_____. *Lafayette.* New York: John Wiley & Sons. 2002.
Urban, Sylvanus, ed. *Gentlemen's Magazine and Historical Chronicle* 59, 60. London: John Nichols, 1789 & 1790.
U.S. Congress. House of Representatives. Committee of Revolutionary Claims. *Report on Settlement of Accounts of Silas Deane.* House Report 952, to accompany S. 155, 27th Congress, 2nd Session. Washington: Government Printing Office, 1842.
U.S. Congress. Senate. Committee of Revolutionary Claims. *Report Made by Mr. Smith of Connecticut.* Senate Report 201, to accompany S 155, 26th Congress, 2nd Session. Washington: Blair & Rives, 1841.
Utrilla, J.F. Yela. *Espana ante la independencia de los Estados Unidos.* 2 vols. Lerid, 1925.
Van Doren, Carl. *The Secret War of Independence.* New York: Viking, 1941.
Van Dusen, Albert E. *Connecticut.* New York: Random House, 1961.
Van Powell, W. Holland. *The American Navies of the Revolutionary War.* New York: 1974.
Van Tyne, C.H. "French Aid Before the Alliance of 1778." *American Historical Review* 31 (1925).
Van Tyne, Claude H. "French Aid Before the Alliance of 1778." *American Historical Review* 31 (October 1925).
_____. "Influence Which Determined the French Government to Make the Treaty with America in 1778." *American Historical Review* 31 (October 1925).
Van Vlack, Milt. "In Celebration of George Washington Bicentennial: Washington's Masonic Ideals Live on Two Centuries Later." *Boothbay Register,* August 26, 1999.
_____. *Silas Deane: Early Connecticut Leaders.* A Multimedia Instructional Kit. Hartford, CT: Hartford Board of Education, 1968.
_____. "Silas Deane, 1737–1789: A Strange Patriot from Groton." *Connecticut Circle,* September/October 1965.
Van Vlack, Milton C. "The Influence of John Adams Upon the Peace Negotiations of 1779 to 1783." Bachelor's thesis, Bates College, 1953.
_____. "North Canaan's Place in Connecticut History: An Eighteenth Century Iron Country Village." *North Canaan Connecticut Western News,* May 22, 1958.
_____. "A Survey of Writings Concerning the Controversial Envoy Silas Deane, 1776–1789." Master's thesis, Trinity College, 1958.

Vansittard, Peter. *John Paul Jones: A Restless Spirit.* London: Robson Books, 2004.
Ver Steeg, Clarence L. *Robert Morris: Revolutionary Financier.* Philadelphia: 1954.
Vickers, Daniel. "The Northern Colonies: Economy on Society." In *The Cambridge Economic History of the United States.* Edited by Stanley L. Ehigerman and Robert E. Gallman. Cambridge: Cambridge University Press, 1996.
Villers, Patrick. *Le commerce colonial atlantique et la guerre d'indépendence des élats unis d'Amérique, 1778–83.* New York: 1972.
Volo, James M. *Blue Water Patriots: The American Revolution Afloat.* Lanham, MD: Rowman & Littlefield, 2006.
Wadsworth, Jeremiah. Papers. Unpublished Box 129, Collections of the Connecticut Historical Society.
Wagner, Frederick K. *Robert Morris: Audacious Patriot.* New York: Dodd, Mead, 1976.
Warner, Jessica. *The Incendiary: The Misadventures of John the Painter, First Modern Terrorist.* New York: Thunder's Month, 2004.
_____. *John the Painter: Terrorist of the American Revolution.* New York: Thunder's Mouth Press, 2004.
Watkins, Susan Finlay. "The Webb-Deane-Stevens Museum." *Antiques,* March 1996.
Watson, Elkanah. *Tour in Holland in 1784.* Worcester, MA: Isaiah Thomas, 1790.
Watson, Winslow C., ed. *Men and Times of the Revolution, or, Memoirs of Elkanah Watson, Including His Journal of Travel in Europe and America, from the Years 1777 to 1842.* New York: 1861.
_____, ed. *Men and Times of the Revolution, or, Memoirs of Elkanah Watson.* 2nd ed. New York: Dena, 1857.
Watts, Edward, and David Rachels, eds. *The First West: Writing from the American Frontier, 1776–1860.* New York: Oxford University Press, 2002.
Weaver, Glenn. *Hartford: An Illustrated History of Connecticut's Capitol.* Woodland Hills, CA: Windsor, 1982.
_____. *Jonathan Trumbull: Connecticut's Merchant Magistrate, 1710–1785.* Hartford: 1956.
Webb, James Watson, ed. *Reminiscences of General Samuel B. Webb of the Revolutionary Army.* New York: Globe, 1882.
Webber, Ralph E. *United States Diplomatic Codes and Ciphers, 1775–1938.* Chicago: President, 1979.
Weider, Lois M. *A Pleasant Land, A Good Heritage: First Church of Christ in Wethersfield, Connecticut, 1635–1985.* Wethersfield, CT: Wethersfield First Church of Christ, 1986.
_____. *The Wethersfield Story.* Stonington, CT: Pequot Press, 1966.
Weintraub, Stanley. *Iron Tears: America's Battle for Freedom, Britain's Quagmire, 1773–1783.* New York: Free Press, 2005.
Wethersfield Post. "The Man Called Silas Deane." August 20 1993.
"Wethersfield's Silas Deane Received the News from Concord with Great Calm." *Hartford Times,* April 29 1965.
Wharton, Francis, ed. *The Revolutionary Diplomatic Correspondence of the United States.* 6 vols. Washington DC: Superintendent of Documents, Government Printing Office, 1889.
Wilkinson, Henry C. *Bermuda in the Old Empire.* New York: 1950.
Willard, John. *Willard's Wethersfield.* Wethersfield, CT: West Hartford, 1975.
Williams, Alan. *The Police of Paris, 1718–1789.* Baton Rouge: Louisiana State University Press, 1979.
Williams, William Appleman. "Samuel Adams: Calvanist, Mercantilist, Revolutionary." *Studies on the Left* 1 (Winter 1960).
_____, ed. *The Shaping of American Diplomacy.* Chicago: Rand McNally, 1956.
Williamson, Joseph. "The Conduct of Paul Revere [and Dudley Saltonstall] in the Penobscot Expedition." *Collections and Proceedings of the Maine Historical Society* 3, 2nd series (1892).
Williard, Howard Jr. *Historic Structure Survey.* Wethersfield, CT: 1980.
Wood, Gordon S. *The Radicalism of the American Revolution: How a Revolution Transformed Monarchial Society into a Democratic One Unlike Any That Had Ever Existed.* New York: Alfred A. Knopf, 1992.
Worthy, R.L. *The Founders Façade: Christianity, Democracy, Freemasonry and the Founding of America.* London: Kornerstone Books, 2004.

Wright, Louis B. *Everyday Life in Colonial America*. London: 1965.
Yates, Frances A. *The Rosicrucian Enlightenment*. Roullege and Kejar Paul, 1972.
York, Neil L. "Burning the Dockyard: John the Painter and the American Revolution." *The Portsmouth Papers*. Vol. 71. Portsmouth: Portsmouth City Council, 2001.
_____. "Freemasons and the American Revolution." *Historian* 55 (Winter 1993).
Zamoyski, Adam. *Holy Madness: Romantics, Patriots and Revolutionaries, 1776-* . New York: Viking-Penguin, 2000
Zeichner, Oscar. *Connecticut's Years of Controversy, 1750–1776*. Chapel Hill: University of North Carolina Press, 1949.

Index

Adams, John 13, 38, 46, 55, 69, 88, 117, 154, 163, 170, 189
Adams, Samuel 18, 37, 44, 45, 46–49, 62, 138, 189, 194
Allen, Ethan 8, 52–53
Amphitrite 102–103, 109, 125, 131, 151
Arnold, Benedict 4, 8, 29–30, 35, 36, 41, 42, 44, 50, 52–53, 165, 179, 189, 197
Atkin, James 97, 99–101
Austen, Jonathan Loring 144–145

Bancroft, Edward 18, 81, 89, 90–91, 99–101, 125, 127–129, 141, 143, 147–15, 152, 160, 162, 176, 177, 178, 182–183, 185, 186, 189, 191, 194, 196
Beaumarchais, Caron de 4, 86–89, 92–93, 97, 102–103, 105, 108–109, 113–115, 118, 120, 123, 126, 129, 130–131, 133, 144, 148, 151, 158–160, 162, 166, 169, 174–175, 189, 191
Bermuda 59–60, 82, 89, 90, 155
Betsy 82, 85, 86, 89, 90
Broglie, Duc de 106–110, 124, 190

Canaan 11
Carmichael, William 97, 109, 121, 123, 125, 128, 129, 131, 134, 136, 139–140, 144, 158, 166, 167, 189, 191
Chaumont, Jacque Donatien le Ray de 92–93, 115–116, 127–130, 133, 137, 142, 152, 164, 171, 174, 189, 193
Committee of Foreign Affairs 72, 122, 126, 158, 192
Committee of Secret Correspondence 72, 73, 80, 86, 92, 97, 158, 169, 190, 191, 192, 195–196
Continental Congress 4, 5, 7–9, 37, 39, 40–50, 54, 58, 59, 68, 156, 190, 191, 192, 193, 194, 197
Conyngham, Gustavus 133–135, 136–137, 141, 189–190

Deane, Mehitabel Nott (Webb) 22, 23, 26, 172, 190
Deane/Franklin Navy 123, 197–198
Deane House 4, 23, 31, 32–33, 187
Declaration of Independence 87, 88, 98, 107, 168, 191, 193, 194
De Kalb, Baron 84, 101, 102, 106, 107, 108, 109, 110, 190
D'Estaing, Admiral 152, 160, 161, 163, 165, 190
Douceur 112
Dubourg 73, 76, 81, 88–89, 90–91, 92, 94, 113, 114, 118, 120, 123, 126, 151, 195
Du Coudray 96–98, 101–103, 105–106, 109, 131, 190
Dumas, Charles W.F. 73, 81, 95, 121, 126, 139, 141, 157, 190, 196
Dunkirk Pirate 134–136, 141, 189–190
Dyer, Eliphalet 36, 39, 41, 42, 48, 55, 57–58, 65–66, 67, 68, 190

Farmer's General 89, 120
Franklin, Benjamin 4–7, 13, 16, 35, 54, 58–62, 64, 69, 72–82, 83, 86–92, 94, 95, 97, 99, 101, 105, 111, 113–114, 115–118, 120–145, 146–163, 166, 170, 174–175, 177–178, 189, 190, 191, 195–196, 197–198

Gérard, Conrad Alexandre 91–92, 105, 109, 111, 118, 120, 125, 129, 132, 134, 142, 143, 146–147, 150–151, 153–154, 156, 159, 160, 163, 165, 169, 170, 191
Ghent 176, 177, 178, 180
Grand, Ferdinand 119, 123, 129–130, 137, 143, 157, 163, 174, 191
Grand, George 119, 123, 157

Henry, Patrick 45, 50, 171
Hodges, William 126–127, 133–136, 137, 179, 191
Hortalez & Co. 92, 143, 148, 158, 162

229

Hynson, Captain Joseph 123–124, 129, 142, 164

Izard, Ralph 128, 150, 162, 167, 170, 191

Jay, John 5, 43, 45, 55, 66, 72, 79, 113, 117, 156, 168, 169, 170, 178, 183, 191, 195–196
"John the Painter" 99–101, 127, 148, 182

Lafayette. Marquis de 101, 102, 103, 106–111, 133, 148, 182, 190, 192
Lake Champlain 8, 16, 52, 53, 179, 181, 197
Laurens, Henry 165, 166, 168, 169–171, 180–181, 192
Lee, Arthur 3–5, 8, 9, 47–48, 76, 81, 86–88, 92, 93, 97, 111, 115, 116–117, 118, 122, 123, 125, 126, 128, 130, 133, 137, 138, 143–144, 149, 150, 151–159, 160, 162, 163, 167, 168, 169, 170, 171, 178, 181, 186, 192, 196
Lee, Richard Henry 69, 86, 126, 138, 158–159, 166, 167, 168, 169, 171, 178, 181, 186, 192
Lenoir, Jeanne Charles 113, 125
Lexington 133, 135, 140–141, 144
Louis XVI 84, 86, 88, 101, 106, 108, 111, 118, 129, 132, 137, 159, 163, 192

Maurepas, Comte de 108, 109, 110, 126, 140, 162, 192
Morris, Robert 4, 5, 60, 61–63, 67, 72, 73, 74–78, 80, 81–82, 85, 112, 113, 117, 122, 133, 136, 139, 140, 151, 162, 169, 171, 172, 178, 180, 192, 195–196, 197, 198
Morris, Thomas 112–113, 122, 126, 132, 133, 135, 139–140

Nine Ladies Lodge 94

Old Mill Prison 126, 141

Passy 116, 127, 128, 129, 140, 143, 144, 147, 149, 151, 152, 153, 155, 158, 160, 167, 175
Penobscot Expedition 172–173, 193
Privateer Commissions 67–68, 70, 123, 133, 134
Putnam, General Israel 34, 37, 45, 51, 57–58, 68, 107, 193

Recall 5, 47, 158–159, 164, 165–173
Reprisal 85, 122, 135, 140,
Rivington Royal Gazette 176
Ross, John 139–140, 193

Saint Eustatia 61, 94, 112
St. Lawrence River 179, 181
Saltonstall, Captain Dudley 70, 124, 173, 193
Saratoga, Battle of 8, 144–145, 146, 168
Sartine, Antoine-Raymond-Gualbert-Gilbert de 85, 109, 120, 131, 134, 138, 144, 156, 160, 162, 193
Sherman, Roger 37, 39, 41–42, 48, 50, 55, 57, 58, 60, 64, 65–68, 190, 193
Sons of Liberty 7, 30, 34, 35, 41, 43, 52, 193
Stueben, Friedrich Wilhelm, Baron von 130–131, 193
Stormont, Ambassador 90, 97, 103, 109, 110, 112, 118, 120, 122–123, 125–126, 128, 130, 131, 134, 136, 140, 141, 143, 148, 149, 158, 177, 193

Tallmadge, Benjamin 7, 72, 79, 176, 178, 194

Valentois 128, 129, 133, 141, 143, 144, 155, 163, 174, 175
Vandalia 125
Vergennes, Charles Gravier Comte de 4, 5, 73, 74, 76, 81, 84, 86–88, 90–94, 96–97, 98, 99, 100, 103, 105, 108–109, 111, 113, 114, 116–120, 122–123, 125, 127–134, 136–138, 140–143, 145, 146–148, 150–164, 174, 175, 189, 191, 192, 195–196
Versailles 88, 91, 92, 94, 100, 106–108, 114, 116–118, 122, 125, 126, 129, 141, 144, 145, 146–147, 155–156, 159, 163, 170, 193
Victoire 109, 110
"volunteers" 97

Washington, George 5, 6, 7, 16, 35, 43, 46, 47, 55–57, 59, 62, 63, 65, 72, 73, 74, 79, 81, 87, 89, 96, 98, 101, 102, 108, 111, 112, 121, 124, 130, 132–133, 139, 141, 144, 145, 151, 166, 169, 175, 176, 181, 183, 190, 192, 193, 194, 197, 198
"water borne" 121–122
Webb, Samuel 30, 41, 42, 58, 157, 181, 194
Wentworth, Paul 99, 101, 142, 146–152, 158, 177, 194
West Indies 9, 15, 16, 18, 20, 22, 23, 26, 27, 28, 30, 31, 38, 50, 59, 60, 61, 62, 71, 74, 76, 77, 84, 85, 89, 90, 94, 111, 119, 121, 123, 132, 146, 154, 157, 182
Wickes, Captain Lambert 85, 122–123, 125, 129, 134, 135, 137, 141

www.ingramcontent.com/pod-product-compliance
Ingram Content Group UK Ltd.
Pitfield, Milton Keynes, MK11 3LW, UK
UKHW041943140426
5217IPUK00014B/631